# TWELVE S

BY

## WILLIAM ROUGHEAD
WRITER TO THE SIGNET

## THE MERCAT PRESS
EDINBURGH

First published by William Green & Sons in 1913
Reprinted 1995 by The Mercat Press
at James Thin, 53 South Bridge, Edinburgh EH1 1YS

ISBN 1873644 396

Printed in Great Britain by The Cromwell Press
Broughton Gifford, Wiltshire

TO

# H. B. IRVING

IN APPRECIATION
IN FRIENDSHIP

# PREFACE

THESE adventures in criminal biography, begun at the suggestion of the late Mr. Andrew Lang, with his kind encouragement were completed shortly before his death. Mr. Lang read them in manuscript. He was good enough to approve them, and had promised to write an Introduction when they came to be published. Thus, by his sudden passing, which has left literature so much the poorer, the reader is deprived of what would have been the most attractive feature of the book.

Dickens has noted the exclusive nature of a true professional relish, as shown in the enthusiasm of Mr. Dennis; and while, personally, I find the people of our *causes célèbres* more "convincing" than those of many popular and prolific writers, it is quite possible that the reader may not share my taste. I know the disadvantages under which the subjects of these studies labour in competition with their rivals of the circulating library. The fact that they were real men and women, who sinned and suffered in their day, and whose stories are unfortunately true, is alone enough to alienate the sympathy of a fiction-loving public. Yet here we have characters and incidents as curious, and problems in psychology as perplexing, as any wherewith the modern novelist delights his votaries; and although the fitness of my rascals to adorn a tale may be questioned, their ability to point a moral is beyond dispute. So I venture to hope that, if their regrettable actuality be overlooked, they may even afford some measure of entertainment.

The selection of the cases dealt with is purely arbitrary. They were chosen as being unfamiliar, and, in my view, worthy of rescue from orthodox interment in the official records and the pages of old historians, or less hallowed burial in the files of bygone newspapers. Whether or not the result will sustain my judgment is for the

PREFACE vii

reader to say; it may at least be claimed that in each instance
the best available sources of information have been consulted,
and no pains spared to make the several narratives faithful and
complete. So far as my subject permitted I have sought to lighten
its technical obscurities and to garnish the unpalatable fruits of
research, but, as Sir Thomas Browne has observed, with greater
occasion, "A work of this nature is not to be performed upon one
legg and should smel of oyl, if duly and deservedly handled."

A certain historical, even romantic, interest attaches to the earlier
trials; and if, in the course of time, the original colours have somewhat
faded, the figures are still sufficiently distinct. The Reverend John
Kello and Lady Warriston, who flourished in the reign of our sixth
James, were justified (as the phrase went) for solving their marital
difficulties in similar savage fashion, and enjoyed an equal notoriety
by reason of their edifying confessions and godly ends. Major Weir,
the covenanting wizard, needs no introduction; his presence
confers distinction upon any company, however evil. Philip Stanfield
(who aggravated his other crimes by boring Mr. Lang) played with
much success the part of the Prodigal Son, but overacted it at last by
slaying, in the year of the Revolution, "his natural and kindly parent,"
his guilt being established by supranormal means. The Sergeant's
ghost, that temerarious spirit, vainly seeking to convince a jury
of David Hume's fellow-citizens, succumbed to scepticism, and
so was laid for ever. For the rest, the cases of Katharine Nairn
and Keith of Northfield are in themselves remarkable, and throw a
strange light upon the domestic manners of Scottish society towards the close of the eighteenth century. The next three
exemplify the use of the verdict Not Proven, "that Caledonian
*medium quid*" hated by Sir Walter Scott. No account of the
Dunecht mystery or of the Arran murder has hitherto been published,
and, as cases of such importance should not remain unchronicled,
an attempt is here made to supply the want.

W. R.

8 Oxford Terrace, Edinburgh,
*April*, 1913.

# CONTENTS

PAGE

THE PARSON OF SPOTT, 1570 . . . . . . 1

THE DOOM OF LADY WARRISTON, 1600 . . . . 16

TOUCHING ONE MAJOR WEIR, A WARLOCK, 1670 . . . 41

THE ORDEAL OF PHILIP STANFIELD, 1688 . . . . 63

THE GHOST OF SERGEANT DAVIES, 1754 . . . . 85

KATHARINE NAIRN, 1765 . . . . . . 106

KEITH OF NORTHFIELD, 1766 . . . . . . 136

"THE WIFE O' DENSIDE," 1827 . . . . . 160

CONCERNING CHRISTINA GILMOUR, 1844 . . . . 191

THE ST. FERGUS AFFAIR, 1854 . . . . . 221

THE DUNECHT MYSTERY, 1882 . . . . . 248

THE ARRAN MURDER, 1889 . . . . . . 273

# THE PARSON OF SPOTT

N.B.—No mischief but a woman or a priest in it,—here both.
*—The Journal of Mr. Groves,* 1788.

THE criminous clerk is a character but seldom impersonated by what may be called the stock company of the Justiciary Opera. The part has been long a popular one on the Continent, and France especially has produced many eminent players. " From the consummate Riembauer, so graphically described by Feuerbach, through Mingrat and Contrafatto, down to the Abbés Boudes and Bruneau of our own day, the crimes of priests have possessed an atrocity all their own." Thus Mr. H. B. Irving, in his admirable *Studies of French Criminals of the Nineteenth Century.* But the Roman Catholic clergy do not possess the exclusive right of representation ; Protestant England, for instance, is secure in the supremacy of Dr. Titus Oates in the rôle, and very capable performers have been furnished from time to time by a variety of sects. In Scotland, however, we must go back more than three centuries to find an actor of outstanding merit.

So remote is the period that only a glimpse of this old-time tragedy is now obtainable from a brief entry in the official record, and from certain scanty notices by contemporary historians of the Kirk, who, as is their wont in dealing with such scandals, devote more space to the culprit's contrition than to the particulars of his crime. The murderer's own confession, fortunately, has been preserved. "The Confessione of Mr. Johnne Kello, minister of Spott ; together with his earnest repentance maid upon the scaffald befoir his suffering, the fourt day of October 1570," was "imprinted at Edinburgh be Robert Leckprivicke " in that year. It is reprinted with some variations both in the *Journal* and *Memorials* of Richard

1

Bannatyne, secretary to John Knox, and also in Calderwood's *History of the Kirk of Scotland*. Though doubtless edited for behoof of the godly, it remains a human document of rare interest, and such facts of the case as have survived sufficiently prove that the Reverend John Kello was no whit inferior to his clerical rivals of other days and climes.

The time was the year of grace 1570. Calvinism had triumphed, and the cause of Queen Mary and the "Auld Faith" was lost. That unhappy lady was safely in Elizabeth's parlour, the gallant Kirkcaldy still kept the flag of his Royal mistress flying on the castle of Edinburgh, and the ambition of her ambiguous brother, the "Good Regent," had lately been abridged by the bullet of Bothwellhaugh at Linlithgow. The scene was the hill parish of Spott, on the eastern slope of the Lammermuirs, near the coast town of Dunbar. The little East Lothian village, with its ancient church and manse, lies remote from the highroad of history, but echoes of its name are sometimes heard among the crash of great events. A son of Home of Cowdenknowes was rector at the Reformation. George Home of Spott, tried for the murder of Darnley, was himself one of the assize on the trial of Archibald Douglas for the same crime. He was murdered by his son-in-law, James Douglas of Spott, who in 1591 helped Francis, Earl of Bothwell, to beset Chancellor Maitland at Holyrood, when they "made a stour" that nearly frightened King James out of his princely wits. In 1650 General Leslie pitched his camp upon the summit of Doon Hill before the battle of Dunbar, which he lost by abandoning that strong position at the command of the prophets who accompanied his army; and Cromwell himself is said to have spent the night after his victory at the house of Spott. The parish is celebrated, too, as being the scene of the last witch-burnings in Scotland, for so late as October 1705, only two years before the Union, the minutes of the Kirk Session significantly record : " Many witches burnt on the top of Spott Loan."

In the sixteenth century a strange fatality attached to the incumbency of this quiet rural parish, the church of which, previous to the Reformation, was a Prebend of the Collegiate Church of Dunbar. Robert Galbraith, parson of Spott, who afterwards attained the dignity of a Senator of the College of Justice—a post no longer open to the established clergy—was murdered in 1543 by one John Carkettle, a burgess of Edinburgh. The next rector, John Hamilton, brother of the Regent Arran, succeeded Cardinal Beaton in the See of St. Andrews, and was the Archbishop Hamilton of Queen Mary's reign. He was taken prisoner at the capture of Dumbarton Castle in 1571, and was hanged at Stirling for complicity in the assassination of the Regent Moray, his captor being that Crawford of Jordanhill who kept such careful note of what passed between Mary and Darnley at Glasgow. The fate of the archbishop's successor in the manse of Spott, the first minister of the new and purified Kirk, forms the subject of the present study.

The Reverend John Kello is mentioned by Calderwood among those who were " thought apt and able to minister " by the first General Assembly of the reformed Kirk of Scotland, held on 20th December 1560. Owing to " the raritie of pastors in the infancie of our kirk " the list was something of the shortest. The names were given in by the ministers and commissioners within their own bounds, and Mr. John was probably nominated by George Home of Spott, who was a member of assembly. Kello was a parson of the new school, a man of humble origin but great ambitions, married, and, by all accounts, an eloquent and powerful preacher. " I was brocht up from my youth," he tells us in his confession, " in exercise of learning, and imployed my mynd so diligentlie to the meditatione of vertue that I was not esteamed in the leist sort of thai that did minister Godis word into this realme. And the treuth is, that I myself had nocht only the testimonie of a trew preicher in the countreis whair I did travell, but lykwayis of ane sinceir and uncorrupted conversatioune." No

doubt he considered these gifts inadequately rewarded by the
ministry of Spott, the stipend of which in 1567, as we learn
from Scott's *Fasti Ecclesiæ Scoticanæ*, amounted to £100 Scots—
£8, 6s. 8d. of modern money. He had chosen a wife from
his own station in life, one Margaret Thomson, by whom he
had three children, but, although an affectionate and loyal helpmate, she does not seem to have been an ideal partner for a
rising young man bent on achieving at any cost social and
professional advancement. The chroniclers concur in testifying
to her many virtues : " a woman sa loving of him and of his
estait as any woman could have bene reportit to have favorit or
obeyit hir husband in all respectis "; and Mr. John himself, when
displaying in public for the last time his powers of eloquence
on the scaffold, described her as one who had never given him
any just cause of offence. " For wer it possible," said he, " that
the course of my aige mycht be renewed, and the tyme spent
brocht bak agane, thair is no fleshe I wold rather chouse to
be associat with in mariage then hir." During the lady's life,
unfortunately, this feeling was in abeyance, and he came to
regard his amiable but plebeian consort as a stumbling-block in
the path of his future career.

" I had anis ane litle portione of money in my owin hands,"
he informs us, " which I bestowit in Linlythgow upon proffeit."
The investment turned out well, for Mr. John " did wickedlie
resave some gaines and filthie ocker [interest] therby ; ane
thing (alace !)," he laments, " ower meikle used in this countrey."
Like many a wiser man he was emboldened by this first success
to try his luck further, or, in his own words, " This maner of
dealing kindled in me ane desyre of avarice, whiche the apostle
Paull, nocht without caus, termit ' the route of all evill.' " At
the time, however, he took a less moral view of the result, and
having raised money on his Linlithgow property he bought
some land at Spott. This speculation does not seem to have
prospered, and he contracted further debt. Then his relations
with the authorities of the infant Kirk proved unsatisfactory ;

he complains of being " disappointed of the ordinar provisione for preiching of the Word, and not weill entreated of thame whois dewtie was to have taken cair of me." His position would be rendered less agreeable when he recalled the very different fortunes of his Episcopal predecessor. The affairs of the popular preacher became involved, he suffered much from mental worry, and his perplexities " openede ane reddie window to the tentatiounes of the Enemie." He describes with curious callousness how he reviewed the situation. If he were a single man, " without ane pairtie," he might the more " easilie " spend his time ; then, in case he should marry again, he might join himself with such an one as should have friends in the country to maintain him in his possession and procure his further advancement. Plainly he had the second Mrs. Kello in his eye; no less a lady, it seems, than the daughter of the laird. " Thir wer the glistering promises whairwith Sathan, efter his accustomed maner, eludit my senses." On his own showing the motive which induced him to murder his faithful and devoted wife was the peculiarly base one of making a better marriage : " Nather did ony uther thing move me to this wicked interprise but the continwall suggestione of the wicked spreit to advance myself farther and farther in the world."

If the late ingenious Dr. Pritchard had told the truth, which he never so far forgot himself as to do, we should probably find that in destroying his wife he also was moved by a similar purpose. The doctor, by the way, attributed his crimes to the influence of ardent, not evil, spirits.

Mr. John, having satisfied himself of his grounds for action, with diabolic subtlety " did spreid abroad ane rumoure of hir that sche was tempted terriblie in the night, that it mycht thairefter appeir hir self to have bene the author and murtherer of hir owin self." As an additional precaution the wily man made a will, therein appointing his widow to have " the whole cair of my geir " and the upbringing of his children, which testamentary intentions he casually communicated to the neighbourhood. The train thus laid, he spent forty days awaiting " onlie upon the oportunitie of tyme " for achieving his nefarious end, and though "sometymes having the commoditie offered," he was stricken with " sic terrouris " that his heart failed him and the deed was still to do. On the expiry of that period he was himself " visited with seiknes and grit disease," which, after his conviction, he perceived to be " messengeris of God," but at the time were contrived by him to further his design. Under pretence that his wife might also suffer from the like indisposition he " laboured secretlie to have taken hir away by poysone." The strength of the lady's constitution, or, as he puts it, " the cleannes of hir stommocke," enabling her to " reject that violence," some other means had to be devised. During his illness the reverend sufferer availed himself of the professional services of Mr. Andrew Simpson, the first minister of Dunbar after the Reformation, to whom he imprudently related a remarkable dream which was later interpreted by that prophet with telling effect, as we shall presently see. So soon as the invalid felt himself sufficiently restored to health and strength he decided to carry through his scheme without further delay.

On the morning of Sunday, 24th September 1570, when his wife was performing her devotions in her own chamber, Mr. John Kello at length perceived the long-looked-for opportunity, embracing which he strangled her, as she knelt, with a towel. "In the verie death," he admits, "she could not beleive I bure hir ony evill will, bot was glaid, as sche than said, to depairt, gif hir death could doe me ather vantage or pleasoure." Verily it is difficult to write with patience of the Reverend John. The willing victim sacrificed, he tied a rope round her neck and hung the body from a hook in the ceiling of her own room. He then locked the front door of the manse, leaving the key on the inside, and went out by the back. As he says, "Efter I had strangled hir, I left the keyis

within, and escapit by ane back dure of my studie, which was
not accustomed to be opened." The murderer's next act is
unique in the criminal annals of any country. It is best
described in the quaint words of the contemporary author of
the *Historie of King James the Sext:* "For he stranglit hir in
hir owin chalmer, and tharefter closit the ordinar dur that
was within the hous for his awin passage, and sa fynelie
semit to cullor that purpose efter that he had done it, that
immediatelie he past to the kirk, and in presence of the people
maid sermon, as thoght he had done na sik thing. And when
he was returnit hayme, he broght sum nychtbours in to his
hous to vissie his wyffe, and callit at the ordinar dur, but na
answer was maid; then he past to another bak passage with
the nychtbours, and that was fund oppin, and she hinging
stranglit at the ruf of the hous. Then with admiratioun he
cryit out, as thoght he had knawin na thing of the purpose,
and thay for pitie in lyke maner cryit out." The inviting of
some of the congregation was obviously in furtherance of his
preconceived plan; they had been prepared by his false reports
of Mrs. Kello's mental condition. "Vissie" may either mean
simply to visit, or alternatively to make a particular scrutiny.
The murderer himself gives no details of the crime. "I was
alwayes preissed fordward be the tentatioune of the Enemie till
I had performed that crewell fact with my handis against hir"
is all that he says, and the official record of his conviction
merely states that the deed was "committit be him within his
awin lugeing in the toun of Spot for the tyme, be strangling
of hir with ane towale, upon the xxiiij day of September last
bypast, befoir noyne [noon]."

The Rev. John Thomson, writing in 1836, gives in the *New
Statistical Account of Scotland* a slightly different version of the
facts, probably from local tradition: "The murder was committed on a Sabbath. Having before divine worship suspended
his wife behind a door in the manse, he repaired to the church,
where, in the course of the service, he was remarked to have

delivered a more than usually eloquent sermon. The services being over, and the congregation dismissed, he went to the residence of a neighbour, stating to the lady of the house that his wife (Mrs. Kello) had for some time been rather in a depressed state of mind, and that he had called to request that she would kindly come over and join them in their family dinner, and endeavour to cheer her up. The request was at once complied with. On arriving at the manse, to the seeming amazement of both, the doors and windows of the manse were found barricaded. After some little time Mr. Kello contrived to effect an entrance. A few moments after he came running to a window, exclaiming to the lady who accompanied him, ' My wife, my wife, my beloved wife is gone !' "

This is the only instance on record of a murderer going red-handed into church and conducting public worship to the edification of the faithful. The Reverend John was no common criminal ; as he himself modestly remarks, " the caice is rair."

The incident is referred to both by Froude and Hill Burton, and later Mr. Andrew Lang has woven the strange facts into a picturesque tale, as told in vivid Scots by a supposed spectator —one Archibald Dunbar, from whose narrative the following passage may be quoted : " About this time it chanced to be the Sabbath day, a fine sunny day in September, and the kirk bell was jowing. I was not then under conviction, but rather inclined to hang off from the preaching of the Word. For I had no clearness that Daniel, and Haggai, and the other Prophets of old, did no one thing but threip against our Sovereign Lady, Queen Mary, now in an English prison, in sore fear of her life. But so Mr. Kello laid it down, every Sabbath, in the preaching place, and so I was stravaguing but slowly and no very well pleased, to the kirk. Then the bell stopped jowing, and I saw the minister, that aye was in the vestry before exercise began, come running out by a back door of his study which was not accustomed to be opened. He ran across the little green to the kirk door, and spanged up the pulpit stairs, wiping his brow with a fine lawn napkin, while he went peching through the first prayer. But when it came to the sermon, having had a bit rest in the psalm singing, he yoked to Aholah and Aholibah, that were other than good ones, and, in the application, he made it clearly to appear that the King's mother was both the one and the other of these limmers. His wife was not in the kirk with the bairns, that sat glowering at their father, feared like, for he was under a very great gale." The dramatic scene after the sermon was over, when the elders returned with the minister to the manse, may be read by the curious in the story (*Longman's Magazine*, February 1901).

The political tone of the good man's discourse, as reported by his imaginary hearer, has warrant in his own confession: "Nather was thair ony of my vocatioune within this realme of Scotland that detestit moir from the hart, and publictlie in the chayre of trueth, the abhominable murtheraris of Harie Stewart, king of this land, and my Lord Regent, laitly murthered, declaring out of the buike of God that the plages shuld never ceis quhill [until] the land were purgit, and the inventaris, conspyraris, [and] pertakeris proponit [proposed] ane publict exemple of Godis seveir judgmentis." Such an "exemple" the preacher himself was soon to furnish, little though he foresaw it at the time. Whether the poor woman was in fact buried according to the dreadful manner of suicides in those days, as Archibald Dunbar in the tale relates, we do not know; but it seems certain that no suspicion at first attached to her husband regarding her death, and that Mrs. Kello was believed to have taken her own life in a fit of mental depression. "When the bruite [rumour] did aryse that sche had murthered hir self," says the reverend rogue, "for the gude opinione that everie ane had alsweill [both] of my doctrine and conversatioune maid no man to suspect my innocencie," he pretended that his sole anxiety was for her salvation in view of the presumed manner of her taking off. He disputed with those who came to comfort him in his bereavement whether it were possible that she who had thus laid hands upon herself "could be under the protectioune of God," and speculated as to the probability that, "being under so terrible tentatioune, sche could anes sob [once cry] for Godis mercie!" The opinion of the comforters being unfavourable to the deceased's chances in this regard, the disconsolate widower, in order, as he says, that his "affectione towardis hir mycht appeir the greitter," denied in plain terms the existence of a God who suffered so innocent a creature to give place to the "tentatioune and rage of Sathan." Such sentiments from an approved saint must have been painful hearing, but no doubt the godly excused them by reason of the greatness of his grief. "Which thingis," he explains, "I passed about most craftelie to conceill," and, for the time, with apparent success.

If Mr. John Kello had been content to let well alone he might in due course have married again, if not with a clear conscience at least with the approval of the righteous; but with a fatuity fortunately common in criminals he needs must consult his reverend colleague of Dunbar, Mr. Andrew Simpson, in the matter of his wife's suicide and his own religious scruples thereanent. Whether that astute divine was already on the alert, having heard some "sough" of suspicion from the neighbouring parish, or whether Mr. John, with professional enthusiasm, overacted his part for this experienced critic, does not appear, but something transpired at the performance which enabled Mr. Simpson to assume the rôle of Nathan the prophet, with equally startling results. "Brother," said he, "I doe remember quhan I visitate yow, in tyme of your grit seiknes, ye did open to me that visione; that ye war caried be ane grym man befoir the face of ane terrible Judge, and to escaip his furie ye did precipitate your self in ane deip river, when his angelis and messingeris did follow you with two-edged swordes; and ever quhan thai struike at you, ye did declyne and jowke [dodge] in the water; while in the end, by ane way unknowin to you, ye did escape. This visione I do so interprete that ye are the author your self

of this crwell murther, then consaved in your hart; and ye are
careit befoir the terrible judgmentis of God in your owin conscience, which now standis in Godis presence to accuse you; the
messingeris of God is the justice of the countrie, befoir the
whitche ye sall be presented; the water whairin ye stude is
that vaine hypocrisie of your owin, and feanezead [feigned]
blaspheming of Godis name, whairby ye purpose to cullour
your impietie.  Your delyverance sal be spirituall, ffor, albeit
ye have utherwayis deservit, yit God sall pull you furth of the
bandis of Sathan, and caus you to confes your offense, to his
glory and confusione of the Enemie.  Nather do ye in ony
wayes mistrust in Godis promises, for you sall find no sinne,
almost, committed be the reprobat, but ye sall find the childrene
of God to have fallin in the lyke; and yit the same mercies of
God abydis you, gif from your hart ye acknowledge your offence
and desyris at God pardon."

   This prophetic achievement earned for Mr. Simpson a more
than local fame.  Nicol Burne, " Professor of Philosophie in S.
Leonardis College, in the Citie of Sanctandrois," who, proposing
to defend the old religion in debate before the General Assembly
of the Kirk, was imprisoned in the Tolbooth of Edinburgh in
1580, published at Paris in the following year his *Admonition
to the Antichristian Ministers in the Deformit Kirk of Scotland*,
in which he refers to the incident as follows:—

   Symson of Dunbar, quhat sall I say of thee?
   I know thow waittis Lieutenentis place to have;
   I grant thy wisdom soleid for to be,
   As Kellochis dreame bearis witnes ouer the lave.
   Sa may thow baldlie ane hear [higher] place cum crave,
   War not thou seis [essayest] full ill the band to leid:
   The less experience hes thow thy flock to save:
   Kilt up thy connie, to Geneve haist with speid.

   The cryptic phrase in the last line may be rendered, " Pack
up and be off," but time has blunted the point of the topical
allusions.  Simpson, who, as was not uncommon in those days,

combined the offices of parish minister and master of the grammar school at Dunbar, was by birth a Catholic, and is said to have been led to adopt the new faith by reading the poems of Sir David Lindsay. When seven years later the prophet, emboldened by his palpable hit in the matter of the dream, foretold the loss of the fishing fleet wrecked off Dunbar, he was grieved to find his gift less generally acclaimed.

The Reverend John did not at once capitulate. He tells us, with characteristic caution, "I discovrsed within my owin hart what thing ratherest to doe for my owin releife"; whether to flee the country forthwith, or, in modern parlance, to stay and face the music. The first course was open to the objection that he would live in constant terror and bear the mark of Cain wherever he might go, besides leaving "a perpetuall infamie upon the Kirk of God, whairof befoir I was compted ane member, albeit unworthie." He then considered whether, having privately repented, it was necessary to publish his shame before men. Mr. Simpson, however, pursuing his advantage, "did so lyvlie rype furthe the inward cogitatiounes" of the sinner that in the end Mr. John says, "I persuadit my self God spak in him." In addition to the interpretation of the dream, "utheris notable conjecturis which he trwelie deduced befoir my eyes" finally clinched the business.

The author of the *Historie of King James the Sext* says: "He [Kello] differrit na langer tyme with counsall and convoy of this wyse godlie man, that he immediatlie came to Edinburgh, and thair delatit his turpitude to the Juge criminall, and to certayne uther preachers, and how willing he was to suffer puneishment tharefore. Brieflie, be his awin confessioun being clearlie convict, he was condamnit to be hangit, and his bodie to be cassin in the fyre, and brynt to ashes, and so to dee without buriall." No account of the proceedings of the trial has been preserved, but the following is the official record of the sentence, under date 4th October 1570: "For the quhilk he was adjugeit be dome pronounceit, to be hangit to the deid, and thairefter his body to be cassin in ane fyre and brint in assis; and his gudis and geir quhatsumevir (pertening to our soveran lord) to be confiscat, &c." The latter part of the sentence, relating to the confiscation of the convict's property to the Crown, was remitted, as appears from an entry in the Register of the Privy Seal, of date 5th October, to the effect that Bartilmo, Barbara, and Bessie Kello, "sone and dochteris to umquhile [the late] Mr. Johnne Kello," got a gift of his escheat "throw the said umquhile Mr. Johnne being convict and justifeit to the deid for the crewell and odious murthure of umquhile Margaret Thomesoun, his spous."

Mr. John was allowed but short shrift, as we see from the following entry in Lamont's *Diary*: "1570, Oct. 4. Mr. John Kellok, minister of Spot, hangit in Edinb. for murder of his wyfe." In accordance with the etiquette of the time the culprit delivered from the scaffold an address to "ane grit multitude" assembled to witness his execution, wherein he expressed in common form his contrition for the crime of which he had been convicted. He also touched on the political aspect of his fate, and expressed a pious anxiety lest "the enemies of the Evangle, with oppin mouthis," should find in his own lapse an excuse for the failings of his sovereign lady, Queen Mary. "What mervell is it, will thai say, that ane waike veshell, brocht up in pleasouris, had not the feir of God befoir hir eyes, when ane minister, nocht of smallest reputatioune, hes sa trespassed?" Superstition was rampant in Scotland after the Reformation, and belief in witchcraft was a foremost article of the new creed. Every crime was considered to be the result of direct negotiations with the devil himself, and fortunate was that criminal who had not to answer for other than real offences. In the present case it is evident that the Reverend John, who, as we have seen, laid the "wyte" of his wickedness on Satan, had not escaped the popular accusation. "For as concerning the uther whairof I am slanderit," he protests, "I take God and his angellis witnessis in the

contrare, that nather had I any ingres in the wicked practises
of the Magicienis, nather was farder curious to understand then
God had manifested in his Word." Little wonder that so rigid
a professor resented the imputation of the sin of witchcraft.
In conclusion he gave his hearers this sensible advice:
"Measoure not the treuth of Godis word altogether be the
lyvis of sic as are apointed pastouris ower you, for thei beir
the self same fleshe of corruptioune that ye doe, and the moir
godlie the charge is whairunto thai are called, the readier the
Enemie to draw thame bak from Godis obedience." Finally, as
he perceived that his voice was "not able to straicht the self
unto the earis of the multitude heir convenit," he would be
content to leave "ane short memoriall" against himself of his
own offence. "And thus," says the author of the *Historie*, "he
departit this lyfe with ane extreyme penitent and contreit hart,
bayth for this, and all uther his offences in generall, to the
great gude example and comfort of all the behalders."

The editor of the posthumous confession explains that he
doubted the wisdom of publishing it to the world, and that
personally he "wald rather have wished the memorie thairof
to have been buried, then be ony manis industrie and labouris
sa wicked exemple continowed to the posteritie"; his reason
being that, as regards the godly, his pen "culd serve nothing
towardis thame but to ingraffe greater dolour and lamentatioune
in thair hertis," while by the wicked it would be received with
"contempt and mockage." But he was inclined to publish the
true facts of that painful case from the knowledge "that sundrie
of the poysonet sect of the Antechrist had not only written in
uther cuntreis of this murther, but lykwayes be diverse licen-
tious and ungodlie picturis, labored to withdraw the simple
from Godis obedience, and irreverantlie spake of the servantis
of God." Plainly the doings of the Reverend John had given
occasion for the enemies of the Kirk to blaspheme; but the
editor challenges them "gif thay be able to make thair proffeit
farther of this tragedie than Sathan himself, whais counsallis

be his [Kello's] godlie repentance was confoundit, and the pray
which he had in ane maner devored, be [by] Godis providence
preservit from his tyrannie.   Gif God disapointed the Father
of Iniquitie, how can his childrene erect this baner to the
mainteanance of his kyngdome?"   Still, one would like to
have seen those "picturis."

In considering the case of this singular divine we are struck
by the fact that so cool and crafty a miscreant, having successfully accomplished his purpose, should prove such an easy con-
quest for the prophet of Dunbar.   That many persons in his
age voluntarily charged themselves with the commission of
incredible crimes, inviting thereby the direst penalties, is undeniable, and raises the question whether after all it is not
possible that the man himself was mad, and had nothing to do
with his wife's death.   But when we remember the making of
the will, the spreading of reports as to her incipient mania, the
ingenious setting of the scene of the supposed suicide, his
amazing appearance in the pulpit immediately after the deed,
and, further, that he expressly disclaimed those dealings with
the devil which are an invariable feature of such self-accusa-
tions, little doubt remains that he was guilty of his wife's blood.
In any view the Reverend John Kello was a type of parson
with whose unusual gifts his Kirk was well able to dispense.

"What a pity that R. L. S. did not write on Mr. K., who
seems to have been really a bad one," wrote Mr. Lang to me a
few days before his lamented death; and all who have walked
with Gordon Darnaway in Sandag Bay or met Thrawn
Janet by Dule Water in the gloaming, will heartily agree with
him.

In January 1913 the great beech tree which adjoined the
site of the old manse of Spott was blown down; the "new"
manse, built across the road about a hundred years ago, has no
connection with Mr. Kello and his crime.

# THE DOOM OF LADY WARRISTON

Doun by yon garden green
Sae merrily as she gaes ;
She has twa weel-made feet,
And she trips upon her taes.

She has twa weel-made feet,
Far better is her hand ;
She's jimp about the middle
As ony willy-wand.
*—The Laird of Waristoun.*

THE house of Warriston crowns a swelling rise among lawns
and shrubberies, overshadowed by goodly trees, within a mile
of Edinburgh, midway between the city and the Firth.   From
this vantage ground it commands a noble prospect: to the
north, beyond the estuary of the Forth, the coast and hills
of Fife; to the south the terraced buildings of the New Town,
climbing one above another towards the lofty ridge where
Auld Reekie sits supreme.   Westward lie the woods and
pleasant slopes of Inverleith; eastward is Warriston Cemetery,
wherein "a certain archway, a formidable but beloved spot,"
seemed to the child Stevenson the veritable "Death's dark
vale" of the Scots metrical psalm, in the illustration of which
his uncanny fancy employed other places in the immediate
neighbourhood familiar to his early years.

To-day the cable cars clank past the old-world lodge gates
of Warriston, and the city, advancing steadily across the con-
quered fields, beleaguers it on every side.   A few more years,
and of house and policies, transformed by the masonic arts of
the speculator, nought shall survive except a name.

The house itself, though of a respectable antiquity, has in
its turn supplanted a more ancient place or fortalice—that

"gloomy house of Warristoun hanging over a deep black pool"
—which in the seventeenth century yet occupied the site.  At
the period in question, between the lands of Warriston and the
Firth lay the wind-swept waste of Wardie Muir, bordered by
the Water of Leith on its course to the sea, with here and
there some solitary homestead, the very names of which, as
Windlestrawlee and Blaw Wearie, strike comfortless upon
the ear.  On the edge of the muir, nearer the water than the
present house, stood the old mansion of Inverleith, no trace of
which remains save the pillars of the gateway, surmounted by
heraldic monsters, flanking the entrance from St. Bernard's
Row.  Down the avenue that winds by the side of the water,
and between these stony guardians, in the golden days of Auld
Reekie's past "the mulberry-coloured coach" of Mrs. Rocheid
of Inverleith was wont to convey that magnificent dame to the
Assembly Rooms of the Old Town, a harbour of ceremonious
fashion, as Henry Cockburn relates, into which she would "sail
like a ship from Tarshish, gorgeous in velvet or rustling in
silk," to the admiration and envy of beholders.

Sterner memories cluster about the house of Warriston.  In
the latter half of the sixteenth century the estate, which like
its neighbour of Inverleith has often changed proprietors,
belonged to a branch of the Kincaids of that ilk, an ancient
Stirlingshire family.  On 15th June 1577, as appears from
the Justiciary Records, John Kincaid of Warriston was one of
the assize (jury) on the trial of John Sempill of Beltries, the
husband of Mary Livingstone of the Four Maries, accused "of the
treasonable conspiracy of my Lord Regent's Grace's slaughter"
—an attempt upon the life of the Regent Morton.  On 20th
November 1579 certain Dalmahoys of that ilk, with two of the
Rocheids and others, were tried for besieging William Somervell,
apparently a tenant of the Kincaids, "within his dwelling-place
of Warriston," and were acquitted of the charge "of the shooting
and bearing of pistolets in the month of July, and thereafter
coming to the house and asseiging thereof and shooting of

2

pistolets thereat, and hurting and wounding Barbara Barrie."
On 27th May 1591 Robert Cairncross, "callit Mekle Hob,"
and three other miscreants were charged " of art and part of the
rapt and ravishing [abduction] of Jean Ramsay, Lady Warriston,
against the Acts of Parliament and laws of this realm made
thereanent, committed the XIX. day of March last by-past."
The victim of this outrage was, according to Fountainhall, a
member of the Dalhousie family.

The tragedy which has secured for the house of Warriston
a place in the criminal and domestic annals of Scotland occurred
on Tuesday, 1st July 1600. Two contemporary writers have
briefly noticed the crime and its consequences. Robert Birrel,
"Burges of Edinburghe," in his quaint and valuable *Diary*
records on the 2nd of that month : — " Johne  Kincaid  of
Waristone murderit be hes awin wyff and servant man, and
her nurische being also upone the conspiracy. The said gentil-
woman being apprehendit, scho wes tane to the Girth Crosse
upon the 5 day of Julii, and her heid struk fra her bodie at
the Cannagait fit ; quha diet verie patiently. Her nurische
wes brunt at the same tyme, at 4 houres in the morneing, the
5 of Julii." Calderwood, the historian, also refers to the case :—
" Upon Fryday [Saturday] the 4 [5] of July [1600], the Lady
Warristoun, daughter of the Laird of Dunipace, was beheaded in
the Cannongate, for the murther of her husband. The Nurse
and ane hyred woman, her complices, were burnt in the Castlehill of Edinburgh. The horse-boy fled, being guiltie."

The only authorities now available are the official record of
the trial and condemnation of " the horse-boy," Robert Weir,
and an authentic and very remarkable *Memorial of the Conversion of Jean Livingston, Lady Waristoun, with an Account of
her Carriage at her Execution, July* 1600, privately printed by
Charles Kirkpatrick Sharpe in 1827, from the original among
the Wodrow MSS. in the Advocates' Library, Edinburgh.

The tragic story was of course enshrined in the popular
ballads of the day under the title of *The Laird of Warriston.*

No less than three variants have been preserved in print, and Pitcairn, writing in 1833, says that "several are still sung and recited in various parts of Scotland." One, printed by Jamieson, was taken down by Sir Walter Scott from the recitation of his mother, the others were first published respectively by Buchan and Kinloch. All three versions are included in the collections of Maidment and of Professor Child.

Few of the surrounding facts of the case have come down to us, and tradition, as exemplified by the ballads, gives these in varying forms; but across the darkness of three hundred years a lurid light is thrown upon the actual deed by the brief account of Weir's trial, while the spiritual feats of the fair penitent have been chronicled with a particularity which makes one wish that the pious reporter had spared among his windy paragraphs some space for the cause and circumstances of her crime.

The property was at that period in the possession of John Kincaid, called the Laird of Warriston, a landed proprietor and a person of some consideration in Edinburgh, whose family, the Kincaids of that ilk, then owned extensive estates in the counties of Edinburgh, Linlithgow, and Stirling. His wife, Jean Livingstone, by Scots courtesy Lady Warriston, the young and beautiful daughter of John Livingstone of Dunipace, in the county of Stirling, was born in 1579. Both husband and wife were related to many of the first families in Scotland. It is generally assumed that the laird was well advanced in years, and it has even been said that he was thrice married, but in the contemporary Latin epitaph on the lady, printed by Sharpe, both the parties are described as having been married very young and against their inclinations, *invita invito subjuncta puella puello*, with results disastrous to both—*nihil in thalamo nisi rixæ, jurgia, lites*.

How long they had been married does not appear. "For I have been your wife, These nine years running ten," says the lady in the ballad; but the fact that she was executed for her

husband's murder in her twenty-first year renders this statement unlikely.    In one version she thus apostrophises her
spouse, who is referred to as "the young lord" :—

> O Warriston, O Warriston,
>     I wish that ye may sink for sin !
> I was but bare fifteen years auld,
>     Whan first I enter'd your yates within.

Another makes the match one of interest on the girl's part :
" For he married me for love, But I married him for fee."
Be the fact as it may, the marriage was certainly an unhappy
one, whether from disparity or inadequacy of years, the singular
character of the lady, the laird's alleged brutality, or other
causes, we have now no means of judging, and the unfriendly
relations of the pair appear to have been notorious.    That the
young wife was grossly ill-treated by her husband is as much
an article of faith with the ballad-makers as are her remarkable
physical charms, but in view of her subsequent conduct we
may assume that the faults were not wholly on his side.

The indictment of Weir for the murder of John Kincaid
describes the " Guidwife of Waristoun " as having " conceived
ane deadly rancour, hatred and malice " against her husband
" for the alleged biting of her in the arm and striking her
divers times."    In two of the ballads her resentment originates
in a quarrel at the family dinner-table, when, in return for an
answer that "wasna good," the laird, with regrettable impetu-
osity, threw a plate at his wife, which cut and bled her mouth.
The incident recalls Mrs. O'Dowd's description of the Poskys'
*ménage:* "They say they've come to broken pleets."    Doubly
hurt, the lady withdrew to her chamber, where " Man's Enemie,"
recognising his opportunity, appeared to her in person and
instructed her how she might be " avenged."    In the third
ballad the injury done to the lady, though a purely moral one,
was much graver : " Whae's aught that bairn on your knee ?
. . . This bonny bairn is not mine."    She had, in fact, an infant
son at the time of the murder.

In the more prosaic version of the indictment, the evil genius of Lady Warriston was her nurse, Janet Murdo, the "fause nourice" of the ballad and a darker spirit than Juliet's famous attendant, with whom she consulted as to the best means of getting rid of her husband.

Her father, John Livingstone, who according to tradition enjoyed the precarious favour of his Sovereign, James the Sixth —"The Laird o' Dunipace," as the ballad has it, "Sat at the King's right knee"—was in attendance on His Majesty at the Palace of Holyrood House, where the Court was then in residence. Among his servants was one Robert Weir, "the horse-boy" or groom whom the nurse proposed as a suitable person to execute the dead. "I shall go seek him," said this resolute dame to her young mistress, whose cause she vigorously espoused, "and if I get him not, I shall seek another; and if I get none, I shall do it myself!" Weir, however, proved equal to the dreadful task, although the balladists, from a mistaken sense of chivalry, assign the leading part to the lady. "The said Robert" accordingly came down twice or thrice to the place of Warriston in the month of June with a view to arranging the necessary details, but, somewhat unaccountably, "he could get no speech of her." On Tuesday, 1st July, Lady Warriston again sent the nurse to Holyrood, "desiring him of new to come down to her," and that afternoon, on the arrival of Weir, a conference was held in the laird's own house "concerning the cruel, unnatural, and abominable" project. In one of the ballads the lady, by instructions of the Tempter, induces the laird that evening to exceed his usual quantity of wine:—

> So at table as they sat,
> And when they drank the wine,
> She made the glass aft gae round,
> To the Laird o' Warristoun.

The circumstances of the murder are thus described in the words of Weir's indictment, the quaintness of the ancient style aggravating the horror of the scene:—"And for performeance thairof, the said Robert Weir was secretlie convoyit to ane laich [low] seller within the said place, quhairin he abaid quhill [until] mydnycht; about the quhilk tyme he, accompaneit with the said umq$^{le}$ [late] Jeane Levingstoun, cam furth of the said laich seller up to the hall of the said place, and thairfra cam to the chalmer quhair the said umq$^{le}$ Johnne was lyand in his bed, takand the nychtis rest; and haifing enterit within the said chalmer, persaveing the said umq$^{le}$ Johnne to be walknit out of his sleip be thair dyn, and to preise ouer his bed-stok [front of his bed], the said Robert cam than rynnand to him, and maist crewallie with thair faldit neiffis [clenched fists] gaif him ane deidlie and crewall straik on the vane-organe [jugular vein], quhairwith he dang [drove] the said umq$^{le}$ Johnne to the grund out-ouer his bed; and thaireftir crewallie strak him on his bellie with his feit; quhairupoun he gaif ane grit cry. And the said Robert, feiring the cry sould haif bene hard, he thaireftir maist tyrannouslie and barbarouslie with his hand grippit him be the thrott or waisen [weasand], quhilk he held fast ane lang tyme quhill he wirreit [strangled] him; during the quhilk tyme the said Johnne Kincaid lay struggilling and fechting in the panes of daith under him. And sa the umq$^{le}$ Johnne was crewallie murdreist and slain be the said Robert."

It is noteworthy that the murderer anticipated by more than two centuries the methods whereby the miscreant Burke unwarrantably achieved the distinction of adding a new word to the dictionary.

The indictment of Weir infers that the lady was present and assisted in the deed, but says nothing either of the participation of the nurse or any other accomplice therein.

The part played by Lady Warriston in this midnight tragedy is thus described by herself to her spiritual adviser, as set forth by him in his *Memorial* of her conversion: "I think I hear presently [now] the pitifull and fearfull cryes which he gave

when he was strangled; and that vile sin which I committed
in murdering mine own husband is yet before me. Alace!
I pityed not his cryes then, but God has pityed my cryes since;
and albeit I would give him no mercy, yet my God hath given
me mercy. . . . When that horrible and fearfull sin was done,
I desyred the unhappy man who did it—for my own part, the
Lord knoweth I laid never my hands upon him to do him evil,
but as soon as that man gripped him and began his evil turn,
so soon as my husband cryed so fearfully, I leaped out over
my bed and went to the hall, where I sat all the time till that
unhappy man came to me and reported that mine husband was
dead—I desired him, I say, to take me away with him, for I
feared tryall; albeit flesh and blood made me think my father's
moen [influence] at Court would have saved me. Yet he
refused to take me with him, saying, 'You shall tarry still;
and if this matter come not to light, you shall say he died in
the gallery, and I shall return to my master's service. But
if it be known, I shall fly and take the crime on me, and none
dare pursue you.'" Weir seems to have been a magnanimous
assassin.

The ballad contains no allusion to this man's share in the
murder; the protagonists are the lady and her nurse, with the
personal assistance of the Evil One:—

> The Foul Thief knotted the tether,
>     She lifted his head on hie,
> The nourice drew the knot,
>     That gar'd Lord Waristoun die.

Discovery and retribution followed swiftly upon the deed.
How information of the fact reached the authorities in Edinburgh we do not know—

> But word's gane doun to Leith,
>     And up to Embro toun,
> That the lady she has slain the laird,
>     The laird o' Waristoun.

Next morning, however, the officers of justice entered the house of Warriston, where they found the body of the murdered laird, and apprehended the widow, together with her nurse, Janet Murdo, and two " hyred women," her domestic servants. Weir, aware that the murder was discovered, fled, and for four years evaded the penalty of his crime. Lady Warriston told her confessor : " At first, that I might seem to be innocent, I laboured to counterfeit weeping ; but do what I would, I could not finde a tear." The four women were then removed in custody to the Tolbooth, the old prison of Edinburgh, famous in fact and fiction as " The Heart of Midlothian."

By an ancient charter under the Great Seal from King James the Third the Provost and Magistrates of the city were granted an ample criminal jurisdiction as Sheriffs within their burgh, in pursuance of which they had been in use, as appears from their records, "to take tryall of Murthers and Slaughters committed within their bounds." By a subsequent statute of James the Fourth the four pleas of the Crown were exempted from their jurisdiction, a Sheriff being only entitled to judge a case of murder, in the words of that eminent authority, Sir George Mackenzie, " If the Murtherer was taken Red-hand, that is to say immediately committing the Murder, in which case he must proceed against him within three Suns."

In the circumstances of the present case, therefore, the trial took place before the Magistrates of Edinburgh instead of the Lords of Justiciary. That this course was adopted is unfortunate for students of criminology, as the greater part of the criminal records of the city of Edinburgh are lost. Even the researches of the indefatigable Pitcairn, whose mother, Maidment says, was a daughter of Kincaid of that ilk, and well acquainted with the family traditions, failed to discover any trace of the proceedings.

With regard to the guilt of the nurse and servants Lady Warriston in the *Memorial* before mentioned expresses herself as follows : " As to these weemen who was challanged with me, I will also tell you my mind concerning them. God forgive the nurse, for she helped me too well in mine evil purpose; for when I told her what I was minded to do, she consented to the doing of it; and upon the Tuesday when the turn was done, when I sent her to seek the man who would do it, she said, 'I shall go seek him, and if I get him not, I shall seek another; and if I get none, I shall do it myself.'" The author of the *Memorial* states that "this the nurse also confessed, being asked before her death." "As for the other two weemen," continues Lady Warriston, "I request that you neither put them to death nor any torture, because I testify they are both innocent and knew nothing of this deed before it was done and the mean time of the doing of it; that which they knew they durst not tell for fear, for I had compelled them to dissemble."

The trial, which, as we have seen, had to take place "within three suns," was fixed for Thursday, 3rd July, the third day after the murder. At ten o'clock that morning, according to the reverend author of the *Memorial*, "Our sermon being ended, one came to me, saying that this lady was in an evil estate, hardened in her sin, without any remorse, and therefore desired me to visit her and to deal with her as the Lord should give me power, to see if I could draw her to a confession and sorrow for what she had done." This duty the good man willingly accepted, apparently to the eternal welfare of the prisoner and certainly to the enrichment of psychologic literature, of which his contribution forms an astounding chapter. The result was recorded by him in a manuscript bearing the breathless title: " A Worthy and Notable Memorial of the great Work of Mercy which God wrought in the Conversion of Jean Livingston, Lady Warriston, who was Apprehended for the vile and horrible Murder of her own husband, John Kincaid, committed on Tuesday, July 1, 1600, for which she was Execute on Saturday following. Containing an Account of her obstinacy, earnest repentance, and her turning to God; of the odd

Speeches she used during her Imprisonment; of her great and marvellous Constancy, and of her Behaviour and manner of her Death, observed by one who was both a seer and hearer of what was spoken."

The authorship of this wondrous document is attributed by Sharpe to Mr. James Balfour, then minister of the north-west part of Edinburgh, whose colleague, Mr. Robert Bruce, the celebrated leader of the Presbyterians, was, as we shall see, called in at a later stage to consult upon what at first appeared to be a hopeless case.

> They've taen the lady and fause nourice,
>   In prison strong they hae them boun';
> The nourice she was hard o' heart,
>   But the bonny lady fell in a swoon.

So runs the ballad; but by the time of the minister's visit he found "the bonny lady" in anything but a passive condition. He describes her as "raging in a senseless furry, disdainfully taunting every word of grace that was spoken to her, impatiently tearing her hair, sometimes running up and down the house [chamber] like one possessed, sometimes throwing herself on the bed and sprawling, refusing all comfort by word, and when the book of God was brought to her, flinging it upon the walls twice or thrice most unreverently." The admonitions of her visitor "she scorned in a headfull laughter," and called his ghostly counsel "Trittle Trattle." When he pictured the blessed state of the elect she flippantly remarked, "I was never in Heaven to see that!" adding, "with a mocking laughter, 'If I go to Heaven, I go'"; nor was she more moved by his forecast of her future in another place. "I regard not," she said, "I will die but once: I care not what be done with me." This, says the reverend author, "she spoke very desperately and therewith teared her hair out of her head."

The minister had brought certain disciples to witness his treatment of this difficult case. "One standing by"

personally recommended the lady to repent of her sin, to whom
she made the pertinent rejoinder, "You will not dye for it:
I must answer for it myself," which the minister characterised
as "beastly stubborness." "However you rage and fret now
at every word I speak to you," said he, "promising yourself
impunity from the deserved punishment of your sin, yet within
a few hours, when you shall hear the sentence of death pronounced against you, you will be better tamed and the pride
of your heart will be broken in another manner." To this the
lady made no answer, " but incontinent called for a drink," and
having drunk, appropriately enough, " to contentment," threw
the cup on the floor and turned her back upon her visitor.
So he left her, expressing the hope that their next meeting
" should be more comfortable."

Shortly after his departure Lady Warriston was led out
to her trial, and, having been duly found guilty of the murder
of her husband, was condemned to die. Upon what evidence
she was convicted we cannot tell. Certainly she did not plead
guilty. We do not even know whether she was indicted as
the chief actor or merely as art and part in the crime. Weir,
the actual perpetrator, had for the time escaped, the nurse was
manifestly not of the stuff of which informers are made, and
she as well as one of the "hyred women" was also condemned.
It may be that the other servant, who does not seem to have
been brought to trial, turned King's evidence against her
mistress, or yielded to the pressing arguments of "the Boot,"
whereby in those days the prosecutor seldom failed to obtain
the requisite testimony. The lady faced the ordeal of her trial
with singular courage, and, as the minister was informed by an
eye-witness, "it was a wonder to see how little she was moved,
in so far that when the sentence of death—that she should
be hanged at a stock and afterwards burnt to ashes — was
pronounced against her, she never spoke one word, nor altered
her countenance." This horrible form of death — burning
after being "wirreit" (strangled) at the stake—was then the

usual punishment for women in such cases; in atrocious instances the criminal was "brunt quick" (burnt alive). Lady Warriston, however, was to escape this dreadful doom.

So soon as she was brought back to the Tolbooth from the place of trial the condemned woman sent for the minister whom she had treated so cavalierly in the morning. When he returned to the prison he found that his prophecy had been amply fulfilled. The lady was indeed "better tamed," whether by the workings of conscience or the extinction of her hopes we can only conjecture. Her father's interest, if exerted in her behalf, which, as we shall see, is unlikely, had failed to save her from the physical penalty of her sin. That she had relied on his influence enabling her to escape with her life would sufficiently account for her altered mind, but the minister claimed that her change of mood was truly miraculous. At a later stage of their conference, however, when he inquired the reason of her former obduracy, she answered very pitifully: "The love of this natural life, which I made ever too great estimation of, whereof I was then put in hope, notwithstanding of the evil turn I had done. The Lord forgive them that furthered me or made me loath either to confess or take upon me any guiltiness; but now, I thank God, I am otherwise minded." Here the reverend author unwittingly lets the cat out of the bag.

"Such an odd mercy, such deep feeling, and such high measure of grace," says the delighted divine, "saw I never in any creature as I saw in her, considering the ignorance and profanity of her whole life before, who had profited more in knowledge and feeling in the space of thirty-seven hours—for no longer time was between the moment of her first conversion and the time of her execution: the Lord began to work with her in mercy upon Thursday at two hours in the afternoon, and she gave up her soul to Him in peace upon the Saturday following at three hours in the morning—nor, alace! over many has done in thirty-seven years, yea, all their lifetime."

He invites the reader himself to repentance, " that this silly creature, being but a woman and a bairn of the age of twenty-one years, be not a witness against the hardness and security of our hearts."

She saluted him " very lovingly," wherein he quaintly admits he perceived a great alteration, " in respect we had parted so hardly before noon," and informed him that she found a spark of grace beginning in her.  Full of joy, the good man prayed with her at considerable length, after which she remarked: " The spark I was telling you of is grown to a great height; and immediately uttered these words : ' Lord, for mercy and grace at Thy hand for Thy dear Son, Jesus Christ His sake, to the glory of Thy mercy and the safety of my silly soul !'  This prayer had she afterwards ever in her mouth as a common proverb, that I may say she uttered five hundred times before her death."

The minister, finding the interesting penitent in so hopeful a case, " desired to hush the house that we might be keeped quiet, and so might have a better occasion to confer, being about one afternoon, from which till eight at night we were well and spiritually occupied."  During this period she dictated to him her will.   " This done, she subscribed that which I wrote; and thereafter we entered into a conference of sin, of God's mercy, and the joys of Heaven," which the lady discussed in a spirit vastly different from that exhibited by her earlier in the day, " sometimes for joy smiling, sometimes for sorrow weeping, uttering many heavenly sayings and words of great assurance," of which the minister regrets he did not make notes at the time.

At eight o'clock he withdrew for an hour's rest, and returning, found her " very joyfull at her supper, mixing her bodily feeding with words of spiritual comfort, to the great joy and contentment of very many who heard her."  The meal over, they " went to prayer " again till midnight, " at which time she desired to sleep."  The minister then left her, promising to return early in the morning, when the execution was expected to take place at nine o'clock.

Between four and five on the Friday morning the energetic pastor was back at the Tolbooth, and found that the lady was still asleep. On being assured by " them that had walked with her " that she had manifested a visible growth of grace during the night he forbore for the nonce to interrupt her slumbers, and turned his attention to the nurse. She seems to have proved a tougher subject, for he found her " very evil," and says nothing of the result of his ministrations; so, thinking that her mistress had " sleeped too long," he " caused waken her," and resumed his more fruitful labours.

The worthy minister was sufficiently human to desire that his famous colleague, Mr. Robert Bruce, should witness the triumphant result of his converting zeal, so at his suggestion that eminent man was summoned forthwith. The doughty champion of the Presbyterians was soon to make a figure in history by refusing to preach his belief in James the Sixth's incredible narrative of what occurred at Gowrie House on the afternoon of 5th August following, exactly a month after Lady Warriston's death. Rarely was " King Jamie the sapient and sext " so taken to task as by the indomitable divine, who gave " but a doubtsome trust " to that unreliable monarch's princely word.

Mr. Robert came and marvelled, as well he might. He who was soon to brave unflinchingly the wrath of an incensed Sovereign was moved to shed tears of joy. A little before his coming the lady had asked to see her infant child. Her ghostly counsellors at first were " loath to it," fearing " least the sight of him should draw her heart again after him and make her wae to leave him;" but upon her assurance to the contrary they relented, and the child was brought to her. She kissed the unconscious infant for the last time, " desired Mr. Bruce to over see him that he should be trained up in the fear of God, and sent him away without any sorrow." The minister then escorted Mr. Robert out of the Tolbooth, and presently returned with the welcome news that the prisoner's doom was altered, and that she would not be burnt, but be beheaded. This mitigation of her sentence was probably due to the social rank of her family, the "Maiden" being deemed a more genteel instrument than the stake.

None of Lady Warriston's own relatives visited her while in prison. As persons of position and influence they appear to have deeply resented the disgrace which she had brought upon them, and not only did they allow the law to take its course, but, according to Pitcairn, they had first intended and applied for the unusual hour of nine o'clock on Friday evening as the time for her execution, with a view to avoiding publicity. This, however, was overruled. Her cause must have been wholly indefensible, otherwise they could hardly have been so anxious for her speedy death.

Her father seems to have made no effort to save her life. That he possessed both influence and opportunity sufficient to do so if he had wished, appears from the statement of Mr. Gibson, in his history of the Lairds of Dunipace, that John Livingstone had been in attendance on James the Sixth since that King's earliest years, and was his intimate friend and favourite. James stayed with him at Dunipace in the following year, and subsequently gave his host a knighthood. In the ballad "the grit Dunipace" harshly repudiates his erring daughter—

> Up spak the Laird o' Dunnypace—
> Sat at the King's right knee—
> Gar nail her in a tar barrel
> And hurl her in the sea.

In one version His Majesty himself, moved by the youth and beauty of the fair criminal, offers to grant her life— "because you are of tender year"; but this the lady refuses, only asking that the form of her death may be changed—

> Cause tak' me out at night, at night,
> Lat not the sun upon me shine,
> And tak' me to yon heading-hill,
> Strike aff this dowie head o' mine.

King James grants the boon, but "a sorry man was he"—

> I've travell'd east, I've travell'd west,
> And sailed far beyond the sea,
> But I never saw a woman's face
> I was sae sorry to see dee.

Doubtless the ballad-makers exaggerate the royal sensibility, which was in no way remarkable where the sufferings of others were concerned.

On receiving the intelligence that her doom was changed Lady Warriston underwent, according to her enthusiastic confessor, a veritable transformation. "The heavenly beauty of her face at that time shined far beyond the naturall beauty that ever I saw in her heretofore," which he attributed to the Holy Spirit "decoring and beautifying His own temple as a presage of that glory she was going to." The hour of the execution was still unknown to the person chiefly interested, and as the strain was beginning to tell upon her, the minister considerately "suffered her to sleep about the space of half an hour." At mid-day, having awakened her and lifted her out of bed, he "set her on a stool," and until two o'clock continued "in heavenly exercises without intermission," during which time the lady "cast such flours of grace out of her mouth" that those who heard her "weept" for joy and admiration. "Sundry honest men, to the number of fifteen," had been invited to witness this improving spectacle. "Alace!" exclaimed the reverend exhibitor, "that we should be such unprofitable hearers of so great grace in this dear saint, that we should let so many precious words fall to the ground!" Whereupon he began to make notes of the "holy and wise sentences" uttered by "this sweet young woman," upbraiding himself the while for "a sin of grievouse ommission," in that he had "slipped so many pearles of grace which came out of her mouth hitherto." He had, however, little to reproach himself with on that score, as his memory seems to have served him wonderfully well.

The later phases of the conference, wherein the ghostly surgeon and his assistants perform a sort of *ante-mortem* examination upon their hapless subject, savour somewhat too strongly of the moral dissecting-room for non-professional readers.

When it is remembered that this girl, just out of her teens, had in the small hours of Wednesday morning superintended the murder of her own husband in circumstances of singular atrocity, on Thursday had been tried, found guilty, and condemned to a horrible death, and was thereafter for thirty-seven hours continuously exposed to the combined assaults of the ecstatic divine and his fifteen spiritual assessors, only suffered to take brief snatches of sleep from which she was roused to perform further mental gymnastics, and ever stimulated to fresh feats by the rapturous applause of her edified audience, the lay mind is apt to attribute the recorded result to causes less miraculous than natural.

During a temporary lull in these "comfortable speaches" she was reminded that the time of "flitting to God" drew near, and was asked how she was contented with it. "Many days have I lived in this vail of misery," replied the girl of twenty, "and yet had I never a contented heart unto this day. I would not lose the joyes whereof I have presently a sense for all the pleasures in the worlde." She then "fell furth" in prayer again, and afterwards called for refreshment, of which she must have stood in no common need. "I drink," said she, "to all my kind friends, yea, even to my foes, and, chiefly, I drink to all my brethern and sisters in the Lord." The honest men "exorted" her to constancy and courage. "Why should I fear death?" she replied; "I would not lose the life I am going to through this death for a thousand lives in this world."

It was now four o'clock in the afternoon of Friday, and

word came that "immediately was brought down the Maiden, with which she was to be beheaded." This instrument of death —the Scots guillotine—may still be seen at Edinburgh in the Museum of the Society of Antiquaries of Scotland. To the adaptive genius of the Regent Morton, who with much propriety is alleged to have been its first victim, Scotland is said to owe this practical improvement in the administration of justice. One is little surprised to learn that the penitent found the news welcome. Meanwhile she was afflicted by diverse rumours concerning the hour of her execution, "some at 9 a clock at night, others that it would be tymously in the morning," to the reporters whereof she remarked, "You give me many frights, but the Lord will not suffer me to be affrighted."

The fame of this notable conference having spread throughout the city " there came to the door of the prison-house severals of all ranks, who hearing by report of the strange workings of God's spirit in the heart of this saint wer very desirouse to see her and hear herself speak." The penitent was equal even to this new call upon her endurance: " I care not," said she, " who see me, that I may be an example to all both of sin and mercy "; so the multitude were admitted, overflowing the prison, to whom she uttered such " heavenly speaches as made both them that were without and those that were within to lift up our voice and weep, while in the meantime her countenance and behaviour wer most merry in the Lord." Sometimes she walked up and down, that all who came might hear and see her ; sometimes she addressed the crowd from the door—" for the dore and the stair wer never empty, but as one company departed another immediately rushed in, desiring to be comforted by her speaches." One wonders if the Tolbooth authorities had also lost their heads. "Such," says the complacent contriver of this amazing scene, "was the holy and comfortable exercise of this penitent sinner from four of the clock at night till eight of the clock, sometimes lying, sometimes going, to comfort her body, but all the time never ceasing to praise God with her mouth for His loving mercy." The burden of her discourse was that she had been "a silly sinner," who was now assured of salvation.

Presently there arose "a great din" in the street among the people waiting there to witness her execution. She looked down from her window upon the careless crowd, "sporting and taking their pleasure among themselves," and remarked, "These people laugh now; but they have cause to mourn, because not every one of them will get that great mercy and repentance which I have gotten." This she said, we are told, "very heavily"—perhaps the grapes were somewhat sour—and the probing of her lacerated conscience was resumed.

It would seem that certain profane members of the audience ventured to doubt the genuineness of this sudden conversion, as the miracle-worker himself candidly admits. "I grant that these speaches of hers and the great boldness and access which she had in her to God seemed incredible to many, being wrought in such a short time"; but he adopts the explanation of the penitent herself—"It is not I who speaks, but it is the Lord who possesses me that speaketh it within me." "Ther is no temptation of the devil can now get entry in me," she boastfully adds; but the next moment she is showing herself at the window to the people climbing up to the house tops to obtain a glimpse of her, which, in a less saintly person, might savour of the "grievouse sin" of vanity.

When reproached for her former negligence in matters of religion, she deprecated church-going except in the proper spirit, failing which, as she wisely observed, "they will weary more sitting in the kirk one hour than in ten days spent in vice."

At eight o'clock a brief truce was called for supper. "I sup with you this night," said she, "but I will sup with the Lord to-morrow." The entertainment appears to have been excellent, and the appetites of the party suffered nothing by reason of its ominous surroundings. "A more comfortable did I eat never any," is the minister's comment. The spiritual level of the

conversation was maintained during the meal, "as the question
fell in concerning the malice of the Tempter." On its conclusion
the guests arose from the table for public prayer, after which
the lady returned to her wonted exercises, "casting furth such
flushes of grace to us as God gave her occasion to utter." At
ten o'clock she retired, but not to rest, for the pastor and his
disciples, with some lack of taste, remained in the chamber.
"Notwithstanding, she lay not idle in her bed, but still delighted
us with her holy speaches."

About midnight she conferred apart with her confessor,
when "many things wer spoken to and fro." Here for the
first time they condescended to mundane affairs. "She purged
herself very sincerely from many scandalouse things she had
been bruitted with, that she might clear herself from those
false reports that her house was charged with." This evidently
has reference to some scandal of the nature alluded to in one
of the ballads—her alleged infidelity to her husband, perhaps
with Robert Weir. She then gave the minister the account of
her own share in the murder which has been already quoted.
With regard to her intention to make her escape with Weir
when the deed was done, she said, "Now if I had fled with that
unhappy man at that time, what would have become of me?
No doubt I should have born about a heavy sin whereof I am
now relieved in God's mercy. And what would have been mine
estate? No doubt I should have been a vagabond and drawn
to harlotry and many other sins." It seems probable that there
was something unexplained in the relations between Lady
Warriston and her husband's murderer.

At three o'clock in the morning of Saturday, 5th July, this
wonderful conference was abruptly closed by the arrival of
the Magistrates of Edinburgh, who were "brought into the
prison by her friends" (relatives) to take her out to her death.
Some of these, in the minister's opinion, were "too earnest to
hast her away that she might be execute before any should
know of it." Her family, as has been mentioned, had shown

throughout an indecent anxiety to get their erring kinswoman quietly and expeditiously despatched, and having failed as to the Friday night, this was their latest move. The pastor opposed it on religious grounds: "Will you deprive God's people of that comfort which they might have in this poor woman's death? Will you obstruct the honour of it by putting her away before the people rise out of their beds?" The magistrates were willing that she should "stay till sunrising, but her friends were so importunate, that it was not granted." Her husband's brother, who was of the party, showed more humanity: he kissed the girl and forgave her before she was led to the scaffold.

On the way to the place of execution, which was at the Girth Cross, the ancient boundary of the Abbey Sanctuary at the foot of the Canongate, she behaved herself "so cheerfully as if she had been going to her wedding and not to her death." When she came to the scaffold, a stage or platform erected in the centre of the street, she looked up at the "Maiden" with "two longsome looks, for she had never seen it before," noting which the minister bade her be not afraid. "This is but a dead enimy," said he, "a piece of wood and iron; there is no death here but a parting, and entering into a better life. . . . You have been those few hours bygone putting on your harnass within the house; now the Lord has brought you to the field to use your weapons. . . . As to your burial and honourable handling of your corps, tell your will to your friends here present and it shall be done." This, he adds, "was done very honourably."

Though it was then barely four o'clock in the morning a great crowd surged around the scaffold, to whom, from each of the four corners in turn, she addressed her last speech and dying confession, which she delivered with such courage and dignity that many said, "This woman is ravished with a higher spirit than man or woman's." This done she bade her friends "good night," and the minister "convoyed her by the arms" to the place of her expiation. Lady Warriston then desired him to give her to God out of his own hand. His final offices in her behalf, which he reports at length, savour, as Sharpe observes, "more of the absolution of a Roman Catholic priest, than the pious and earnest prayers of a Protestant divine." On receipt of these assurances she laughed for joy. The pastor, however, was so affected by her farewell words that he left the scaffold and departed.

She maintained to the end a fortitude in the circumstances truly remarkable, justifying the encomium of Birrel—"quha diet verie patiently." A clean cloth being brought to bind her eyes, "to the fastening thereof she took out of her mouth a pin and gave it out of her own hand"—

> Tak aff this gowd brocade,
> But let my petticoat be ;
> And tie a kerchief round my face,
> That the people may not see.

She submitted "sweetly and graciously" to the executioner s orders, laid her head upon the block, and, holding the hand of one of her friends, calmly awaited the event. During this time, which was long, for the axe was but slowly loosed and "fell not down hastily," she ceased not to pray aloud. "Into thy hands, O Lord, . . . " she cried; and at the pronouncing of the words the axe fell.

At the same hour of that summer morning Janet Murdo, "the fause nourice," and one of the "hyred women" were, in terms of their fearful sentence, duly "wirreit" at the stake and burned upon the Castle Hill. No record of their trial has been preserved. They were at least more fortunate than their mistress, in that their last hours were not made the occasion of such scenes as those by which hers were disfigured. The nurse, as we have seen, was certainly a prime mover in the murder and deserved her fate. The other, who was exonerated by her mistress while in prison, probably suffered as an accessory after the fact. If, as appears to have been the case, their

execution was fixed for the same untimely hour as that of
Lady Warriston at the suggestion of her susceptible relatives,
in order to afford a counter-attraction for the populace, the
device failed, the less lurid spectacle proving the greater
draw.

Not until four years later was Justice able to bring the
absconding "horse-boy" to account. The trial of Robert Weir
took place at Edinburgh in the Justice Court, on 26th June
1604, before Mr. (afterwards Sir) William Hart, the Justice-
Depute, who in 1608 presided at the trial of George Sprot,
the Eyemouth notary, for alleged complicity in the so-called
Gowrie Conspiracy. The indictment, verdict, and sentence are
printed by Pitcairn, but of the circumstances of Weir's arrest
nothing is known. The "Perseweris" or private prosecutors
were Patrick, Thomas, Archibald, and Adam Kincaid, "all
brether to the defunct." Patrick, who is designed as "tutour
of Wariestoune," was no doubt the guardian of his infant
nephew. The indictment sets forth the manner of the
murder, as before related. No witnesses appear to have
been called, and the jury, "in respect of his Confessioun maid
thairof in Judgement," found the prisoner "ffylit" (guilty) of
the crime libelled. Sentence of death was then pronounced
by the mouth of James Sterling, dempster of Court, in terms
so unusual as to warrant quotation:—"Discernit and ordanit
the said Robert Weir to be tane to ane skaffold to be fixt
besyde the Croce of Edinburgh, and thair to be brokin upoune
ane Row [wheel] quhill he be deid, and to ly thairat during
the space of xxiiij houris. And thaireftir his body to be
tane upone the said Row and set up in ane publict place betwixt
the place of Warestoun and the toun of Leyth; and to remane
thairupoune ay and quhill command be gevin for the buriall
thairof. Quhilk is pronouncet for dome."

Pitcairn notes this as the first recorded instance of such
punishment having been inflicted in Scotland, but he himself
has printed in his invaluable work a similar sentence pro-

nounced upon John Dickson, convicted of parricide on 30th April 1591.    This horrible form of execution, which was unknown in England, was borrowed from the practice of France and Germany, and was apparently adopted in these two cases to impress the public mind with a due sense of the exceptional atrocity of the respective crimes.

Birrell thus records in his *Diary* the execution of the sentence:—"The 16 [26 ?] of Junii 1604 Robert Weir broken on ane cart-wheel, with ane coulter of ane pleuche [plough], in the hand of the hangman, for murdering of the guidman of Warriston, quhilk he did 2 Julii 1600."

Thus was the Laird of Warriston at length avenged.  The tragic story, as evidenced by the ballads, caught the popular imagination and assumed the importance of a legend.  The account of the lady's conversion certainly exhibits an interesting case of conscience, and as such is of value to the student of metaphysics, but there is need for the caution given by Sharpe against the mischievous tendency of a work which teaches that a sinner, though stained with the worst of crimes, may be transformed into a "sweet saint of God" in the twinkling of an eye—"then is crime cheap, for penitence is easy." This warning applies with even greater force to the confession of the Black Laird of Ormistoun, one of Darnley's murderers, who, in extenuation of his crimes, remarked that within seven years he never saw two good men nor one good deed, but all kind of wickedness, yet was able, on the day of his hanging, to say that he hoped to sup with God, being "assurit that he was ane of His Elect."

# TOUCHING ONE MAJOR WEIR, A WARLOCK

> In rangles round before the ingle's lowe
>   Frae gudame's mouth auld warld tales they hear
> O' warlocks loupin' round the wirrikow,
>   O' ghaists that win in glen and kirk-yard drear,
>   Whilk touzles a' their tap, and gars them shak wi' fear.
> > —*The Farmer's Ingle*, ROBERT FERGUSSON.

THACKERAY once complained that since the author of *Tom Jones* was buried no writer of fiction has been permitted to depict a man. What, then, must be the plight of him who would show forth a veritable monster ? So I have chosen this old-fashioned title as indicating that it is not here intended to do more than touch the major, and that gingerly, as the phrase goes, and with a nice discretion. But despite these reservations there is much in his strange story worth retelling to such as are interested in the curiosities of psychology, while for the lover of old Edinburgh Major Weir shares with his successor, Captain Porteous, and with Deacon Brodie, the distinction of having preserved, amid so much that has been improved out of existence, if not a local habitation, at least a name.

The major, though in his day a stalwart of the Covenant, and, as Stevenson describes him, " the outcome and fine flower of dark and vehement religion," for obvious reasons finds no place in Presbyterian martyrology. The sources of information regarding his extraordinary career are the official report of his trial in the Justiciary Record; an unpublished MS. of 1670 in the Advocates' Library, Edinburgh, by the Rev. James Fraser, minister of Wardlaw, who knew the major in the flesh; the rare old tract, *Ravaillac Redivivus*, by Dr. George Hickes, Dean of Worcester, published anonymously at London in 1678; and that curious collection of wonderful relations, *Satan's Invisible World Discovered*, by Mr. George Sinclair, "late Professor of Philosphy in the Colledge of Glasgow," and afterwards minister of Eastwood in Renfrewshire, first printed at Edinburgh in 1685. The professor, in his account of Weir, borrows largely and without acknowledgment from Mr. Fraser's "Providential Passages," as above. Other contemporary references are contained in Lamont's *Diary* and in Law's *Memorials*.

"If I were ever to become a writer of romances," said Sir Walter Scott in 1798, sixteen years before *Waverley*, "I think I would choose Major Weir, if not for my hero, at least for an agent, and a leading one, in my production." Unfortunately he never did so, but in these later days the major, suitably draped, has made his appeal to the general reader in an excellent novel bearing his name by another hand.

Thomas Weir, Scotland's most notable wizard, was born at Kirkton, near Carluke, in Clydesdale, in 1599. His father, Thomas Weir of Kirkton, receives unfavourable mention in the *Memoirs* of the Somerville family as a person capable on occasion of domestic treachery, while his mother, according to the confession of his sister Jean, was a sorceress of repute, who bore upon her brow a witch-mark enabling her to tell "the secretest thing that any of the family could do, though done at a great distance." For the matron's peace of mind it is to be hoped that this gift was rarely exercised. Of the boyhood and youth of Thomas we have no record, but from the indictment upon which he was afterwards tried we gather that his earlier years were spent with his family in their "House of Wicketshaw." Mention of him occurs in connection with the granting of a conveyance by his father, with his consent, of part of the lands of Waggetshaw in 1632. He is said to have acted as a lieutenant in the Puritan army under Leslie's command sent by the Scots Estates in 1641 to assist in suppressing the Irish Catholics. He was also an officer in the Covenanting forces during Montrose's campaign of 1644-45, as appears from an entry in the register of the estates quoted by Sinclair, when on 3rd March 1647 the major applied for arrears of pay due to him in respect of "his service as Major in the Earl of Lanark's regiment by the space of twell months, and his service in Ireland as ane Captain-Lieutenant in Colonel Robert Home his regiment by the space of nineteen months." He further craved "that the Parliament wald ordain John Acheson, Keeper of the Magazine, to redeliver to the supplicant the band [bond] given by him to the said John upon the receipt of ane thousand weight of poulder, two thousand weight of match, and a thousand pound weight of ball, sent with the supplicant to Dumfries for furnishing that part of the country." How the petition sped is not recorded.

The year 1649, which saw King Charles the Martyr lay upon the block at Whitehall "that comely head," found Major Weir retired from active service, settled in Edinburgh, and occupying the honourable post of Captain of the City Guard. It has been constantly stated that to this appointment he owed the designation of major, but there is no doubt, as we have seen, he already held that rank. This venerable body of armed police had its origin in the fears besetting the citizens after the fatal defeat of Flodden, but the belief in its extreme antiquity is evidenced by an old Edinburgh legend that some of the Guard were present in Jerusalem at the Crucifixion, and, during the commotion which ensued, carried off from the Temple an original portrait of King Solomon, which long was piously preserved in proof of the tradition ! But once in its lengthy and chequered career does the City Guard emerge from mere local annals into the strong light of history under the celebrated captaincy of John Porteous. The events attending the murder of that unhappy officer, and the utter inability displayed by the guardians of the King's peace to discharge their duty upon that occasion, nearly brought about their abolition. Towards the end of the eighteenth century the strength and prestige of the ancient corps had much declined, and lovers of Fergusson's racy muse will recall his frequent thrusts at "that black banditti, the City Guard." By the year 1817 the last survivors of an outworn system had ceased to struggle against the innovating spirit which permeated the Scottish capital, and, along with many things much worthier of preservation, were swept into the dust-bin of the past.

During his early days in Edinburgh the major lodged for some years with a widow, one Mrs. Grissald Whitford, who dwelt in the Cowgate in a house which, if still standing, cannot now be identified. There, according to Dr. Hickes, "that dishonour of Mankind" had for fellow-boarder the conventicle-preacher, Mr. James Mitchell, assassin and martyr, who was hanged in 1678 for the attempted murder of Archbishop Sharp, as his indictment says, "in the High Street of Edinburgh and in the face of the sun." If we may believe a contemporary rhyming "satyr" on his memory, the character of Widow Whitford's abode rendered it a somewhat singular retreat for a godly young man. Be that as it may, the political and religious views of his companion seem to have stimulated the major's martial spirit, which since the fall of Montrose had no worse opposition to contend with than that of the Edinburgh rabble, for in 1650 he became an eminent promoter of the "Western Remonstrance," though his professional duties prevented his joining its active supporters in arms. "To these principles he stuck as close as to the Devil himself; insomuch that when the Government of the Church was restored, he avowedly renounced the Communion of it, and endeavoured to widen the Schism to the utmost of his power. He could not so much as endure to look upon an Orthodox Minister, but when he met any of them in the Streets, he would pull his Hat over his eyes in a Pharisaical kind of indignation and contempt."

As might be expected in so uncompromising an adherent of the Covenant, when "dressed in a little brief authority," the major enjoyed to the full the advantage which his office afforded of maltreating such unfortunate Royalists as came within his

clutches.  He was " very active in discovering and apprehending
the Cavaliers and bringing them to be arraing'd and try'd for
their lives.   He used to insult and triumph over them in their
miseries, and persecute them with all manner of Sarcasms
and Reproaches when they were led out like Victims to public
execution, as many yet alive can testifie to the World.   This
cruel manner after which he used to outrage the poor Royalists
pass'd among the people for extraordinary zeal, and made them
consider him a singular Worthy whom God had raised up to
support the Cause."   But the proudest moment of the major's
life was when fate delivered into his official hand his old enemy
Agag, the gallant James Graham, who, after his capture in
the north, was brought to Edinburgh to die.   The warding of
prisoners awaiting trial and attendance at their execution
were part of the Town Guard's duties.   How ably these were
discharged by Major Weir in this instance the following contemporary account will show :—" The barbarous Villain treated
the Heroick Marquess of Montrose with all imaginable insolence
and inhumanity when he lay in Prison ; keeping him in a Room
in which was no other light than that of a Candle, and his
lighted Tobacco, which he continually smoked with him, tho'
the Marquess had an aversion to the smell of it above anything
in the World."   That Major Weir was a heavy smoker supplies
an unexpected touch of nature which his Satanic personality
could ill afford so to pervert.   " Nay," continues our author,
" he would even disturb him in his Devotions, making his
very calamities an Argument that God as well as man had
forsaken him ; and calling him Dog, Athiest, Traytor, Apostate,
Excommunicate Wretch, and many more such intolerable names."
This did the major exult after his fashion over the fate of
the great marquess, whom later he escorted to the scaffold ; and
twenty more years of his own flagitious life were yet to run
before the fire was kindled for himself upon the Gallow Lee.

Prominent in any plan of older Edinburgh is the crooked
line of the West Bow, which ran abruptly down from the head

of the High Street, whence it formed the main thoroughfare to the Grassmarket in the valley on the south. Of this curious zigzag descent, which is said to have been one of the most ancient and characteristic streets in the old town, naught but the name has escaped the "improving" mania of our fore-fathers. The Bow was long the peculiar domain of the white or tinsmiths, and so godly was the repute of its indwellers at the time of which we write, that they had earned for them-selves the title of the Bowhead Saints. The denizens of this favoured quarter must have hailed with holy joy the arrival among them of Major Weir, when, on an unascertained date, he withdrew his patronage from the dubious widow of the Cowgate and pitched his tent within "the sanctified bends of the Bow."

The records of the Town Guard preserved in the City Chambers unfortunately do not extend so far back as to in-clude the period of the major's service, which seems to have lasted for at least two years. After his resignation or dismissal, having ceased to interfere in the wordly affairs of his fellow-citizens, he had the more leisure to devote himself to their spiritual concerns. Then, as now, people were to a large extent appraised at their own valuation, and as the major was an imposing personality in more senses than one, and laid claim to phenomenal sanctity, his pre-eminence among the Bowhead Saints was speedily assured. "He became," says Mr. Fraser, "so notoriously regarded among the Presbyterian strict sect, that if four met together, be sure Major Weir was one." His deportment, we are told, was marked by a formal gravity "and demureness in his looks," a prodigious memory enabled him to quote Scripture with fluency and ease, while his gift of extem-pore prayer was deemed miraculous, both before and, as we shall see, after his exposure. He had acquired, says Dr. Hickes, "a particular gracefulness in whining and sighing above any of the sacred clan, and had learn'd to deliver himself upon all serious occasions in a far more ravishing accent than any of their

Ministers could attain unto." Soon no "house-conventicle" of
the elect could with propriety be held unless the wonderful
major presided, and indeed so great became his popularity
that it was said, "Happy was the Man with whom he would
converse, and blessed was the Family in which he would vouch-
safe to pray." But the business instincts of this inspired
professor were too shrewd to let custom stale his infinite
variety. He would pray only in the families of such as were
"Saints of the highest Form," with the gratifying result that
" the Brethern and Sisters of those Precincts would strive who
should have him to exercise in their Houses," and " To meet
Major Weir" would insure the acceptance of any invitation.
Gradually the fame of his signal gifts outgrew the narrow limits
of the Bow, and people would come forty or fifty miles to have
the happiness to hear him pray. "Conceived prayer" was the
major's speciality. He never undertook to preach, "for fear of
invading the Ministerial Province," which certainly would have
kindled the wrath of the Kirk. The fact that the supplicant
"could not officiat in any holy duty without his Rod in his hand,
leaning upon it," was remarked at the time, but the full extent
of the major's dependence upon his famous staff was not appreciated till later. He was thought more angel than man, says
the contemporary minister, Mr. Fraser, whose criticisms are
perhaps not without some slight leaven of professional jealousy,
and by some of the holy sisters was happily named Angelical
Thomas. The same authority gives us the only impression we
have of Major Weir's personal appearance, a sketch which took
captive the imagination of Stevenson: "His garb was still a
cloak, and somewhat dark, and he never went without his staff.
He was a tall black man, and ordinarily looked down to the
ground; a grim countenance, and a big nose."

We have two pictures of the tenement hallowed by the
occupancy of this choice spirit, which of old rose upon the east
or left-hand side of the street at the first turn in descending
the West Bow, and was long known as Major Weir's *Land*—the

quaint etching by Skene of Rubislaw, representing the sup-
posititious turret of the major's dwelling as viewed from the
Bow, and the bald little woodcut in Chambers's *Reekiana*,
showing the actual house, seen from the inner court. The
entrance to the front building from the street was by a stone
turnpike stair—once so common a feature of Edinburgh archi-
tecture—the door of which bore the inscription, "Soli deo
honor et gloria," with the date 1604; but a low vaulted *transe*
or passage immediately adjoining led through the tall *land*
to a narrow court behind, in which, sinister and solitary, stood
the wizard's dread abode. It is said that he had cast a spell
upon the neighbouring turnpike stair, despite its pious motto,
to the effect that whoso attempted the ascent felt as if, instead
of mounting, he were descending the steps. "No other story
of witchcraft and necromancy," says Sir Daniel Wilson, "ever
left so deep-rooted an impression on the popular mind as that
of Major Weir; nor was any spot ever more celebrated in the
annals of sorcery than the little court at the head of the Bow,
where the wizard and his sister dwelt."

As to this unfortunate woman, criminal and lunatic, we must
now say a word. Her Christian name has been a matter of
dispute. Sinclair and Law refer to her as Jean, which Dr.
Hickes renders Jane for his English readers; Fraser, the contemporary authority before quoted, calls her Grizel; but she
was indicted and tried in the name of Jean Weir, which settles
the point. It is generally said that the major never married,
but from the record of his trial we find that he was formerly
married to a widow named Mein, who had a daughter, Margaret,
by her first husband. The major's behaviour to his stepdaughter
was the subject of one of the charges in his indictment. Probably he had been long a widower, and for many years his sister
lived with him and kept his house. In view of their subsequent
trial it is necessary to add that their relations were those of
Hilarion and Palmyre Bouteroue, in Zola's *La Terre*. Jean was
an indefatigable spinster. Day by day during her evil life the

hum of her necromantic spinning vibrated through the dark chambers, and for years after her shameful death the midnight wayfarer down the Bow would be arrested at the Bends by the rhythm of that ghostly wheel.

Few men are so individual as to present on inspection a single personality; in the most blameless of Jekylls there too often lurks some strain of the indigenous Hyde—" which makes this speckled Face of Honesty in the World." Like the celebrated Deacon Brodie, Major Weir's life was lived variously in diverse sorts of company; but whereas the deacon was merely a capable cabinetmaker by day, and by night but an indifferent burglar, the major's complex character enabled him to play simultaneously three distinct parts, each of which he sustained for many years with equally marked success. With Weir the saint we have already dealt, of Weir the sinner it is not proposed to treat, but Weir the warlock has still to be considered. Of the manner in which the major in his second rôle abused the confidence of the holy sisters as their spiritual director, of his more recondite gallantries and astral amours, and of his other manifold and great impieties we cannot here speak, but one incident may be referred to as explaining the immunity from punishment which he so long enjoyed. It appears upon his own confession that a certain damsel, in consequence of what she observed of his conduct in a field "at New Mills in the West Country," whither the major had ridden from Edinburgh "to a solemn meeting," complained of him to Mr. John Nave, the minister of New Mills, at whose instance he was brought back to the place by some soldiers, " but was there dismissed for want of further probation [proof]; and the woman that delated him for the fact near New Mills was, by order of the magistrates of Lanark, whipped through the town by the hand of the common hangman, as a slanderer of such an eminent Holy Man "! Her fate was little calculated to encourage talebearing to the saint's detriment. Twenty years later, however, the lady had her revenge, when she gave evidence for the

4

prosecution at the major's trial, and she was probably an interested spectator of the subsequent ceremony at the Gallow Lee, of which he was the central figure.

The ability displayed by Major Weir in his several capacities was explained as the result of a compact with the Prince of Darkness, who, in consideration of the price customary in such bargains, had engaged to warrant the other party to the trans- action against all mortal dangers "except one burn." How the devil, according to his wont, paltered with the major in a double sense will presently appear. In support of this theory Sinclair records that upon one occasion during Weir's captaincy of the Town Guard, while going his nightly rounds to inspect the ports—the old city gates of mediæval Edinburgh—he found the waiters (gatekeepers) at the Nether Bow absent from their post and the port unguarded. The major unearthed the delin- quents from an adjacent cellar, where they were " taking a cup of Aile," and sharply reprimanded them for their neglect of duty. They pleaded as excuse that they had but abandoned their charge for the moment in order to have a drink "with their old Friend and Acquaintance, Mr. Burn." "At which word," continues the narrator, "he started back, and casting an eye upon them, repeated the word 'Burn' four or five times." The major, white and trembling, retired precipitately home, and kept the house for some weeks afterwards. It was also observed that when going in company to Liberton " he shunned to step over that Water-brook which is ordinarily called Liberton Burn, but went about to shun it." Evidently the major believed that by taking thought he could still get the best of the bargain, but his spoon was not long enough for those who, as warned by the proverb, would sup with the Enemy unscathed.

The end came with startling and dramatic suddenness. On a certain day of obligation among the Bowhead Saints, in the early spring of the year 1670, the gloomy audience chamber of their high priest was thronged by a great gathering of the faithful. The company included a brother of Professor Sinclair,

the discoverer of Satan's invisible world, one "Maister John
Sinclaire," a conventicle-minister of Ormiston, who probably
attended in the hope of gleaning some professional hint from
the methods of the popular prophet.  Major Weir was then
in the seventieth year of his treble life, a failing man, long
"harassed below a mountain of duplicity," and still pursuing
in despite of time the course of his incredible vices.  The pre-
liminaries over, amid an inspiring hush Angelical Thomas
rose to address his complacent disciples for the last time.
Whether the "Magical Staff," upon whose diabolic aid his
eloquence depended, suddenly failed him; whether his conscience, seared by unnumbered crimes, suffered some tardy
pang; or whether, as is most likely, his reason reeled beneath
the intolerable burden of such prolonged hypocrisy, we cannot
tell; but, instead of the usual "Enthusiastical phrases, Extasies,
and Raptures" wherewith he was wont to transport his silly
flock, the unhappy man poured forth a full confession "of his
particular sins which he was guilty of, which bred amazement
to all persons, they coming from a man of so high a repute of
Religion and Piety."

Picture the scene in that crowded upper room, the theatre
of so many former triumphs—the smug self-righteousness of
those burgher faces smitten as by a thunderbolt into horror
and dismay, the once angelic voice offending silence with the
items of that monstrous category, while spurred by some
unknown power the terrible old man stripped off relentlessly,
rag by rag, the cloak of his spurious sanctity.  How the ears
of the holy sisters must have tingled!  Idols have been cast
down ere now by the devotees of rival gods, or have fallen by
mere neglect of their own worshippers, but here was one voluntarily overthrown, and shattered into nameless fragments by
his single act.

"Before God," cried the miserable wretch, "I have not told
you the hundred part of that I can say more, and am guilty
of!"  But the congregation had heard enough.  Measures were

at once concerted "with all possible care and industry" to bury the knowledge of this "confounding scandal" within the bosom of the elect. It was given out that the saint had been seized with illness—and little doubt he was a broken man. For several months the affair was screened successfully from the profane. The "godly plants of the Bowhead" had now the whip-hand of their oracle, and the reputation of the Bow might yet be saved. But the major's infernal creditor was not to be balked of his due so easily. One of the ministers—was it he of Ormiston?—actuated, as regrettably appears, by professional spite, denounced the unveiled prophet to Sir Andrew Ramsay of Abbotshall, then Lord Provost of Edinburgh, who in the following year became a Senator of the College of Justice. His lordship, "judging humane nature uncapable of such horrid crimes as the Minister told him the Major had confessed," considered the case as one calling rather for medical than criminal treatment. He therefore sent certain physicians of his acquaintance to visit the patient "and Physick him for his distempered Brain." The doctors, however, having seen him, reported to the provost that the major was in good health, "that he was free from Hypocondriack Distempers," and that his "Intellectuals" or mental faculties were perfectly sound. They found him suffering from "only an exulcerated Conscience," which, in their opinion, could not be relieved till he was brought to justice, "as with cryings and roarings he desir'd to be." The provost was still unwilling to believe the worst. He requested "some Conventicle-Ministers" to inquire into the major's condition and to report. These spiritual physicians, "finding it was impossible to disguise the matter which now was Town-talk," concurred in the views already stated by their medical brethren: "The terrors of God which were upon his Soul urged him to confess and accuse himself." Official ignorance of the scandal could no longer be maintained, so the provost sent the Town Guard to apprehend their old officer and his sister Jean, who was implicated in his confession, and to carry them both to the

Tolbooth, the Bastille of Auld Reekie. The arrests were effected "in the night time," in presence of two of the magistrates. When the prisoners were seized, Jean urged the bailies to secure the major's staff, as, if he once had it in his hand, "he would certainly drive them all out of doors, notwithstanding all the resistance they could make." So the wizard's wand was duly impounded, as also were certain sums of money found in the house, wrapped "in several clouts" (rags).

"This Magical Staff," says Dr. Hickes, " was all of one piece, upon which were Engraved certain Symbols in the shape of Centaures, with a crooked head of Thorn-wood. She said he received it of the Devil and did many wonderful things with it; particularly that he used to lean upon it in his Hypocritical Prayers; and after they were committed she still desired it might be kept from him, because if he were Master of it again he would certainly grow obdurate, and retract the Confessions he had so publickly made. Apollonius Thyaneus had such a Magical Staff as this, which I am apt to believe was a Sacramental Symbol which the Devil gave to the Major, and the Court were not without some apprehensions of it for it was ordered by the judges to be burnt with his Body; and it was afterwards observed that his body did not fall into the Flames till that staff had first done so." The major, when in prison, acknowledged his indebtedness to this familiar, and confessed that he never " bow'd the knee at his own or other men's prayers," but stood always leaning upon his staff, a practice which had been long noted by his disciples.

When they had seen their prisoners safely under lock and key, the two bailies adjourned to a tavern in the West Bow, taking with them the major's money, which was there put into a bag and the clouts thrown into the fire. These, "after an unusual manner, made a circling and dancing" as they burned. Another cloth containing "a certain root," also found in the warlock's den, was similarly disposed of, "which circled and sparkled like Gunpowder, and passing from the Funnel of the

Chimney, it gave a crack like a little Cannon, to the amazement of all that were present." The money was taken home by one of the bailies and laid by in a closet, but the family could get no rest "for a terrible noise within the Study like the falling of a house," so the accursed coins were sent to the other bailie's, where they caused a like disturbance. Probably he broke the spell by spending them, for we hear no more of the matter.

While the major lay in the Tolbooth awaiting his trial, all sorts of clerical artillery was brought to bear upon him, from the great guns of the establishment, like my Lord Bishop of Galloway and the Dean of Edinburgh, to irregular sharpshooters of his own persuasion. But the major since his downfall was indifferent even to sectarian shades. "Sirs," said he to his reverend visitors, "you are now all alike to me." He was willing enough to horrify them with personal reminiscences, but firmly withstood their exhortations to repentance, remarking that he was already damned, and that the united prayers of all the saints in heaven and earth would be vain if offered in his behalf. "One minister (now asleep) asking him if he should pray for him, was answered, 'Not at all.' The other replied in a kind of holy anger, 'Sir, I will pray for you in spite of your teeth and the Devil your master too.'" Finally the prisoner thus adjured the well-meaning divines: "Torment me not before the time"; and they threw up the case as hopeless. Law says in his *Memorials* that the major's obduracy was due to characteristic craftiness; "that now since he was to goe to the Devil he would not anger him."

Jean Weir, though equally impervious to ghostly counsel, was more communicative than her inscrutable brother as to their Satanic dealings. She had inherited, she said, her witchcraft from her mother, together with an unholy mark upon her brow, which she exhibited to the ministers then present. "She put back her head-dress, and seeming to frown, there was seen an exact Horse-shoe shaped for nails in her wrinckles "— "terrible enough, I assure you, to the stoutest beholder," says an eye-witness. She added that her brother having on one occasion "desyred her to claw his back," she found upon his shoulder "that which they call the Devil's Mark." Sir Walter Scott, by the way, borrowed Jean Weir's horse-shoe frown for *Redgauntlet*, and bestowed the major's name upon Sir Robert's "great, ill-favoured jackanape." Jean admitted that she and her brother had made a compact with the devil, "and that on the 7th of September, 1648, they were both transported from Edinburgh to Musselburgh and back again in a Coach and six Horses, which seemed all of fire, and that the Devil then told the Major of the defeat of our army at Preston in England, which he confidently reported several days before the news had arrived here"—a prophecy the fulfilment of which much enhanced the major's reputation with the godly. Other accounts refer the major's special intelligence to the battle of Worcester, with which, however, Jean's date does not agree. "She knew much of the inchanted Staff, for by it he was enabled to pray, to commit filthinesse not to be named, yea even to reconcile Neighbours, Husband and Wife, when at variance." This latter property must have proved a valuable antidote to the major's personal influence in the marital affairs of his flock, which tended rather in the opposite direction. She further confessed "that when she keeped a school at Dalkeith and teached childering"—how Mr. Squeers would have appreciated such "a educator of youth"!—a tall woman came to her house when the children were there, with the request that she should "spick for her to the Queen of Fairie, and strik and battle in her behalf with the said Queen." This royal lady "is that very Mab" who, under the style and title of Quene of Elphane, figures for the first time in our criminal records at the trial of Alison Pearson for witchcraft on 15th May 1588. Next day a little woman came, who gave the schoolmistress "a piece of a tree or root"—perhaps the identical root whose explosion had so amazed the bailies—telling her that as long as she kept it "she would be able to doe what she should desyre." After certain necromantic ceremonies, not the least important of which was the delivery to her visitant of "all the silver she hade," the woman departed, and Jean, sitting down to her spinning-wheel, "did find more yearn upon her pirne [spindle], and good yearn, nor [than] she thought could be spun in so short a time." Yet, despite this miraculous gift, the devil cheated her after all, as he did the major, "for her Weaver could not make cloath thereof, the yearn breaking or falling from the Loom."

On Saturday, 9th April 1670, the wicked old couple were placed at the bar of the Justice Court before "that learned Civilian, Mr. William Murray, and Mr. John Preston, Justice-Deputes." The prosecution was conducted by the Lord Advocate, Sir John Nisbet of Dirleton, the author of the historic *Doubts*, but no counsel seems to have been bold enough to undertake the defence of the prisoners. They were tried together upon separate indictments, that of the major laying more stress upon his dealings with creatures of flesh and blood than with the occult powers of darkness; his sister Jean, in addition to another crime, was charged with specific acts of sorcery. Both libels having been read and duly found relevant, "The King's Advocate caused interrogate the Major judicially anent his guilt, who answered, he thinks himself guilty of the foresaid Crimes and cannot deny them; and the King's Advocate takes Instruments that he refuses to answer posatively." In view of this, as there was nothing against the pannels except their extrajudicial confessions, the Lord Advocate proceeded to lead evidence for the Crown. Four witnesses deponed that they were present when Major Weir made his memorable statement and heard him confess the crimes libelled, while many others gave damning testimony to his actual misdeeds. The Reverend Mr. Sinclair, who had been throughout very busy in the case, swore that the major sent for him from the Tolbooth "of purpose to confess his sins to him," and had also solicited his prayers, which, in view of other evidence as to the major's then

frame of mind seems, to say the least, unlikely. A new item of
iniquity was alleged to have been elicited from the penitent by
this conventicle-confessor, namely, "that he had converse with
the Devill in the night time." Arnot, commenting in his
*Criminal Trials* on this incident, justly remarks, "I leave it to
casuists in religion to determine as to the efficacy of auricular
confession in the salvation of the soul; but I cannot help
thinking that for a priest to reveal this confession in a
criminal court to the destruction of the body, deserves to
be placed nigh at the top of the scale of human depravity."
In the end the major, seeing that the game was up, judicially
acknowledged the truth of the charges. His sister followed
suit, and confessed to the Court "all the Sorcerys as in the
lybell." So the jury found them both guilty, and sentence
of death was pronounced as follows: Major Weir to be taken
on Monday the 11th inst. to the Gallow Lee between Leith and
Edinburgh, and there, "betwixt two and four hours in the afternoon," to be strangled at a stake till he was dead and his body
to be burnt to ashes; Jean Weir to be hanged at the "Grass
Mercate of Edinbr." on Tuesday following. "Which were
accordingly execute," as we learn from a contemporary note on
the record, "and the said Major not being able to travell for
age, was dragg'd on a sled, the horse being led by the hangman,
and died in despair, declaring that he had no hopes of mercy;
and the woman died folishly." "Thus," observes the Reverend
Robert Law, "did the holy justice of God eminently shyne
furth in detecting such wreatched hypocrites."

The Gallow Lee, the scene of the major's expiation, was a
spot situated upon the declivity of Greenside in Leith Walk,
opposite the end of York Place, and lying towards the Calton
Hill. The parish church of Greenside now occupies the site.
It is recorded that when the rope was about his neck to prepare
him for the fire, for the last time the major was implored to
pray. "Let me alone," he replied: "I will not. I have lived
as a Beast and I must die as a Beast." Such was Major Weir's

epitaph. "In the flames along with him," says Sinclair, "was consumed his conjuring staff, carved with heads like those of Satyrs, without which he could not pray nor work many of his other diabolical feats. Whatever incantation was in it, the persons present own that it gave rare turnings and was long a-burning, as also himself." "I have been told," adds Dr. Hickes, "by very credible persons that the Body of this unclean Beast gave manifest tokens of its impurity . . . as soon as it began to be heated by the Flames"—from which the horrid inference has been drawn that the criminal was burned alive.

The major at least paid the last penalty with composure; not so his sister, who, as has been said, "died folishly." After his execution was over, one of the ministers waited upon her in the Tolbooth to cheer her with an account of the ceremony. She seemed more concerned, however, as to the fate of the staff, which, when she heard, "notwithstanding of her age"— she was some ten years her brother's junior—"she nimbly and in a furious rage fell on her knees, uttering words horrible to be remembered." Some inquisitive bystanders pressed for certain particulars of her crime, but the minister prudently stopped her disclosures, observing that the speculation of such iniquity was in itself a sin. She intimated to him that in the morning she proposed to die "with all the shame she could," which at the time the good man mistook for a sign of contrition. Next day in the Grassmarket, however, it appeared that her words bore a meaning less commendable. Lamont, the contemporary diarist records, "On the scaffold she cast away hir mantell, hir gown tayle, and was purposed to cast of all her cloaths before all the multitude; bot Bailie Oliphant, to whom the business was intrusted, stoped the same and commanded the executioner to doe his office. While he was abowt to throw hir ovir the leather [ladder], she smote the executioner on the cheike; and hir hands not being tyed when she was throwen ovir, she labored to recover hirself, and put in her head betwixt two of the steps of the leather, and keiped that powster for atyme, till she was put from itt." These shocking details are here transcribed in order to remove from the reader's mind any shadow of doubt as to the madness of this unhappy creature. Major Weir, however, was possessed by a more evil spirit. For him, in view of the physicians' verdict, the plea of insanity in the general sense cannot be urged, except in so far as in the light of modern science all such criminals may be regarded as insane.

The abode of the wizard in the West Bow, which survived its owner by more than two hundred years, stood for upwards of a century after his death dark and tenantless in the midst of the superstitious city. Its reputation as a place of dread was early established. "The facts struck the public fancy," says Stevenson, "and brought forth a remarkable family of myths." One of the first and quaintest of these is the story of a certain "gentlewoman" who, attended by her maid with a lantern, was returning at midnight from the Castle Hill, "where her husband's niece was laying-in of a child." About the Bowhead she perceived "three Women in windows, shouting, laughing and claping their hands"—an unseemly but not necessarily supranormal sight. The gentlewoman, however, "went forward" and fared worse, for just at Major Weir's door "there arose as from the street a Woman above the length of two ordinary femells." The courageous dame, "not as yet excessively feared," ordered her maid to approach the phantom, "if by the Lanthorn they could see what she was"; but as they advanced "this long-legged Spectre was still before them, moving her Body with a vehement Cachinnation, a great unmeasurable Laughter." In this order they descended the slope "till the Giantiss came to a narrow lane in the Bow, commonly called the Stinking-closs, into which she turning, and the Gentlewoman looking after her, perceived the closs full of flaming torches and as it had been a great multitude of People, stentoriously laughing and gapping with Tahies of laughter."

This was too much for the lady's nerves, and followed by her maid she fled home, where she related to the family, " but more passionately to her husband," her terrible experience.  Perhaps she had relied upon having his manly escort, the rather that it was upon his relative's affair she had been abroad so late.

The winds that swept over Greenside from the " Craigs of Caltoun," and scattered the ashes of the warlock and his wand upon the Gallow Lee, could not cleanse Auld Reekie of their unholy memories.  As time went on, these assumed ever more marvellous proportions in the public mind.  The " Magical Staff," it was said, used formerly to run upon its master's disreputable and secret errands, and was wont of old to answer the long-closed door, behind which it still lurked, a diabolical porter, to perform its ancient functions; and when in the mirk night the wicked major would sally forth on nameless business, it flamed before him up the Bow like some infernal link-boy.  The major himself, in spite of stake and faggot, became, in Chambers's phrase, "the bugbear of the Bow."  Jovial roisterers from Lawnmarket *howffs*, negotiating in the small hours that critical descent, beheld the wizard, mounted on a headless charger, burst from the Stinking Close and gallop furiously away "in a whirlwind of flame."  Decent burgesses, returning with their wives from solemn or sociable meeting, saw the windows of the deserted house ablaze with lights as for some eldritch festival, while, to the accompaniment of unearthly music, fearful shapes flitted wildly athwart the broken panes; and trembled to think, as they hastened by to their respectable beds, what manner of company the major and his sister kept that night.  But perhaps the most popular of these manifestations, as it was the legend longest associated with the locality, was that which, in the chill unchancy hour before the dawn, startled the sleepers of the Bow, when down that ill-paved alley, with clatter of hooves and groaning axles, thundered the six coal-black horses and fiery coach of the " Muckle Deil himsel'," and drew up with a resounding crash

before the warlock's door.  Then would some bolder spirit rise,
and, peering awfully into the shadows of the street, behold
through the flaming glasses the dead damned face of Major
Weir.  This agreeable fancy for many years survived in nursery
lore, and was often told to Stevenson's father in his childhood
by judicious guardians, as his son relates.

" About fifty years ago," says Chambers, writing in 1869,
" when the shades of superstition began universally to give way
in Scotland, Major Weir's house came to be regarded with less
terror by the neighbours, and an attempt was made by the proprietor to find a person who should be bold enough to inhabit
it."  Such an adventurous tenant was found in one William
Patullo, an old soldier of reprobate and drunken habits, who,
professing to hold materialistic views, but probably tempted by
the lowness of the rent, agreed to beard the warlock in his den.
The news excited much interest in the neighbourhood, and
the issue of the hazardous experiment was eagerly awaited.
Accordingly, on the appointed day Patullo and his wife,
with their exiguous chattels, " flitted " into the haunted house.
That night, the old soldier's scepticism notwithstanding, the
couple lay long awake.  When the last embers of their scanty
fire were cold, and silence and darkness held possession of the
Bow, " they suddenly saw a form like that of a calf, which came
forward to the bed, and setting its fore-feet upon the stock
[bed-foot] looked steadfastly at the unfortunate pair."  After
contemplating them thus for some time, the vision gradually
vanished.  This emanation from the major's past was too much
even for the godless old campaigner ; next day " that eligible
family residence " was again to let, and remained so for another
half-century.

In later years it was occupied at divers times, not in-
appropriately, as a brazier's shop and as a magazine for lint,
but no human family ever sought to make a home beneath that
accursed roof.  At length there came a time when Satan was
hoist with his own petard.  In the spring of 1878 the Improve-

ment Commissioners, whom he had long so happily inspired, rebelled against him, and with cynical ingratitude razed his infernal fortress to the ground.

Since that date the peace of Edinburgh has not been broken by the visible presence of the evil twain, but Mr. Lang informs me (1912) that three years ago Major Weir and his sister were seen again in Lanarkshire, in the haunts of their uncanny childhood.

# THE ORDEAL OF PHILIP STANFIELD.

In a secret Murther, if the dead carkasse be at any time thereafter
handled by the Murtherer, it will gush out of blood ; as if the blood were
crying to Heaven for revenge of the Murtherer.

*—Dæmonologie*, KING JAMES THE SIXTH.

As one of the four parricides recorded in Scottish criminal
annals, and the last person convicted in that country upon the
ancient ordeal of *Bahr-recht* or Law of the Bier—the bleeding
of the slain corpse at the murderer's touch—Philip Stanfield
has attained some eminence of infamy. He has pointed a moral
for Wodrow and furnished footnotes for Sir Walter Scott, who
doubted the evidence of his guilt. He has his part in Howell's
dismal repertory. More recently he has adorned a tale by Mr.
S. R. Crockett, in which he plays the villain for the circulating
libraries at some sacrifice of truth, and, despite an undeniable
gibbet and dismemberment, continues by the author's favour
his criminous career. The contemporary report of his trial at
Edinburgh in 1688 is appreciated by the bibliophile, but to
the general reader the facts of his strange story are unknown.
It is a tragedy of old years of blood and superstition; grim,
indeed, but with here and there quaint glimpses of the ghostly
marvellous, wherein we perceive malice domestic incite to
midnight murder, and in the end the guilty designated by
the manifest finger of God.

Philip Stanfield—the name is variously given as Stansfield,
Standsfield, and Stamfield—was the eldest son of Sir James
Stanfield of New Mills, in East Lothian. A Yorkshireman by
birth, the elder Stanfield is said to have held the rank of colonel
on the Parliamentary side in the Civil War. He settled in
Scotland after Cromwell's victory at Dunbar, having purchased

certain lands lying on the south bank of the river Tyne, a mile
east of Haddington, formerly belonging to the local abbey,
There he established a cloth manufactory upon the site, some
thirty years earlier, of a similar undertaking.  Colonel Stanfield's enterprise enjoyed the patronage of the Protector, and
after the Restoration he was further encouraged by divers
privileges granted to him by the Scots Parliament.  Later he
received from Charles II. a knighthood, presumably in recognition of his mercantile rather than his military achievements.
In 1681, with the approval of James, Duke of York, then
resident in Scotland, proposals were made for establishing a
cloth manufacturing company on a large scale, to compete with
the English industry.  Among the promotors of this patriotic
scheme was Sir James Stanfield, and from him the new
company acquired upon liberal terms a lease of " that great
manufactory stone house on the south side of the village of
Newmylnes," with the offices thereof, " which are many, great
and spacious."

At this time Sir James was a wealthy man.  The cloth
manufactory had prospered, and we learn from the decisions
of the Lords of Session that in addition to his estate of New
Mills he owned other lands at Hailes and Morham in the same
county.  But he was more blessed in his business than in his
home.  Lady Stanfield was no ideal helpmate, while Philip, his
son and heir, was a prince of prodigals.  Sir James complained
to his friends that " he had no comfort in his wife and family,"
whom he described as " very wicked," observing that it was
" sad that a man should be destroyed by his own bowels."
His chief cause of anxiety was the conduct of his elder son, of
whose misdeeds a lurid account is given in the indictment upon
which Philip was convicted of the murder of his long-suffering
sire.  Apart from that catalogue of iniquities we know little of
Philip's youth, but an anecdote preserved by Wodrow shows
him to have been a student of St. Andrew's University.  While
at that seat of learning, he one day attended the preaching of

John Welsh, the great-grandson of Knox, and, disliking his doctrine, " threw somewhat or other at the minister, which hit him." Mr. Welsh promptly prophesied that " there would be more present at his [Philip's] death than were hearing him preach that day." This retort seems to have been a favourite one with outraged prophets. Similar predictions are recorded of Captain Porteous and others, the seers being justified by the event.

It is stated in the indictment that, notwithstanding the advantages of an excellent education, Philip, " being a profligate and debauched person, did committ and was accessory to several notorious villainies both at home and abroad." He had, it is said, " entered a souldier in the Scots Regiment," but most of his time was spent in retirement in the Marshalsea and the public prisons of Brussels, Antwerp, Orleans, and other places on the Continent. At Treves he was condemned to death, but managed to escape. From these retreats he was time and again released by his father's liberality; but so far from exhibiting either gratitude or sign of amendment, it was his habit " most wickedly and bitterly to rail upon, abuse, and curse his natural and kindly parent," and on two occasions he actually attempted his father's life. On the first of these he " did chase and pursue his father upon the King's highway at Lothian-burn, and did fire pistols upon him "; on the second he " did attempt to assassinate his father for his life at Culterallors," by similar methods.

Some years before the murder, Philip, married, was living with his wife at the house of New Mills, as appears from a case reported by Lord Fountainhall, a contemporary judge. In 1682 an action was raised in the Court of Session by an Edinburgh merchant against Philip, for payment of £1100 Scots for clothes " taken off" by himself and his wife in two years' time. Sir James was also called as defender on the ground that although his son was major and married at the time of the furnishing, yet the young couple were then living *in familia* with him, and

5

had no separate estate, so that he was bound to clothe and aliment them. The Lords decerned against Philip, but assoilzied (discharged) the father, "because he made it appear that he had paid 5000 merks of debts contracted by Philip during that very space, and that his son was a prodigal waster."

Sir James, finding his pecuniary affairs embarrassed by the unnatural encroachments of his family, proposed, in 1686, to sell "the houses and lands of Newmilns" to the cloth company. The negotiations were interrupted by his death in the following year, but were shortly thereafter completed. Meanwhile he had decided to disinherit the peccant Philip in favour of John, his second son. But Jacob, of whom "he had some comfortable hopes," was little less unsatisfactory than Esau, and "several times came in drunk as the other."

In this unhappy situation it is not surprising that Sir James at times exhibited a certain lowness of spirits, which the wicked Philip artfully attributed to mental derangement. So far, however, from being driven mad by his troubles, it appears that Sir James bore his afflictions with fortitude, and though he suffered in mind, body, and estate, his reason was unimpaired.

Matters reached a crisis in November 1687. On Saturday the 27th of that month Sir James Stanfield rode into Edinburgh for the last time, and having transacted his business there, returned in the evening to his house of New Mills, accompanied by a friend, one John Bell, "minister of the Gospel, aged 40 years," who was to occupy the pulpit of the neighbouring church at Morham next day. This divine was probably Mr. John Bell, parish minister of Gladsmuir, the learned contemporary author of certain treatises on witchcraft. They supped together after their long ride, and according to Mr. Bell Sir James's discourse was rational and pertinent, both before and after supper. At ten o'clock Sir James, having conducted his guest to his chamber, went to bed. The minister's experiences of the night must be described in his own words: "I declare that having slept but little, I was awakened in fear by a cry (as I supposed), and being waking, I heard for a time a great dinn and confused noise of several voices, and persons sometimes walking, which affrighted me (supposing them to be evil wicked spirits); and I apprehended the voices to be near the chamber-door sometimes, or in the transe [passage] or stairs, and sometimes below, which put me to arise in the night and bolt the chamber-door further, and to recommend myself by prayer, for protection and preservation, to the majestie of God; And having gone again to bed I heard these voices continue, but more laigh [low], till within a little time they came about to the chamber-window; and then I heard the voice as high as before, which increased my fear, and made me rise again to look over the window, to see whether they were men or women; but the window would not come up for me, which window looked to the garden and water, whither the voices went on till I heard them no more; only towards the morning I heard walking on the stairs, and in the transe above that chamber where I was lying. I told the women who put on my fire in my chamber that Sabbath morning that I had rested little that night, through dinn I heard; and that I was sure there were evil spirits about that house that night."

Next morning Sir James Stanfield was missing. The maid-servant found his bed "better spread up than it used to be, and the curtains more drawn about it."

Some distance behind the house of New Mills the river Tyne flowed beneath a steep bank upon the south. Early that Sunday morning a stranger named John Topping, going from Monkrig to the village by the water-side, saw Philip standing "at the brink of the brae," his eyes fixed upon the body of a man floating in the pool below. Topping asked whose body was in the water, but received no reply; when he came to New Mills he learned the answer to his question. About an hour after daybreak Philip entered the minister's chamber and inquired if he had seen his father that morning, adding that he himself had been seeking him by the banks of the water.    Mr. Bell "having gone without the gate and up the cawsey that leads to the manufactory, one came running and said they had found Sir James in the water."    The minister then left to perform his Sabbath duties at Morham, remarking, "If the majestie of God did ever permit the Devil and his instruments to do an honest man wrong, then Sir James Stanfield has received wrong this last night, which the Lord will discover in his good time."

Umphray Spurway, the manager of the cloth mills, was a fellow-countryman of Sir James.    Their relationship was intimate and friendly, and Umphray was often consulted by Stanfield in his unhappy domestic troubles.    Apprised of his master's disappearance, he was leaving the mills to go up to the great house when he encountered Philip.    The latter expressed wonder at the cause of his father's "discontent, that he should thus leave his lodgings"; whereupon Umphray plainly told him that in his view his (Stanfield's) family were responsible for what had happened.    The search was then begun, and presently Sir James's body was discovered floating, face downwards, among the ice in a pool of still water some five feet deep, "a little by-west the town [village]."    It was observed at the time that the ground at the water's edge nearest the body was "all beaten to mash with feet and the ground very open and mellow, although a very hard, frosty morning."    When the dead man was carried by his servants to his own house, Philip met the bearers in the doorway, and "swore that the body should not enter there, for he had not died like a man but like a beast."    It was accordingly deposited in an outhouse.

"The presumptions here were very pregnant against Philip," says Fountainhall, "for though other children in such dubious cases do ever ascribe their father's death to murder, yet he, being asked his opinion, asserted he thought he was not murdered, but rather took pains to persuade all that he was *felo de se* and his own executioner."

Philip's expressed opinion that Sir James had taken his own life was at first generally shared. Within an hour of the recovery of the body, the son ransacked his father's repositories, secured his valuables, and, appropriately enough in the circumstances, removed the silver buckles from the dead man's shoes and put them on his own.

When Mr. Bell returned to New Mills on the Sunday evening, he was informed by Philip that he had advertised several friends in Edinburgh of what had happened, and was expecting their arrival that night. The minister commended his prudence, deeming it highly desirable that the body should be "sighted" by the physician and friends of the deceased, for, from his midnight experiences, he was inclined to think it not a case of suicide, but "a violent murder committed by wicked spirits." In the morning he found to his astonishment that by Philip's orders the body had been secretly buried in the night. "They had very hastily buried him," says Fountainhall, "pretending that they would not have his body to be gazed upon and viewed by all comers."

Meanwhile "the fame of the country did run" that Sir James had been strangled by his son or servants, and Umphray Spurway, suspecting that all was not right, had, through a friend in Edinburgh, communicated with the Lord Advocate, Sir John Dalrymple (afterwards the first Earl of Stair). His lordship replied by letter, recommending that the body be viewed by Spurway, "along with two or three discreet persons," and if they saw no reason to suppose Sir James had met with foul play, that it should then be buried "privately and with as little noise as could be." When the messenger returned on the Sunday night, however, he was intercepted by Philip, who suppressed the letter.

At three o'clock on the Monday morning Umphray Spurway was awakened, and looking out from his own house at the mills saw horses and "great lights" about Sir James's gate. He arose, and going down to ascertain the cause met one of his men, who told him that Philip, "having received orders from my Lord Advocate for that purpose," was taking the body for interment to Morham churchyard. Umphray did not offer to join the funeral convoy to the lonely burial-place on the Lammermuirs some three miles off, where, in the black winter night, lit only by the torches of the murderer and his satellites, a grave was hastily dug in the frost-bound earth. He prudently went back to bed; but next day "the Englishmen in the manufactory, who were acquainted with the Crowner Laws, made a mutiny anent the burial."

On the following night Spurway was again aroused from sleep, and found at his door two Edinburgh surgeons, named Crawford and Muirhead, and three other gentlemen from the city (one being Mr. James Row, a relative of the deceased), who exhibited an order from the Lord Advocate for the exhumation of Sir James Stanfield's corpse. He accompanied them to the churchyard forthwith. Mr. Andrew Melvil, minister of the parish, with whose services Philip on the former occasion had dispensed, attended in his official capacity. Sir James's brief rest was broken, and the body was carried into the church, where the surgeons conducted their examination by torchlight. Philip himself was present, how unwillingly and with what feelings may be imagined.

The autopsy concluded, the surgeons requested the relatives to assist in replacing the body in the coffin. It afterwards appeared from Sir George Mackenzie's address to the jury that this was done deliberately, with a view of subjecting Philip to the ordeal by touch. In accordance with the Scots custom the son lifted his father's head, but no sooner had he done so than the horrified onlookers "did see it darting out blood through the linen from the left side of the neck which the pannel [prisoner] touched." Philip, astounded, let the head fall with a loud crash upon the "furm" [bench], staggered back, wiping his bloody hands upon his clothes, and crying lamentably upon his Maker for mercy, fell fainting across a seat. The watchers, "amazed at the sight," looked at one another in awe. They had witnessed the immediate interference of the Deity— "God's revenge against murder."

In due course Philip Stanfield was arrested and brought to justice. His trial took place before the High Court of Justiciary at Edinburgh upon 6th, 7th, and 8th February 1688. George, Earl of Linlithgow, Lord Justice-General, presided, the other judges being Sir John Lockhart, Lord Castlehill; Sir David Balfour, Lord Forret; Sir Roger Hogg, Lord Harcarse; and John Murray, Lord Drumcairne. The prosecution was conducted by Lord Advocate Dalrymple and Sir George Mackenzie, the "Bloody Mackenzie" of Presbyterian tradition. Dalrymple had succeeded Mackenzie in the office of Lord Advocate a year before; within a month the political whirligig was again to bring about a similar exchange of parts. Sir David Thoirs, Sir Patrick Hume, William Moniepenny, and William Dundas appeared for the defence. The usual debate upon the relevancy of the libel, the formidable and unwieldy indictment of former times, setting forth at portentous length all (and sometimes more than) the Crown expected to prove, occupied the first day. Stripped of the cumbrous verbiage of their "qualifications," the crimes charged were three in number—(1) high treason, as having drunk confusion to the King; (2) cursing of parents; and (3) murder under trust, each of which was at that date equally punishable by death. The copious arguments of counsel were, according to the old practice, reduced to writing and are printed in the trial. We cannot here enter these learned labyrinths, abounding in quaint subtleties and citations from Carpzovius, Mattheus, and other ancient jurists. Fountainhall, who gives a curious abridgment of the pleadings, observes, "It was alleged, against the parricide, that the presumptions libelled where not relevant, such as his [Philip's] preceding threats, his hasty burying of him, the corps bleeding when he touched them, . . . and that his [Sir James's] murder might be ascribed to other causes, seeing it is notour [publicly known] that he was once mad, and that it can be proven that he was once melancholy and hypochondriac thereafter, and that he used to tell himself that in one of these fits he rode towards England with a design never to have returned, but his horse stopped and would not go forward, which he looked upon as the finger of God, and returned home again; that once he was throwing himself out at a window at the Nether Bow if Thomas Lendall had not pulled him in by the feet; and that the very week before his death he desired George Stirling to let blood of him because his head was light." The Lords, however, found the libel relevant, and repelled all the defences.

Next day a jury was empanelled, and the prosecutor adduced his proof. The charge of treason need not detain us. It was proved that Philip, in the kitchen of New Mills, had proposed to five persons the comprehensive toast of confusion to the Pope, Antichrist, the Devil, and the King, "and did menace the witnesses with a great Kane that he would beat and brain them if they told it." The cursing of his father upon many occasions was fully established. For instance, Sir James's own servant deponed that, when asked to come to dinner with his father, Philip's ordinary answer was, " The Devil damn him and you both, and the Devil rive him, for I will not go to him, and if he [Philip] had a sixpence a day he would not go near him, for his father girned upon him like a sheep's head in a tongs." On another occasion, Philip having obtained some tobacco from a shop in the village without paying for it, the vendor hinted that Sir James might do so; whereupon Philip rudely retorted, " The Devil take him and his father both, for there never came an honest man out of Yorkshire "—a graceful allusion to his parent's original domicile.

With regard to the cause of Sir James's death Mr. James Muirhead, one of the surgeons who made the post-mortem, was examined, but, curiously enough, only as to the miraculous

bleeding of the corpse. The joint medical report stated that
there was upon the neck "a large and conspicuous swelling,
about three inches broad, of a dark red or blae colour, from one
side of the larynx round backwards to the other side thereof,"
which, on incision, was found to be full of bruised blood. The
neck was dislocated. Otherwise the body presented a healthy
appearance, and was entirely free from water. Mr. Muirhead
deponed that when he and the other surgeon were "putting on
the clean linens and stirring and moving the head and craig
[neck], he saw no blood at all." There were also produced for
the Crown separate reports of the Chirurgeons of Edinburgh
and the College of Physicians, based on the post-mortem
appearances as reported, to the effect that strangulation, not
drowning, was the cause of death.

It was proved that father and son were upon the worst of
terms; that Philip had repeatedly threatened to take his
father's life if he was disinherited in favour of his brother,
"though he should die in the Grass Mercat for it," *i.e.* on
the gallows; and that Sir James went in great fear of him,
having twice narrowly escaped assassination at his hands. Mr.
Roderick Mackenzie, an Edinburgh advocate and the old gentleman's friend, deponed that he met him in the Parliament Close
eight days before his death, when "the defunct invited him to
take his morning draught." While enjoying their "meridian"
in an adjacent tavern, they discussed the unhappy situation of
Sir James's domestic affairs. Mr. Mackenzie hinted that he had
heard this was partly due to the disinheriting of the heir.
"The defunct answered, 'Ye do not know my son, for he is the
greatest debauch in the earth; and that which troubles me
most is that he twice attempted my own person.'"

It further appeared that within a month of his father's
death Philip had several times boasted that he would be "laird
of all before Christmas," and would then "ride in their skirts
that had been ill to him"; also that during this same period
Lady Stanfield, being sick, said to him: "You will shortly

want your mother, which will be a gentle visitation to Sir
James," when Philip rejoined, "By my soul, mother, my father
shall be dead before you!"

Lady Stanfield herself was not free from the dreadful
suspicion of having been accessory to her husband's murder.
That the relations between husband and wife were most
unhappy, and that in the family quarrels she espoused the
cause of her prodigal son, was clearly proved. Fountainhall
records that "the mother had the dead-clothes all ready,"
that is, before the occasion for their use arose. "Some
alleged that she was concerned in the murder"; and he adds
an even more shocking accusation. In the opinion of Sir
Walter Scott some countenance is afforded to these horrible
rumours by the evidence given at the trial.

The manner of the murder, according to the prosecution,
was in this wise. Philip, though young in years, was "old
in—everything else." A married man, as we have seen, he
carried on an intrigue with one "Janet Johnstoun, spouse to
John Nicols," who lived in the village of New Mills. With
the aid of this woman and of two other profligate companions,
George Thomson, significantly named "The Devil's Taylour,"
and Helen Dickson his wife, Philip was alleged to have com-
passed his father's death, producing incidentally those manifestations which caused the minister's "affrightment in the
night." These three accomplices, we learn from Fountainhall,
had been examined before the Privy Council on 8th December,
"and tortured with the thumbikins but confessed nothing;
which criminal lawyers say does purge and elide, at least
debilitates and extenuates, all the former *indicia* and presumptions against themselves, if not those also which militated
against others." For this reason they were not produced
upon the trial, either in the witness-box or, more suitably,
at the bar. The servants at New Mills had also been "questioned" regarding their knowledge of the facts in the practical
manner of the Crown authorities of that day, for we find that

on 13th December " Sir James Stanfield's servants are tortured,"
apparently with negative results, so far at least as their
testimony was concerned.

It appeared from the proof that Janet Johnstoun and the
Thomsons had been closeted with Philip in his chamber the
night before the murder; that Janet, though a woman of
infamous repute, " who was his own concubine and his father's
known enemy," was alone entrusted by him with the duty
of " woonding " (laying out) the old man's corpse; that she and
Lady Stanfield quarrelled next day " about some remains of
the holland of the woonding-sheet " (winding-sheet), when
Philip bade his mistress hold her peace, " for he would reward
her well for the kindness she had done to him at that time ";
and that Thomson the tailor, bringing " the mournings " to
the great house and learning that the body was to be raised,
said it was the blackest news that ever he heard in his life,
and " he would sew no more in the house of New Mylns for
the world."

As these adminicles of evidence hardly went the length
of sustaining a charge of murder, the Lord Advocate proposed
to examine two children, James Thomson, son of " The Devil's
Taylour," and Anna Mark, daughter of Janet Johnstoun, aged
respectively thirteen and ten.   In view of their tender years
the Court refused to receive them as witnesses, but allowed
their declarations to be taken " for clearing of the assize,"
which came to much the same thing.   Their depositions are
very interesting and full of curiously vivid touches, which a
brief summary necessarily pretermits.

The boy Thomson deponed to the following effect: Philip
and Janet came to his parents' house on the night of the
murder between nine and ten.    Drink was sent for, but as
Philip had no small change " the ale was taken on upon trust."
The boy, who had been beaten and sent to bed, heard Janet's
daughter Anna call with a request for her mother to go
home to nurse her child.   He heard Philip say, " God damn

his own soul if he should not make an end of his father, and
then all would be his, and he would be kind to them." Philip
and Janet went out about eleven, and shortly afterwards the
boy's father and mother followed. In about two hours his
mother returned alone and "came softly to bed." His father
came in some time later, and called to him to know if he
were awake, but he feigned to be asleep. The wife asked
the husband, "What had stayed him?" and he replied, "That
the deed was done; and that Philip Stanfield guarded the
chamber door with a drawn sword and a bendet pistol, and
that he never thought a man would have died so soon; and
that they carried him out towards the waterside and tyed
a stone about his neck." After some discussion, however,
the murderers had thought it better to throw the body into
the river without the stone, to produce the appearance of
suicide. The boy added that, when his father received from
Philip the coat and waistcoat found upon the body, his mother
"was affrighted, for she thought that some evil spirit was
in it"; and from that time she was afraid to be alone after
nightfall.

The girl, Anna Mark, deponed that on the night in question
Philip was at her mother's house, and sent her to see if Sir
James had returned from Edinburgh. On learning that he had
done so, Philip and her mother went out about eleven. Her
"good-father" sent her to bring her mother back to nurse her
child, and she found her with Philip at the Thomsons' house.
Her mother, however, did not come home till about two in the
morning, when Anna heard her "good-father" say, "—— and
——, where have ye been so long?" Her mother answered,
"Wherever I have been, the deed is done!" and after that she
heard them speak softly together, "but could not know what
they said." Since that night Janet, like Mrs Thomson, "was
feared, and would not bide alone," a peculiarity also exhibited
by Philip after his father's death.

The testimony of these two children concluded the evidence

for the Crown; but Fountainhall states that the prosecution had
certain affidavits from London, not mentioned in the report of
the trial, "being the oaths of the keepers of the prisons where
Philip, the pannel [prisoner], had lain, who deponed that he
often cursed his father for not relieving him and boasted that
if he were out he should dispatch him; and that one Betty
Dolbry, being with child to him [Philip], had followed him
to Scotland and might possibly be on the plot; but this was
not produced to the assize."

No witnesses were adduced for the defence. Indeed, as
appears from Sir George Mackenzie's address to the jury, the
prisoner's counsel took the unprofessional course of throwing
up their brief before half of the evidence for the prosecution
had been led. The case for the defence, as disclosed upon the
pleadings, was that Sir James had committed suicide "in a
frainzie or melancholy fit," to which he was alleged to be subject.
But even if he were in fact suffering from depression, it is, as
Sir George pointed out, hard to believe that "after he had
strangled himself and broke his own neck, he drown'd himself."
No proof was offered in support of the allegations of his previous
insanity and attempted suicide.

It is very rarely that one finds the addresses of counsel to
the jury reported in a Scottish criminal trial even of a hundred
years later, but here we have a full and excellent report of
Sir George Mackenzie's speech for the Crown, probably a
unique example of his forensic oratory, at which we can now
only glance. "You will discern," said he, "the finger of God
in all the steps of this probation as evidently as Philip's guilt;
and this extraordinary discovery has been made as well to
convince this wicked age that the world is governed by Divine
Providence, as that he is guilty of this murder." The motive
alleged was Philip's desire to prevent delivery of the disposition
or conveyance of his property made by Sir James in favour of
his younger son, "after which settlement Philip could gain
nothing but the gallows by killing his father." Sir George

noted in passing the affinity between the two crimes first libelled: "for to pray confusion to the King, who is *pater patriæ*, is a cursing of our great parent"; and, dealing with Philip's former attempts upon his father's life, he described that "innocent and obliging Gentleman" as flying from his unnatural offspring like "a trembling Partridge pursued by a Haulk." The charge of treason was not pressed, but the learned counsel made the most of his trump card, the miraculous bleeding of the body, whereby "the Divine Mejesty, who loves to see just things done in a legal way, furnished a full probation in an extraordinary manner." Therein, said he, "God Almighty himself was pleased to bear a share of the testimonies which we produce : that Divine Power which makes the blood circulate during life, has oftimes in all nations opened a passage to it after death upon such occasions." And this was specially remarkable in the present case, where the incision had been carefully bound up, and the body "designedly shaken up and down," having been some time buried, "which naturally occasions the blood to congeal"; yet at the murderer's touch the blood "darted and sprung out, to the great astonishment of the chirurgeons themselves, *who were desired to watch the event.*" Then, with regard to the hardly less marvellous discovery "by the mouths of babes and sucklings," Sir George observed, "If you had seen this little boy upon his knees begging his father to confess with so much affection, so much judgment, so much piety, you had needed no other probation." This refers to the confronting of the wicked parents with their accusing children before the Privy Council. The peroration is as follows: "If, then, such amongst you as are Fathers would not wish to be murdered by your own children, or such of you as are Sons would not wish the World to believe that you are weary of your Fathers, you will all concur to find this miscreant guilty of a crime that God has taken so much pains to detect and all mankind has reason to wish to be punished. May the Almighty God, who formed your hearts, convince

them; and may this poor Nation cite you as the remarkable
curbers of vice to all succeeding ages."

At the conclusion of Sir George's address, the Lord Advocate, to "mak sicker," protested for "an Assize of Error against
the Inquest in case they should assoilize the Pannel"; which,
being interpreted, meant that if the jury so far forgot
themselves as to acquit the prisoner they would be fined and
imprisoned for the wilful error of absolving him against clear
evidence! The jury, however, on 8th February, unanimously
returned a verdict of guilty of the first and second, and art and
part of the third charges libelled, and the Court pronounced
sentence of death in the horrible form applicable to his
crimes.

As to the ultimate fate of Janet Johnstoun and of "The
Devil's Taylour" and his wicked wife, history is silent; but in
Mr. Crockett's robustious pages a brilliant future awaited Janet
as the wife of the Spanish governor of the Isle of San Juan de
Puerto Rico.

"The 15th being come and the gallows and scaffold ready,"
says Fountainhall, Philip Stanfield "was reprieved for eight
days longer by the Chancellor at the priest's desire. He craved
by a bill that those already tortured for his father's murder
might be re-examined. This he thought would clear him
on their reiterated denial; but the Counsel refused it, lest
it should harden him." The Lord Chancellor was James
Drummond, Earl of Perth, who had adopted the faith of his
sovereign, James the Seventh. Fountainhall adds that Philip
"had tampered with the Popish priests and professed himself
to be of their religion, hoping thereby to get his life"; but
finding this move unsuccessful, he returned to the Presbyterian
fold.

On the 24th the sentence was duly carried out. At the Cross
of Edinburgh Philip Stanfield was hanged upon a gibbet. The
tongue wherewith he had cursed his "natural and kindly
parent" was cut out and burned upon the scaffold; the right

hand raised by him against his father's life was cut off and affixed to the East Port of Haddington, "as nearest to the place of the murder"; his dead body was hung in chains at the Gallow Lee, between Edinburgh and Leith; his name, fame, memory, and honours were ordained to be extinct; his arms were riven furth and delete out of the book of arms, and all his goods and gear were forfeited "to our Sovereign Lord, to remain perpetuallie with his Highness in property."

He maintained to the last his complete innocence of the old man's blood, and "imprecated a judgment against himself if he was in the least guilty or in the foreknowledge of his father's death."    Two incidents in connection with his execution and the fate of his remains were noted by the superstitious of the day.    At his hanging the knot of the rope slipped, "whereby his feet and knees were on the scaffold (this I Robert Mylne, Writer, saw with my own eyes) which necessitate the hangman to strangle him, bearing therein a near resemblance with his father's death." Application being made to the Privy Council, probably by Lady Stanfield, for permission to bury the body, "Duke Hamilton was for it, but the Chancellor would not consent, because he had mocked his religion."    The recently converted Lord Chancellor evidently found Philip's taste in toasts offensive.

The body, as we have seen, was hung up in chains at the Gallow Lee, among those of other malefactors,

"Waving with the weather while their neck will hold."

It was, however, secretly taken down a few days afterwards and thrown into a neighbouring ditch, "among some water, as his father's corpse was."    Once more the body was hung up by order of the authorities, but it was again mysteriously removed, "and no more heard thereof."

"This," concludes Fountainhall, whose account we have hitherto followed, "is a dark case of divination to be remitted to the great day, whether he was guilty or innocent.    Only

it is certain he was a bad youth, and may serve as a beakon
to all profligate persons." But without seeking to anticipate
that final finding, we may rest assured that Sir James Stanfield died by some hand other than his own, and that Philip,
who clearly was *capable de tout*, was, in Braxfield's classic
phrase, "nane the waur o' a hangin'."

The case of Philip Stanfield attracted the notice of Sir
Walter Scott, who makes reference to it on several occasions.
The earliest of these is in his private note-book, extracts
from which are given by Lockhart, where, under date 15th
March 1797, he writes:—"Read Stanfield's trial, and the conviction appears very doubtful indeed. Surely no one could
seriously believe, in 1688, that the body of the murdered bleeds
at the touch of the murderer, and I see little else that directly
touches Philip Stanfield. It was believed at the time that
Lady Stanfield had a hand in the assassination or was at least
privy to her son's plans; but I see nothing inconsistent with
the old gentleman's having committed suicide." In later years,
when Adolphus, who discovered the identity of the author of
*Waverley* from his works, was visiting him at Abbotsford,
Scott recommended his guest to read the trial, and lent him
his own copy of the original folio for the purpose.

In his notes to "Earl Richard" in the *Minstrelsy*, Scott
discusses the superstitious belief in the bleeding of the
murdered corpse, and instances Stanfield's case as the last
and leading example in Scotland. He also refers to the
trial of Muir of Auchindrane, which took place in 1611, where
a conviction was obtained by similar miraculous means, and
of which he himself made a ballad, "Auchindrane, or the
Ayrshire Tragedy," in 1830.

The last case of the kind in England reported in the State
Trials, and one of the most remarkable instances of touching
as a test for murder, is that arising out of the death of Joan
Norkott in 1628, sixty years before the Stanfield affair. This
woman was found dead in her bed with her throat cut, the

knife with which the wound had been inflicted sticking in
the floor, in a room within that occupied by her husband's
mother, sister, and brother-in-law.  At the inquest these
persons declared that they had slept in the outer room that
night, but heard and saw nothing amiss, and that no one
could have entered the inner room without their knowledge.
The coroner's jury accordingly returned a verdict of *felo
de se.*  In consequence of certain rumours, however, they
afterwards desired that the body should be exhumed, which
was done *thirty days after the death,* in presence of a curious
crowd, including the three relatives above mentioned and
the husband of the deceased, who had been absent on the
night in question.  All four were required to touch the
corpse, " whereupon," in the words of Sergeant Maynard, who
reports the case, " the brow of the dead, which before was
of a livid and carrion colour, begun to have a dew or gentle
sweat arise on it, which increased by degrees till the sweat
ran down in drops on the face.  The brow turned to a lively
and fresh colour, and the deceased opened one of her eyes and
shut it again; and this opening the eye was done three several
times.  She likewise thrust out the ring or marriage finger
three times and pulled it in again, and the finger dropped blood
from it on the grass."

These phenomena were attested by the minister of the
parish and by his brother, who also was in holy orders.
The former had dipped his finger in the supernatural fluid,
and swore that it was blood.

The coroner's jury withdrew their former verdict.  The four
accused were duly tried at Hertford Assizes for the murder,
and, against the expressed opinion of Judge Harvey, who
tried the case, were acquitted.  The miraculous wink was no
better than an ordinary nod to so blind a jury.  On appeal,
the case was re-tried at the Bar of the King's Bench before
Sir Nicholas Hyde, the Lord Chief-Justice, when a less
sceptical jury found the husband and his mother and sister

guilty, but acquitted the brother-in-law. The two former were executed, but made no confession; the sister, owing to her condition, was reprieved.

The fact that the victim's neck was broken, as also was that of Sir James Stanfield, disposed of the suggestion of suicide; while apart from the bleeding of the corpse, "according to God's usual method of discovering murder," to quote Philip's indictment, the circumstantial evidence, as in his case, pointed plainly to the prisoners' guilt.

Echoes of the Stanfield case reverberated in the Parliament House for some years after the murder. On 22nd December 1693 the children of one James Scott of Bristo "pursued" Sir James's creditors, who were in possession of his estates, upon an assignation of his share of the cloth manufactory granted to Scott by him on the day of his death. The deed, duly executed, was found lying on the table in Sir James's room, and directed to Scott, who called for it on the following day. Presumably it had escaped Philip's notice. The question being, Was there delivery of the document in a legal sense? the Lords thought this "a too nice and metaphysical tradition," and held that the deed was undelivered.

On 9th November 1697 Sir James's creditors presented a petition to the Court, stating "that John Stanfield, his son and apparent heir, was *in lecto* dying and had the whole writs of the lands whereof they had raised a summons of sale, and there was hazard of his wife's putting them out of the way." The Lords, "this extraordinary case requiring haste," ordered the title-deeds to be sealed up in the hands of the clerk of Court.

What became of John we are not told, but from the little we know of his habits it is probable that the illness was his last.

In 1713, on the winding up of the cloth company, its property was offered for public sale in various lots, and the lands of New Mills were purchased by the notorious Colonel

Francis Charteris of evil memory, who changed the name to Amisfield, after his family seat in Nithsdale, which they still retain.   Through him the estate passed in succession to the present owner, the Earl of Wemyss.

The stately mansion of the wicked Colonel has superseded Sir James Stanfield's old unhappy home, and the "great manufactory stone house, together with the walkmylne and dying house," even the busy village itself, are among the things that have been.   Only the river is unchanged, and still the eddies circle in the quiet pool where Philip looked long upon his murdered father, that frosty winter morning two centuries ago.

# THE GHOST OF SERGEANT DAVIES

"You must not tell us what the soldier or any other man said, Sir ; it's not evidence."—BARDELL v. PICKWICK.

FEW judicial utterances are better known or more widely quoted than this immortal dictum of Mr. Justice Stareleigh. Yet there was precedent against his Lordship's ruling, for in the year 1754 the High Court of Justiciary had admitted as evidence what was said by "the soldier's" ghost! and so lately as 1831 the testimony of a voice from the other world was accepted in the Assynt murder case by the same tribunal. But English practice was no stricter, and although only two instances of spectral evidence occur in the State Trials, the research of Mr. Andrew Lang has disclosed similar cases. Both of the Scots spirits spoke in Gaelic, which would seem to be an appropriate medium of communication but for the fact that the soldier, an Englishman, while in the flesh had no knowledge of that tongue.

The case first mentioned arose out of the slaying of Sergeant Davies, and the trial of his murderers was privately printed for the Bannatyne Club at the instance of Sir Walter Scott. The time was some three years after the doleful day of Drummossie, the place a solitary hillside at the head of Glenclunie, in the heart of the Grampians. "A more waste tract of mountain and bog, rocks and ravines, extending from Dubrach to Glenshee, without habitations of any kind until you reach Glenclunie, is scarce to be met with in Scotland," writes Sir Walter ; "a more fit locality, therefore, for a deed of murder could hardly be pointed out, nor one which could tend more to agitate superstitious feelings."

The swell following the great gale of the Forty-five had not subsided in the remoter Highlands; and bands of disaffected and broken men still lurked in security among the grim defiles and rugged fastnesses of that formidable land. The disarming of the Highlanders was a farce, as Prestongrange admitted to David Balfour. To stamp out the smouldering embers of the Rising, and to enforce the Disarming Act and that which proscribed the national dress, the Government still maintained garrisons throughout the suspected districts. From these stations small pickets were sent out to occupy various posts, whence they communicated with one another, and constantly patrolled the country.

In the month of September, 1749, Sergeant Arthur Davies, with a party of eight men of the regiment of foot commanded by Lieutenant-General Guise, were quartered at Dubrach, a small upland farm near the clachan of Inverey in Braemar. They had marched thither in the previous June from their headquarters at Aberdeen. Another party of the same regiment, under the command of a corporal, guarded the Spittal of Glenshee, some eight miles off. In the course of patrolling the district, these two parties were wont to meet twice a week at a spot midway between their respective stations. During the three or four months in which Sergeant Davies had occupied the hostile territory, he seems to have discharged his onerous duties with tact and moderation, and though officially unpopular, had managed to obtain the goodwill of his subject neighbours. The private tastes and character of the man were likeable: he was of a genial disposition, a keen and indefatigable sportsman, fearless, thrifty, and particular in his dress. For one in his position his circumstances were prosperous. He had been married for about a year to the widow of a former comrade, and his wife shared the responsibilities of his post. Beyond Dubrach and farther up Strathdee there was at that time no cultivated land, and it was the sergeant's daily custom, combining business and pleasure, to wander by himself with rod or gun among the hills, glens, and streams of those inhospitable and lonely wilds. Though often warned of the risk to which such habits exposed him at the hands of lawless and desperate men, many of whom were then "in the heather," the sergeant laughed at danger, and continued to "gang his ain gait."

His figure was a notable one in so poor a neighbourhood. His ordinary dress was "a blue surtout coat, with a striped silk vest, teiken breeches, and brown stockings." He carried a green silk purse containing his little capital, fifteen and a half guineas in gold, and a leather purse with silver for current expenses. The existence of this green silk purse was a matter of common knowledge, for it was his kindly way, when playing with the children of the clachan, "to rattle it for their diversion." He wore two gold rings, one plain, engraved on the inside with the letters D. H. and the motto, "When this you see, Remember me." This "posie" had reference to the late David Holland, sometime paymaster of the regiment, and the sergeant's predecessor in the lawful affections of his spouse. It would appear that he had no sentiment in such matters, for his brogues were enriched with a pair of large silver shoe-buckles formerly the property, and also bearing the initials, of the defunct. The other ring, which plays a part in the story, was of curious design, and had "a little lump of gold" in the form of a heart raised upon the bezel. The sergeant, further, wore silver buckles at his knees, a silver watch and seal at his fob, two dozen silver buttons on his waistcoat, and carried in his pocket a penknife of singular form. His "dark mouse-coloured hair" was tied behind with a black silk ribbon, and his silver-laced hat, with a silver button, had his own initials, misplaced, cut on the outside of the crown. A gun with a peculiar barrel, given to him by a brother officer, completed his usual equipment.

Thus accoutred and adorned Sergeant Davies, very early on the morning of Thursday, 28th September 1749, bade farewell to his wife at the house of Michael Farquharson, where they

lodged, and set forth in advance of his men to meet the patrol
from Glenshee. Four of his party followed him soon after.
This arrangement was not unusual, and on the return journey
he would often "send the men home and follow his sport."
An hour after sunrise he was seen and spoken to in Glenclunie
by one John Growar, whom he had occasion to reprimand for
wearing a coat of tartan, in contravention of the Act. With
characteristic good-nature, Davies "dismissed him, instead of
making him prisoner." The four soldiers from Dubrach duly
met the corporal's guard from Glenshee; on their way they
had a distant glimpse of the sergeant still pursuing his sport,
and heard him fire a shot. They marched home in the afternoon without seeing anything further of him. After the
patrols had separated, the Glenshee party encountered the
sergeant at the Water of Benow, half a mile from the rendez-
vous. Davies informed the corporal "that he was going to
the hill to get a shot at the deer." The corporal thought it
"very unreasonable in him" to venture on the hill alone, as he
himself was nervous even when accompanied by his men. To
which the sergeant answered "that when he had his arms and
amunition about him, he did not fear any body he could meet."
Whereupon they parted company; and from that hour Sergeant
Davies vanished from among living men, and his place knew
him no more.

Next day the news spread throughout the district that
the sergeant had disappeared. The captain of the garrison
at Braemar Castle sent a party of men on the Sunday to
Dubrach, and on the Monday the whole countryside was
raised to search for the missing man. After four days of
fruitless labour, the search was finally abandoned; no trace
of the sergeant could be found. From the first his wife
was certain that he had met with foul play. As she afterwards said, "It was generally known by all the neighbourhood that the sergeant was worth money and carried it
about with him." She scouted the rumour that he had deserted,

"for that he and she lived together in as great amity and
love as any couple could do that ever was married, and
that he never was in use to stay away a night from her;
and that it was not possible he could be under any temptation to desert, as he was much esteemed and beloved by
all his officers, and had good reason to believe he would
have been promoted to the rank of sergeant-major upon the
first vacancy." Her view came to be the accepted one, and
the opinion of the country was that the sergeant had been
robbed and murdered, and his corpse concealed amid the
desolate high places of the hills.

In June 1750, nine months after the disappearance,
Donald Farquharson, the son of Michael, with whom Davies
had lodged when on earth, received a message from one
Alexander M'Pherson "that he wanted much to speak to
him." M'Pherson was then at his master's sheiling (shepherd's hut) in Glenclunie, some two miles distant from
Dubrach. A few days afterwards Farquharson went to see
him as requested, "when M'Pherson told him that he was
greatly troubled with an apparition, the ghost of the deceased
Sergeant Davies, who insisted that he should bury his bones;
and that he having declined to bury them, the ghost insisted
that he should apply to Donald Farquharson, saying that he
was sure he would help to bury his bones." The spirit's
confidence was misplaced, for Donald at first declined the
office, and "could not believe that M'Pherson had seen such
an apparition." But on the ghost-seer stating that, guided
by his visitant's description, he had actually found the bones
in question, and offering to take him to the spot, Donald
reluctantly agreed to accompany him; "which," as he naively
says, "he did the rather that he thought it might possibly
be true, and if it was, he did not know but the apparition
might trouble himself."

M'Pherson led him to the Hill of Christie, between
Glenchristie and Glenclunie, two or three miles from Dubrach,

and about half a mile from the road taken by the patrols between that place and Glenshee. The body, which lay on the surface of the ground in a peat moss, was practically reduced to a skeleton. The bones were separated and "scattered assunder," but the "mouse-coloured" hair of the unhappy sergeant, still tied with the black silk ribbon, was intact. Fragments of blue cloth, some pieces of striped stuff, and a pair of brogues from which the tags for the buckles had been cut, left little doubt as to the identity of the remains.

M'Pherson told his companion that when he first found the bones, eight days before, they lay farther off under a bank, and "he drew them out with his staff." Donald inquired, "If the apparition had given any orders about carrying his bones to a churchyard?" and learning that the spirit had indicated no preference for any specific resting-place, he agreed to bury the bones on the spot. They accordingly dug a hole in the moss with a spade brought by M'Pherson, and buried therein all that they had found.

Now, though M'Pherson does not appear to have told Farquharson at this time, he afterwards swore that the ghost, being pressed by him to disclose who had slain the sergeant, did, on the occasion of its second appearance, actually name the murderers. To this we shall return later.

Between the discovery of the bones and the communication to Donald Farquharson, M'Pherson had informed John Growar (the man to whom the sergeant had spoken about the tartan coat) both of his spectral visitor and of what he had found. "John bid him tell nothing of it, otherwise he would complain of him to John Shaw of Daldownie." To anticipate this, M'Pherson himself reported the circumstance to Daldownie, who "desired him to conceal the matter, and go and bury the body privately, as it would not be carried to a kirk unkent [unknown], and that the same might hurt the country, being under the suspicion of being a rebel country." Later, M'Pherson showed Growar where he had found the bones. It was not far from the place at which John had met the sergeant on the day of his death.

Notwithstanding the desire for secrecy expressed by all the parties, someone let out the finding of the body, with the result that local interest was directed to the Hill of Christie. James Growar, a relative of John, presently found there the sergeant's gun, and a girl named Isobel Ego picked up a silver-laced hat with a silver button on it, afterwards identified as his. Isobel, who had been sent by her master to the hills to look for some horses, remarked on her return, "That she had come home richer than she went out," and produced her find. Her mistress "had no peace of mind, believing it to be Sergeant Davies's hat, and desired it might be put out of her sight;" so the farmer hid the hat under a stone by the burnside, near his house, and knew no more of it. Some time after, however, "the bairns of Inverey," playing about the burnside, lighted upon the hat and took it to the village. It then passed successively through the hands of Donald Downie, the miller of Inverey, and of James Small, factor on the forfeited estate of Strowan, into the custody of John Cook, barrack-master at Braemar Castle, who four years later produced it at the trial. We shall hear of the Strowan factor again.

The barrack-master afterwards said that within ten days of the sergeant's disappearance "it was reported that he had been murdered by two young men about Inverey." By the following summer not only was the story of the ghostly visitant and the resulting discovery of the bones well known throughout the neighbourhood, but "it was clattered" that the spectre had denounced by name as the murderers two persons then living in the district. These where Duncan Terig, *alias* Clerk, and Alexander Bain Macdonald. Both were men of questionable character and reputed thieves. Clerk lived with his father in Inverey without visible means of livelihood, and Macdonald, who was forester to Lord Braco (the first Earl Fife), resided in Allanquoich. Apart from their supernatural impeachment, many material facts confirmatory of their guilt accumulated against them in the public mind, but four years elapsed before they were brought to trial.  It does not appear from the official record how the tardy sword of justice came to be drawn so long after the event, for not until September 1753 were Clerk and Macdonald apprehended on the charge and committed to the Castle of Braemar.  The Lord Advocate stated in Court that the prisoners "were at last accused by the general voice of the country," and that the cause of delay in bringing them to trial was that "at first the proof against them did not appear so pregnant."  But certain events after the trial throw some light, as we shall see, on how the charge was made.

On 23rd January 1754 the prisoners, being judicially examined before Lords Strichen and Drummore, two of the Lords Commissioners of Justiciary, each gave different and contradictory accounts of their movements upon the day of the murder. Clerk declared that he, in company with Macdonald, was upon the Hill of Gleney the day Sergeant Davies disappeared; that both were armed with guns; that Macdonald fired one shot at some deer; and that at ten o'clock that morning he parted from Macdonald on the hill and returned to his father's house, to which Macdonald came the same evening, and where he stayed all night.  Macdonald declared that he spent the night at his own house in Allanquoich, and did not see Clerk after they parted on the hill about nine or ten o'clock.  For the rest, his declaration concurred with Clerk's.

The trial began before the High Court of Justiciary at Edinburgh on 10th June 1754, the judges being Lord Justice-Clerk Alva, who presided, and Lords Strichen, Drummore, Elchies, and Kilkerran.  The two last named had assisted Argyll, the Justice-General, at the judicial murder of James of the Glens two years before, as immortalised by Stevenson. The Lord Advocate, William Grant of Prestongrange, so vividly portrayed in *Catriona*, Patrick Haldane and Alexander Home, " His Majesties Solicitors," and Robert Dundas, conducted the

prosecution.   The prisoners were represented by Alexander
Lockhart (who ten years later in that Court heroically defended
Katharine Nairn) and Robert M'Intosh, the friend of Scott.

In the debate upon the relevancy, which, as was then usual,
occupied the first day of the proceedings, it was argued for
the pannels that they were persons of good fame, and had no
malice against the sergeant ; that they had a true and warrant-
able cause for being on the hill under arms; and that they did
so openly and avowedly.   It was further objected that though
arrested for the murder as already described, and having almost
" run their letters " without being served with an indictment,
they were again committed for theft, and the time nearly
expiring in that case also, they were detained on a third warrant
for wearing the Highland Dress, and last of all, " upon the mali-
cious information of some private informer," were served with
this indictment.   They offered to prove that after they had left
the hill, the sergeant was seen alive with his party, but in
support of this allegation no shadow of evidence was afterwards
adduced.   The Lord Advocate confidently answered that such
facts and circumstances would come out upon proof as would
satisfy the jury of the pannels' guilt.   The delay complained of
was owing to no intention of his to oppress the pannels—" he
had early information of the murder charged upon and was
very willing and desirous it might come to light "—but was
due to the difficulty of obtaining conclusive evidence against
them, which he hoped he had now done.   The Court found the
libel relevant, and adjourned till the following day.

At seven o'clock next morning (11th June) the trial was
resumed, and a jury, composed of Edinburgh tradesmen, was
empanelled.   Macdonald was allowed to amend his declaration
to the effect that he had spent the night of the murder at the
house of Clerk's father in Inverey.   The Lord Advocate's first
witness was Jean Ghent, the widow of the murdered man, from
whose evidence many of the foregoing facts have been related.
She described the dress and belongings of her husband on that

morning when she last saw him alive, and identified as his the hat and gun found on the hill, as already mentioned. She had seen him cut his initials on the hat, and had remarked to him at the time, "You have made a pretty sort of work of it by having misplaced the letters." The stock of the gun had been altered, but she knew it by "a cross rent" in the middle of the barrel, occasioned, as her husband had told her, by his firing a shot when the gun was over-loaded. While the search party was being organised she had asked the prisoner Clerk, "whom she took to be a particular friend, to try if he could find the body"! The poor woman then little knew how well qualified he was to do so.

Donald Farquharson, whose evidence we have recounted, told how M'Pherson communicated to him the spirit's message, and described the subsequent burial of the remains. He also identified the gun produced, having been present when Davies fired the charge which cracked the barrel. He had seen gold rings, "one of which had a knob upon it," on the fingers of Elizabeth Downie, a girl whom Clerk had married since the murder. It struck him as being like the sergeant's ring, and he questioned her about it, but she said it had belonged to her mother. Macdonald, as Lord Braco's forester, was the only man who had a warrant "for carrying guns for killing of deer," and Clerk was usually associated with him in his expeditions. Clerk was reputed a sheep-stealer. The witness knew nothing against Macdonald "but that he once broke the chest of one Corbie, and took some money out of it." He considered M'Pherson, the ghost-seer, "an honest lad," but it was the general opinion "that all is not to be believed that he says."

Alexander M'Pherson was then called. In the earlier part of his examination he made no reference to the ghost, but merely stated that in the summer of 1750 he found, lying in a moss bank in the Hill of Christie, the bones of a human body, which at the time he believed to be that of Sergeant

Davies. His description of the appearance of the remains agreed with that given by Farquharson. When first discovered, the body was partially concealed, and "by the help of his staff he brought it out and laid it upon the plain ground, in doing whereof some of the bones were separated one from another." He narrated his conversations on the subject with Growar, Daldownie, and Farquharson, described the burial of the bones, and gave the following account of his parleyings with the disembodied sergeant: One night in June, 1750, being then abed in his master's sheiling at Glenclunie, "a vision appeared to him as of a man clad in blue," which he at first took to be "a real living man," namely a brother of Donald Farquharson. The spirit, presumably unwilling to disturb the other sleepers, withdrew to the door of the hut, and M'Pherson arose and followed it outside, when it made the startling announcement, "I am Sergeant Davies!" It added that, in the days of its flesh, it had been murdered on the Hill of Christie nearly a year before, minutely described the place where the body was hidden, and requested M'Pherson to arrange with Donald Farquharson for its interment. Notwithstanding the singular character of the interview, M'Pherson retained sufficient wit to inquire who had done the deed. The spectre made answer that if M'Pherson had not asked, it might have told him, but as he had, it could not. Perhaps to do so was contrary to ghostly etiquette. Thereupon the apparition vanished "in the twinkling of an eye." So exact were its directions as to the position of the body, that M'Pherson "went within a yard of the place where it lay upon his first going out." Although this should have been an absolute guarantee of the ghost's good faith, M'Pherson did nothing further in the matter. A week later, at the same time and place, " the vision again appeared, naked, and minded him to bury the body." M'Pherson repeated his inquiry as to the identity of the murderer, and the spectre, having apparently laid aside its reticence with its raiment, at once replied, "Duncan Clerk and Alexander Macdonald," and vanished as before. Both conversations were held in Gaelic, with which language the sergeant, when in life, was unfamilar. Excepting Growar, Daldownie, and Farquharson, M'Pherson had told no one about the vision, nor did he tell the other folks in the sheiling at that time.

Some whisper of the spirit's purpose must have reached the ear of Duncan Clerk, for that autumn he repeatedly invited M'Pherson to enter his service. Clerk's circumstances had unaccountably improved of late. He had taken upon lease the farms of Craggan and Gleney, and was married to Elizabeth Downie, the damsel with the remarkable ring. At Martinmas, 1750, M'Pherson, yielding to his solicitations, became a member of his household. He noticed that his new master carried a long green silk purse, while his mistress wore a gold ring, "with a plate on the outside of it in the form of a seal," both of which, he heard it reported, had belonged to the murdered man. One day when they were together on the hill, Duncan, "spying a young cow," desired M'Pherson to shoot it. The latter refused to do so, and administered the moral reproof, "that it was such thoughts as these were in his heart when he murdered Sergeant Davies!" Duncan at first used "angry expressions," but M'Pherson sticking to his point, he "fell calm," desired him to keep the secret and he would be a brother to him, offered to help him to stock a farm when he took one, and gave him a promissory note for twenty pounds Scots "to hold his tongue of what he knew of Sergeant Davies." M'Pherson afterwards asked Duncan for payment of the note and failing to obtain it, left his service. That M'Pherson did tackle his master about the murder, is corroborated by John Growar, who reports a conversation between them on the subject, when Duncan, to deprecate exposure, pathetically remarked, "What can you say of an unfortunate man?" After Clerk's arrest, his brother

Donald "solicited" M'Pherson to leave the country, "that he might not give evidence," and offered him "half of every penny Donald was worth" if he would bear false witness at the trial.

Whatever may be thought of M'Pherson's ghost story, it is supported by the testimony of Isobel M'Hardie, in whose sheiling the vision appeared. This lady, who missed the spirit on its first call, deponed that on the night in question she, along with her servants, was sleeping in the hut, when she awoke and "saw something naked come in at the door in a bowing posture." From motives either of modesty or fear, "she drew the clothes over her head," and unfortunately saw nothing further. Next morning she mentioned the matter to M'Pherson, who, having decided to comply with the ghost's request, assured her "she might be easy, for that it would not trouble them any more."

James Macdonald, Allanquoich, stated that, having heard the rumour of the pannels' guilt, he applied to Clerk's father-in-law, Alexander Downie, to know if it were true. Downie admitted that it was so, adding, "What could his son-in-law do, since it was in his own defence?" Macdonald had seen upon Elizabeth Downie's finger after her marriage a gold ring, "having a little knap upon it like unto a seal," which he suspected had belonged to Davies. Peter M'Nab, a neighbour, also saw the gold ring, "pretty massy, having a lump upon it pretty large," and asked Elizabeth how she came by it, to which she answered "that she had bought it from one James Lauder, a merchant." Elspeth Macara, Clerk's servant, had often seen her mistress wearing a gold ring "with a knob upon it of the same metal."

Lauchlan M'Intosh, who had been a servant of the sergeant's landlord, deponed that some two years after the disappearance he saw in the hand of the prisoner Macdonald a penknife resembling one Davies used to carry, which had certain peculiarities known to the witness. He remarked at

7

the time that it was "very like Sergeant Davies's penknife," but Macdonald merely observed "that there were many siclikes."

John Grant, Altalaat, deponed that the pannels lodged in his house on the night of 27th September 1749, that preceding the murder. Next morning, "after the sun-rising," they went out, each with a gun, saying "that they intended to go a deer-hunting." As he left home that morning to attend a fair at Kirkmichael, and did not return for four days, Grant knew no more of their doings. He was corroborated by his son, who saw the pannels start on their shooting expedition, going up the water to the Hill of Gleney, a mile and a half from the Hill of Christie. Clerk was wearing a grey plaid. Jean Davidson, Inverey, stated that "about sun-setting" on the day Sergeant Davies disappeared she saw Clerk, "having a plaid upon him with a good deal of red in it," return from the hill to his father's house in the clachan.

John Brown, ground-officer, Inverey, said that when, by order of the chamberlain, he called out the inhabitants to search for the missing sergeant, Clerk "challenged him for troubling the country people with such an errand, and upon this the witness and the said Duncan had some scolding words."

Such was the circumstantial evidence adduced in support of the charge; but the Crown was in a position to prove by the direct testimony of an eye-witness that Davies undoubtedly met his death at the prisoners' hands. Angus Cameron, a Rannoch man, swore that upon the day of the murder he and a companion named Duncan Cameron, who had since died, were hiding, for political reasons, in the heather. They had spent the previous night on Glenbruar Braes, and were then lying concealed in a little hollow upon the side of the Hill of Galcharn on the lookout for one Donald Cameron, "who was afterwards hanged," and some other friends from Lochaber, with whom they expected to foregather that day. They had lain there since "two hours after sun-rising." The time hung heavily enough upon their hands, and they would welcome any passing incident as a relief to the tedium of their vigil. About mid-day they observed Duncan Clerk, whom Angus knew by sight, and another man "of a lower stature," unknown to him, both with guns, pass the hollow where they lay. Clerk had on a grey plaid "with some red in it." An hour or so before sunset Angus saw a man in a blue coat with a gun in his hand, whose hat was edged with white or silver lace, about a gun-shot off upon a hill opposite to the place where he lay. Coming up the hill towards the stranger were the two men he had seen in the morning. The three met upon the top of the hill, and after standing some time together Clerk struck the man in blue upon the breast, whereupon the man cried out, clapped his hand to his breast, "turned about, and went off." The other two "stood still for a little," and then each of them raised his gun and fired at him practically at the same moment, though Angus could distinguish the separate reports. "Immediately upon them, the man in blue fell." The murderers then approached their victim, and the watcher saw them stoop down "and handle his body." While they were so employed Angus and his companion deemed it prudent to beat a retreat, which they did unobserved, and, without waiting for their companions, left the district.

Not till the following summer did Angus chance to hear of the vanishing of Sergeant Davies, and realise that he had been present at his slaying. Hitherto he had told no one of what he had seen, but he now consulted two Cameron friends as to how, in the circumstances, he ought to act. They advised him to do nothing in the matter, "as it might get ill-will to himself and bring trouble on the country." The two Camerons above mentioned corroborated. When informed by Angus that he had seen Clerk and another shoot a man dressed "like a gentleman or an officer" upon a hill in Braemar, one prudently said he did not want to hear any more on that subject, and the other that it would never do to have such a report raised of the country, and advised Angus "to keep the thing secret." We have already seen how the fear of possible reprisals had sealed the lips of those who long before could have enabled the authorities to bring the murderers to justice.

This concluded the evidence for the prosecution, which we have been thus particular in setting forth in view of the startling verdict thereon arrived at by the jury. The proof in exculpation consisted of the testimony of but three witnesses. Colonel Forbes of New deponed that as justice of the peace he had been instructed to examine Elizabeth Downie (who, being Clerk's wife, was incompetent as a witness upon his trial) touching the nature and extent of her jewellery. She informed him that she was married to Clerk in harvest, 1751; that before her marriage she had a copper ring "with a round knot of the same metal on it," which she gave to a glen-herd named Reoch; that since her marriage she had only possessed two rings, a small brass one, which she produced, and a gold one, which she got from her mother. It will be remembered that to other witnesses Elizabeth had given different and contradictory accounts of her rings. Two witnesses who had been at the shearing in Gleney on the day of the murder, said they had seen Clerk there alone about noon. Gleney is a mile farther up the water towards the hill than Inverey, and is about the same distance from Glenclunie. Both witnesses were very vague as to the hour, which they fixed with reference to their dinner, admittedly a moveable feast.

Reoch, who doubtless had his own reasons for declining to testify concerning the ring with the knob on it, having failed to obey his citation as a witness, was fined one hundred merks, the Court inflicting a similar penalty upon another absenting witness. The jury were then enclosed, and the Court adjourned at four o'clock in the morning of 12th June, having sat for twenty-one consecutive hours. At six o'clock the same afternoon the jury, "all in one voice," found the pannels not guilty of the crime libelled! The Court then "assoilized" Clerk and Macdonald, and dismissed them from the bar.

This amazing conclusion was, one would think, more likely to offend the sergeant's "perturbéd spirit" than the disrespect previously shown to his bones; but whether or not he resented the verdict and troubled in consequence the peace of the jury, we have now no means of knowing. It is highly probable that he had already, by his well-meant intervention, done much to frustrate the ends of justice and bring about his murderers' acquittal; for the supernatural element thus introduced was seized upon by the defence to cast ridicule on the Crown case, and so obscure the very material evidence of the pannels' guilt. Robert M'Intosh, one of their counsel, told Scott that M'Pherson, in cross-examination, swore the phantom spoke "as good Gaelic as ever he heard in Lochaber." " Pretty well," said M'Intosh, "for the ghost of an English sergeant!" But this fact was surely less marvellous than the appearance of the spectre at all; in such matters c'est le premier pas qui coûte. It was Sir Walter's opinion that M'Pherson arrived at his know-ledge of the murder "by ordinary means," and invented the machinery of the vision to obviate the odium attaching to informers. Such also was the view of Hill Burton, who thought Farquharson a party to the fraud. But this theory ignores the testimony of Isobel M'Hardie, and, as we shall find from contemporary evidence, neither of these men did in fact give the information upon which the prisoners were charged. Unless they had themselves seen the deed done or heard Angus Cameron's account of its doing, they knew no more than any of their neighbours, and it does not appear that Angus had then spoken. They certainly displayed little zeal to discover the authors of the crime, for M'Pherson, despite the revelation, took service with the murderer and remained a year in his employment, while Farquharson did nothing whatever in the matter.

The reader will recollect that upon the spirit's first appear-

ance M'Pherson took it for "a real living man, a brother of
Donald Farquharson." It would be interesting to learn more of
this person; where, for instance, he was that night, what were
his relations with the accused, and whether he had not himself
discovered the remains. For it is much more likely that someone, either with a knowledge of the facts or from a desire to
fix public suspicion upon Clerk and Macdonald, the reputed
murderers, assumed the spectral rôle and successfully imposed
upon the credulous shepherd lad, than that the latter would,
in the circumstances, invent and swear to so ridiculous a tale.
Mrs. M'Hardie, on the second visitation, saw a naked figure
enter the low door of the hut "in a bowing posture," which is
more suggestive of a physical than a psychic intruder. Whatever the Lord Advocate may have thought of M'Pherson's good
faith, it is difficult to see how he could ever have expected the
jury to swallow the ghost, but it may be (for the records of
these old trials are confusing) that the spirit was judicially
evoked by Lockhart in cross-examination. Probably, had
M'Pherson and Farquharson confined themselves to the bones
and left the murderers to be named by Cameron, who saw
and knew them, a conviction would have been secured, for
M'Intosh admitted to Scott that both the counsel and agent
of the accused were convinced of their guilt.

It has been conjectured, in explanation of the inexplicable
verdict, that the jury were Jacobites, and as such would
be indisposed to deal very strictly in so trifling a matter as
the removal of a superfluous English sergeant, but the fact
that they were all Edinburgh tradesmen hardly encourages
the supposition. "The whole affair," writes Mr. Lang, "is
throughly characteristic of the Highlanders and of Scottish
jurisprudence after Culloden, while the verdict of 'Not
Guilty' (when 'Not Proven' would have been stretching a
point) is evidence to the 'common sense' of the eighteenth
century."

A curious incident, unnoticed by Scott and Hill Burton,

which arose out of the trial, throws some light on the former
proceedings, and is in itself sufficiently quaint to be recorded.
On Friday, 14th June, two days after the accuseds' acquittal,
Alexander Lockhart, their counsel, presented in his own behalf
to the Lords of Justiciary a petition and complaint against
James Small, late ensign of the Earl of Loudon's regiment, and
then factor upon the forfeited estate of Strowan, whose name, it
will be recalled, had been mentioned during the trial.  According to the petition, Small was "the person upon whose instigation " Clerk and Macdonald had been prosecuted.  He had been
"extremely industrious in searching out witnesses against them,"
and it was alleged that not only did he examine and take
declarations from the witnesses in private, but after they were
cited to give evidence in Court he "dealt with " some of them
not to appear, and endeavoured to intimidate others who did
not say "such strong things " as he expected.  These matters,
said Lockhart, he had thought it his duty to bring to the notice
of the Court and jury at the trial, which he had accordingly
done.  Small, resenting his observations, had, armed with a
sword and attended by two men "of very suspicious appearances," lain in wait for Lockhart in the Parliament Close that
Friday morning.  Upon the arrival of the advocate at his usual
hour for attending court, Small rushed upon him, "made a
claught at the petitioner's nose," and raising his stick, "which
he shaked over the petitioner's head," made the somewhat
superfluous remark that his action was intended as a public
affront, which if Lockhart proposed to resent, "he would be at
no loss to find out where the said James Small lived."  The
petitioner pointed out that no words of his could adequately
represent "the atrociousness of the injury " to the dignity of
the Senators of the College of Justice and the Faculty of
Advocates in general and to himself in particular resulting
from such scandalous behaviour, and that in these circumstances he was induced to seek redress by summary complaint
to the Court "rather than in the way and manner suggested

by James Small." The Court granted warrant for the apprehension of the militant factor, and ordered his committal to the Tolbooth till the next sederunt.

Answers to Lockhart's petition were lodged by Small, who stated that he did not receive any information that Clerk and Macdonald were reputed the murderers until he was instructed to inquire into the case and, if possible, discover the criminals. In December 1753 he assisted the Sheriff-Substitute in making such an inquiry, when it appeared from the precognitions then taken that the accused were the guilty parties, and they were charged accordingly. Had he been called as a witness upon their trial, the objection might validly have been made "that he had given partial counsel in the cause," but though his name was included in the Crown list the point did not arise. Mr. Lockhart, however, in his address, had gratuitously attacked him, with a view to "blacken the petitioner in the most public manner and to fix upon him for ever the basest and worst of characters." He (Small) had been actuated throughout solely by his duty as a good subject and his desire to see justice done, and the strictures of Lockhart upon his conduct, which were well and widely known, so "grieved, vexed, and confounded him by turns" that he was provoked to treat his traducer in the manner set forth in the petition. He protested that in so doing he had intended no disrespect either to the Court or to the Faculty, and though his behaviour "had not perhaps been altogether legal," he hoped the Court would consider his "great and just provocation."

Next day Small was brought to the bar of the High Court of Justiciary. The proceedings took place with closed doors, and the parties were heard by their procurators. The Lords found that the prisoner had been guilty "of a high contempt of this Court, and of a high injury to the Faculty of Advocates and to the complainer, Mr. Alexander Lockhart," and approved of the means taken by the complainer to obtain redress. They ordained Small to be imprisoned in the Tolbooth till Wednesday the 19th, when he must apologise in Court to the injured parties, and find caution to keep the peace for one year, under a penalty of fifty pounds sterling.  Lockhart was ordered "not to resent the injury done to him in any other manner."

On 19th June Small again appeared in custody before the Lords, gave in his bond of caution, and having publicly begged the pardon of the Court, of the Dean and Faculty of Advocates, and of Mr. Alexander Lockhart, was thereafter dismissed from the bar.

Thus was vindicated the outraged majesty of the law, which, if it had signally failed to avenge the slaying of the sergeant, despite the co-operation of his unquiet spirit, could at least see justice done to an advocate's nose.

# KATHARINE NAIRN

Paolo and Francesca in Angus.—ANDREW LANG.

WHEN douce Mr. Thomas Ogilvy brought his young bride home to Glenisla his mother doubtless hailed the event as of happy augury for the house of Eastmiln. Hitherto fortune had frowned upon her family. Her eldest son "grew delirious and hanged himself in '48 in a sheepcot." As the length of the drop was insufficient, "he came down and delved below his feet to make it proper for him," which showed considerable force of character. His brother William "went on board a man-of-war carpenter, and was crushed to death 'twixt two ships." Her husband, who under his chief, Lord Ogilvy, had been out in the Forty-five as a captain of the Prince's army, after the defeat of Culloden was confined in Edinburgh Castle, and, having lain a prisoner in that fortress until 1751, fractured his skull in attempting to escape over the walls "by a net tied to an iron ring." Thomas, the third son, prudently eschewing politics, became by virtue of these calamities laird of the paternal acres. Of her remaining sons, Patrick, sometime lieutenant of the 89th Regiment of Foot, was but newly invalided home from the East Indies, his career eclipsed, while the youngest, Alexander, then prosecuting at Edinburgh his studies in depravity and physic, had just redeemed a nominal celibacy by marriage with a woman of the lowest rank. When therefore, Thomas, at the responsible age of forty, wooed and won Miss Katharine Nairn, a damsel of nineteen, the beautiful daughter of Sir Thomas Nairn of Dunsinnan, old Mrs. Ogilvy (by Scots courtesy Lady Eastmiln) may have believed herself entitled to sing

the Song of Simeon. How far she was justified in the event
the following tale will show:—

The marriage, which took place on 30th January 1765,
would seem to have been on both sides one of affection. The
bride, of a family more rich in ancestry than in money, was
better born than her husband, who was but a "bonnet laird."
Marrying against the wish of her relatives she brought him
at least youth and beauty, whereas Eastmiln (so named by
Scottish custom) was a man of small means who had, moreover, anticipated the modern malady—too old at forty. His
health, as we shall see, was bad; he was somewhat of a
valetudinarian. Mr. Spalding of Glenkilry, the husband of
Katharine's sister Bethia, at whose house Thomas Ogilvy
probably met his future bride, quaintly described him as
wearing "a plaiden jacket and a belt round his middle, much
broader than ever he saw another wear, with lappets of
leather hanging down his haunches, and a striped woollen
nightcap upon his breast, the lower end of which reached
near his breaches." His change of state must have proved
beneficial, for Mr. Spalding adds, "upon his marriage he
took off these happings."

At this time the inmates of the house of Eastmiln were
the dowager, her son and his young wife, Patrick the
lieutenant, and three female servants. From the date of
the marriage until the first of March ensuing all was
apparently well with the family. But on that day —
ominously enough a Friday—there arrived upon the scene
one who was to prove the evil genius of the house and the
harbinger of dishonour and death. This was Anne Clark,
"aged thirty and upwards," a cousin of the laird. Her
private character and professional pursuits, if known, would
necessarily have excluded her from decent society, while as
a guest she laboured under the further disadvantage of being
"a notorious liar and dissembler, a disturber of the peace of
families, and sower of dissension." Her relatives in Angus,

however, knew nothing of all this, and she was received by them "without suspicion, and treated as an equal and a gentlewoman." Miss Clark came ostensibly upon a visit of reconciliation from Edinburgh, where she had been associated with her cousin, Alexander Ogilvy, in the sowing of his wild oats. Jealousy was not among her numerous failings, for after his marriage she had lived with his wife's father. By his alliance with "the daughter of a common porter" Alexander had given great offence to his family, and Katharine in particular had not concealed her opinion of his conduct. Hence the appearance of Anne in her maiden rôle of peacemaker. But it was later alleged that she was actuated by a motive less lovely. Both Eastmiln and Patrick, his heir-presumptive, were in ill health; on their death, should the marriage of the elder prove childless, Alexander the needy would reign in their stead. The first step towards the attainment of this end was to effect an estrangement between the newly-married pair. If such was indeed her scheme Anne had no time to lose. Her mission, genuine or not, had failed. Alexander's entry in the family black books was indelible.

Miss Clark must have had a winning way with her, inviting to confidence. She and young Mrs. Ogilvy had never met before, yet within a fortnight of her coming Katharine told her she disliked her husband, "and said if she had a dose she would give it him." Nor was this a mere isolated indiscretion, for Miss Clark states that thereafter "Mrs. Ogilvy did frequently signify she was resolved to poison her husband." She even consulted Anne as to the best means of procuring the requisite drug — whether "from Mr. Robertson, a merchant in Perth, or Mrs. Eagle, who keeps a seed shop in Edinburgh, upon pretence of poisoning rats." Anne considered this classic formula open to objection, as being apt to bring the purchaser "to an untimely end," but she generously offered to go herself to

Edinburgh "and get her brother, who lived there, to buy the poison." Although a woman with many pasts, Anne, as the cousin of the proposed victim, seems at first sight an unsuitable confidant, but such is her own version of the facts. There for the time the matter rested.

Anne Clark had not been long established beneath that hospitable roof when an ugly rumour concerning Mrs. Ogilivy and her young brother-in-law began to trouble the house of Eastmiln. Anne charitably warned her hostess " to be upon her guard as to her conduct and to abstain from the lieutenant's company." Her well-meant hint, however, proved ineffectual, for on Sunday, 19th May, according to her own account, she obtained indisputable proof of a liaison between them. Katharine, although at once apprised of the discovery by her considerate kinswoman, continued in her evil course with cynical, nay lunatic, effrontery. Anne would fain have supported her story by the testimony of her aunt, but old Lady Eastmiln, who enjoyed the same facilities for seeing and hearing what Anne alleged to have occurred, noticed nothing, despite the fact that her attention was specially called to the matter by her niece at the time. She consented, however, to communicate Anne's " suspicions " to Eastmiln.

It happened that at this time a dispute arose between the brothers "about the balance of a bond of provision resting owing to Patrick Ogilvy," as to which the latter considered himself aggrieved. On Thursday, 23rd May, in the course of a discussion of this vexed question, the laird lost his temper, referred to Anne's allegations, and ordered his brother out of the house. Patrick, indignantly denying the charge, left that afternoon and went to stay with a friend at Little Forter, about three miles distant. That Katharine, whether innocent or guilty, was in the circumstances considerably upset is not surprising. Eastmiln warned his wife that she would injure her reputation "by intermeddling in the differences betwixt him and his brother," which hardly looks as if he took the matter seriously; but the servants swore that they overheard him tell her "that she was too great with Lieutenant Ogilvy, and that they were as frequent together as the bell was to ring on Sunday." Anne says that the laird proposed to leave his own house so as to give the young people a clear field, and that she urged Mrs. Ogilvy to agree, "as she saw little prospect of harmony between them," which, so long as she remained their guest, was no doubt likely enough. Be that as it may, Katharine, with singular imprudence, wrote to the lieutenant begging him to return, which he wisely declined to do. According to Anne's story Mrs. Ogilvy, who had become impatient at her delay in procuring the poison from Edinburgh as promised, told her, after the lieutenant's departure, that "with much difficulty" she had prevailed upon him to furnish it. That same day Anne had an unexplained conversation with a surgeon of Kirriemuir as to the properties and effects of laudanum and the amount of a fatal dose. Whether she shared Rosa Dartle's passion for information or made the inquiry on behalf of Katharine, does not appear.

It is admitted that by the following day husband and wife were so far reconciled that Eastmiln himself wrote to his brother asking him to come back. He sent the letter by a neighbour, to whom he first read it, telling him of Anne Clark's reports, "but that for his [Eastmiln's] part he did not believe them." Patrick, however, still refused to return. He visited various friends in the neighbourhood, and while at Glenkilry, the house of Mr. Spalding, Katharine's brother-in-law he received from her another letter, the contents of which we do not know, unless it be the one produced later at the trial.

On Friday, 31st May, Patrick entertained his brother officer, Lieutenant Campbell, and a friend, Dr. Carnegie, to dinner at an inn in Brechin. He afterwards stated that before he left Eastmiln, Katharine asked him to send her for her own use some salts and laudanum, of which he told her he had a quantity in his sea chest, then at Dundee. Unfortunately for him, Dr. Carnegie proved that at this dinner he delivered to Patrick at his request " a small phial glass of laudanum and betwixt half an ounce and an ounce of arsenic," which latter " he wrapt up in the form of a pennyworth of snuff under three covers." Patrick's reason for wanting the arsenic was, he said, " in order to destroy some dogs that spoiled the game "—which was open to the objection previously taken by Anne to Katharine's hypothetical rats. After paying Dr. Carnegie a shilling for these commodities, Patrick accompanied Lieutenant Campbell to Finhaven as his guest for the week-end.

On Monday, 3rd June, Patrick rode to Alyth to visit his kinsman, Andrew Stewart, who had recently married his sister, Martha Ogilvy. Mr. Stewart had brought the lieutenant's sea chest from Dundee to his own house, and on this occasion he saw Patrick " working among some salts " in the chest. Next day Elizabeth Sturrock, one of the servants at Eastmiln, came to Alyth upon some household matter, and delivered to Patrick a letter from Katharine, to which he returned an answer by her. Mr. Stewart having announced his intention of visiting Eastmiln the following day, Patrick gave him " a small phial glass, containing something liquid which he said was laudanum, and also a small paper packet, which he said contained salts," together with a letter for Mrs. Ogilvy, all of which he requested his brother-in-law to put into her own hands.

Meanwhile Miss Clark states that Katharine told her she had heard from Patrick, who " had got the poison the length of Alyth," and would send it by Andrew Stewart next day. Anne, ever zealous for the family honour, very properly exhorted her to abandon her nefarious purpose, dwelt upon the consequences likely to ensue " both in this world and the next," and asked her reasons for " this strange resolution."

These were that Mrs. Ogilvy did not love her husband, and
that he had used the lieutenant ill upon her account. "How
happy," said she, "could they live at Eastmiln, if there were
none there but the lieutenant, she, and the deponent [Anne]!"
That experienced spinster at once pointed out that in no
circumstances could Katharine marry her brother-in-law, but
was met by the suggestion that they might live abroad.
Still, Anne thought it "a dreadful thing to crown all with
murder." Mrs. Ogilvy desired "to be let alone, for the
conversation was disagreeable to her." Now all this could
have been no news to Anne Clark in June, for on her own
showing she had known since the middle of March both the
nature of Katharine's feelings towards her husband, and her
fell design.

In the forenoon of Wednesday, 5th June, a chapman
(hawker) called and demanded from Eastmiln the price of
some cambric, of which Anne was then making ruffles for
the lieutenant. As he had been told that Patrick himself
supplied the material, the laird was justifiably annoyed, and
repudiated liability for the account. Later in the day Andrew
Stewart arrived at the house of Eastmiln and privately handed
to Katharine the lieutenant's parcel, which she placed un-
opened in a drawer in the spare bedroom. But Anne was
on the alert, and waylaying him, asked if he had brought
anything from Patrick. Mr. Stewart, "because he considered
Miss Clark as a person given to raise dissension in families,"
at first denied that he had done so; but, being persistently
pressed by her, he finally admitted the fact. Whereupon
Anne said "they were black drugs," and that Mrs. Ogilvy
meant to poison her husband. Stewart, shocked at the suggestion, was "very much displeased" with her, the more so
that she proposed to her aunt to warn Eastmiln of his
danger. But "the old lady said it would be improper,"
being, as appears, a stickler for etiquette.

That night the four relatives supped together—a strange

party—at a public house in the Kirkton of Glenisla. Eastmiln told his brother-in-law, Andrew Stewart, that he had
not been well for some time past, and was thinking of con-
sulting Dr. Ogilvy of Forfar. He further said that he was
seized with illness the day before, and "had swarfed [fainted]
on the hill," for which reason he could drink no ale. So he
called for a dram, "which he took, and thereafter seemed
hearty and in good spirits." But Miss Clark's conscience, a
tender plant, still troubled her, and she unobtrusively left
the board in quest of ghostly aid, or, in her own words,
"with a view of being advised by the minister what was fit
to be done in such a case." The minister of Glenisla was
from home, so she rejoined the supper-party without the
benefit of clerical counsel, the nature of which, in a situation
so delicate, one would like to have known. On the way
home Stewart escorted his sister-in-law, the laird following
with Anne, who, availing herself of the opportunity, warned
him that his life was threatened by his own wife, and
begged him to leave home. Eastmiln said he was then too
busy to do so, but promised to take nothing from Katharine's
hands. It is probable that he was not much impressed by
his cousin's solicitude; that he disliked and distrusted her
is certain. Apparently the hour was favourable for con-
fidences; Katharine at the same time was telling her companion that she lived a most unhappy life with her husband,
and "wished him dead, or, if that could not be, she wished
herself dead." This statement, chiming as it did with
Anne's suspicions, somewhat startled Mr. Stewart. When
they reached the house, and after Eastmiln and his wife had
gone to bed, he proposed to Anne Clark and the old lady
"that they should either take Mrs. Ogilvy's keys out of her
pocket or break open her drawers at the back," so as to see
what were the actual contents of the packet. To neither of
these practical suggestions could Anne by any means be
brought to agree, which is the more remarkable in view of

8

the urgent anxiety expressed by her earlier in the evening.
But when Lady Eastmiln, who had gone up to listen at the
door of the connubial chamber, reported "that there was
then more kindness between them than usual," Mr. Stewart
was confirmed in his opinion "that there was no foundation
for Miss Clark's fears."

Next morning, Thursday, 6th June, breakfast was earlier
than common—"betwixt eight and nine"—as Mr. Stewart
was returning that day to Alyth. All the members of the
family were present except the laird, who, having been unwell in the night, was still in bed. Katharine poured out a
bowl of tea from the teapot, put sugar and milk in it, and,
telling the old lady and Stewart that she was taking it up
to Eastmiln, left the room. While she was upstairs the
party was completed by the appearance of Anne, to whom
Katharine, on re-entering the parlour, remarked "that the
laird and Elizabeth Sturrock were well off that morning, for
they had got the first of the tea." Upon which, Anne says
she exclaimed in alarm, "What! has the laird got tea?
and on Mrs. Ogilvy answering that he had, the deponent
said nothing"—like the parrot in the tale. An hour and
a half afterwards, according to Mr. Stewart—Anne says half
an hour—Katharine announced that the laird "was taken
very ill." Anne ran upstairs to the bedroom, and on returning significantly reported that "Eastmiln had got a bad
breakfast." Stewart then went up himself to see what was
the matter, and found his brother-in-law suffering from sickness and other distressing symptoms. The laird expressively
said that "he was all wrong within." Mr. Stewart proposed
to Mrs. Ogilvy to send for Dr. Meik of Alyth, but she
would not consent, saying that "he [Eastmiln] would be
better; and she would not for any money that a surgeon
should be called, as the consequences would be to give her
a bad name from what Miss Clark had said of her."
Later, Mr. Stewart persuaded her to let him summon

Dr. Meik, "a discreet person," and thereafter set out for
Alyth.

Katharine's forecast was so far justified that Eastmiln
presently rose "and went first to the stables to see his
horses fed, and then to the Shillinghill, where he conversed
with some of his tenants." On returning to the house he
became violently sick in the kitchen, and had to be helped
upstairs to bed. Katharine attended to her husband during
the forenoon, but from mid-day until his death Anne Clark
was in possession of the sickroom. She states that Mrs.
Ogilvy refused to remain there unless she (Anne) was dismissed, to which the laird would not agree. Anne and some
of the servants represent that Katharine tried to exclude
people from the room, but it is proved that, apart from
those in the house, Eastmiln was visited by at least five
persons, including his brother-in-law, Mr. Spalding, and the
local precentor, who was summoned by Katharine to pray
with him. The symptoms exhibited by the dying man
were admittedly vomiting, purging, "a burning at his heart,"
pains in his legs, restlessness, and persistent thirst. Anne
gave him repeated draughts of water and of ale, none of
which he could retain; but on her trying him with "a glass
of wine and a piece of sugar in it," the sickness ceased
for about an hour. On cross-examination, she had to admit
that she got the wine from Mrs. Ogilvy. That the laird
had become convinced that his wife had poisoned him is
clear. When Anne Sampson, one of the maids, brought him
a drink of water in the same bowl in which Katharine had
given him the tea, he cried out, "Damn that bowl! for I
have got my death in it already." He said in the hearing
of Elizabeth Sturrock, another servant, "that he was poisoned,
and that woman [his wife] had done it." Lady Eastmiln
reproved him for saying so, to which he answered "that it
was very true, and his death lay at her [Katharine's]
door." Anne, on the other hand, says that the old lady

blamed him for taking anything from his wife, when he replied, "It is too late now, mother; but she forced it on me." He told Andrew Stewart that "he had what would do his turn"; to his friend and neighbour, Mr. Millam, he remarked, "I am gone, James, with no less than rank poison!" At midnight the unhappy man was dead. It was but four months since his wedding-day.

Dr. Meik arrived from Alyth two hours later; it does not appear when he received the summons. He had an interview with the widow, who was apparently "in great grief and concern." She made the remarkable request "that whatever he might think to be the cause of her husband's death, he would conceal it from the world." Patrick Ogilvy, sent for by Mr. Spalding from Glenkilry, where he had been that gentleman's guest, was then in the house, and conducted the doctor to the death-chamber. He struck Dr. Meik as being, like Mrs. Ogilvy, "in great grief and concern." After a brief examination the doctor departed, having, as it appears, come to no conclusion regarding the cause of death.

That morning (Friday, 7th June) the servants, probably at the instigation of the thoughtful Anne, applied certain scientific tests to the fatal bowl, in which they said they had noticed "something greasy in the bottom." The results were negative. They filled the bowl with broth, which was given to a dog, "who eat it up, but was nothing the worse of it." Anne Clark recounts a curious conversation had by her with the lieutenant on his coming from Glenkilry. She told him "she knew the whole affair of the poison," whereupon Patrick admitted sending it to Katharine, but said "he did not think she had so barbarous a heart as to give it."

The funeral was fixed to take place on Tuesday, 11th June, the lieutenant, as his brother's heir, remaining at Eastmiln to make the requisite arrangements. Mr. Millam, the late laird's friend, tells us that when "the mournings came home" Miss Clark complained to him "for want of a mourning apron, adding that she would make it as dear to them [Katharine and Patrick] as if it was a gown!" This was short-sighted parsimony indeed; Anne's silence was worth many aprons' purchase. On Monday, the 10th, Mrs. Ogilvy dismissed her dangerous kinswoman, giving her money in presence of Mr. Millam, both of which facts Anne afterwards denied on oath. Anne further swore that before she left the house she did not communicate to anyone, "by letters or otherways," her belief that Eastmiln had been poisoned. Yet early in the forenoon of Tuesday, the 11th, her old flame Alexander Ogilvy arrived from Edinburgh, and dramatically stopped the burial on the ground that his brother had not died a natural death. The widow resented her brother-in-law's action—reasonably enough in any view of her conduct—and "behaved very ill, weeping and crying, and wringing her hands and tearing herself." Mr. Millam, hearing what had happened, strangely advised Patrick "to make his escape, if guilty"; to which the lieutenant replied, "That God and his own conscience knew that he was innocent." Next morning, at the request of Alexander Ogilvy, Dr. Meik of Alyth and Dr. Ramsay of Coupar-Angus arrived to make a post-mortem examination of the corpse, Katharine and Patrick offering no objection. Alexander, however, refused to allow the body to be opened until Dr. Ogilvy of Forfar, who had been desired by the Sheriff to attend, was also present. The two surgeons, therefore, merely inspected the corpse and left, refusing to wait for Dr. Ogilvy. After they had gone the latter arrived, but declined to open the body in the absence of the other surgeons, on the ground that the autopsy might be attended with personal danger. He, in his turn, made an inspection and departed. We shall see later the result of their several observations.

On Friday, 14th June, Katharine and Patrick were apprehended upon the signed information of Alexander Ogilvy, and, having been examined before Mr. George Campbell, Sheriff-Substitute of the county, were consigned to Forfar gaol. That day Miss Clark returned in triumph to Eastmiln, to assist her old friend Alexander in taking possession. On the 17th, the erstwhile medical student, confident in the assumption of his lairdship, "rouped the stocking upon the farm," *i.e.* sold by auction the cattle, etc., on the false pretence of an authority from Patrick, and appropriated the proceeds of the sale.

On 21st June the prisoners, having been removed to Edinburgh, were examined there before Mr. Balfour of Pilrig, Sheriff-Substitute of Edinburgh—the kinsman of Stevenson's David Balfour—and were committed to the Tolbooth to await their trial. It is said that when they landed at Leith, Katharine was with difficulty rescued from the fury of the populace, so strong was the feeling against her by reason of the rumour of her misdeeds.

It may be convenient here briefly to consider the purport of the prisoners' judicial examinations, so far as these relate to the question of the poison. In her first declaration at Forfar Mrs. Ogilvy deponed, "That before Patrick Ogilvy left his brother's house she asked him, any time he was at Alyth, to buy for her and send to Eastmiln two doses of salts and a little laudanum, as she slept very ill. . . . That she took one of the doses of salts on the Friday after her husband's death and the other on the Saturday; and on the Sunday and the Monday nights she took the laudanum each night, and as she did not use the whole laudanum she delivered back the glass and the remainder of laudanum to the said Patrick Ogilvy on his return to Eastmiln after his brother's death"—which, as regards the laudanum, was afterwards proved to be true. She admitted giving her husband the bowl of tea, which "she carried straight from the low room, where they were at breakfast, upstairs to her husband's room." She further declared that Elizabeth Sturrock got the remainder of the bowl of tea, as Eastmiln "did not drink it out." Patrick Ogilvy the same day declared, "That the said laudanum and salts he brought from the East Indies with him, as a remainder of what he used when his health was bad there and on his passage home. . . . That within these two weeks he was at the town of Brechin, and in company with James Carnegie, surgeon, of that place, *but that he received from him no laudanum or any other medicine whatever.*" He corroborated Katharine's account of her request for the drugs.

While in Forfar gaol, Patrick learned from a friend that Dr. Carnegie had disclosed the purchase of the laudanum and arsenic, "upon which the lieutenant seemed to be under some concern," and expressed a desire to see the Sheriff and amend his declaration upon that point; but this could not be done.

When examined before Sheriff Balfour at Edinburgh upon lengthy interrogatories both prisoners, by advice of their counsel, declined to answer the various leading questions put to them, Katharine refusing even to sign her declaration.

On 1st July, Sheriff Campbell of Forfar proceeded to the house of Eastmiln to search the repositories (which since the laird's death had been locked up by the scrupulous Alexander), and found two letters, obviously written by Katharine to Eastmiln before their marriage, and later so described in the indictment. These were produced at the trial as proof of her handwriting, with reference to an unsigned, unaddressed letter alleged to have been written by her to Patrick on an unknown date, in the following terms:—

DR CAPTIN,—I was sorrie I missed you this day. I sat at the water side a long time this forenoon; I thought you would have comed up here. If you had as much mind of me as I have of you, you would have comed up, tho' you had but stayed out-by, as there was no use for that; there is more rooms in the house then one. God knows the heart that I have this day, and instead of being better its worse, and not in my power to help it. You are not minding the thing that I said to you or [before] you went out here, and what I wrote for. Meat I have not tasted since yesterday dinner, nor wont or you come here; tho' I should never eat any, it lyes at your door. Your brother would give anything you would come, for God's sake come.

This letter was not recovered by Sheriff Campbell on his search of the premises, but was sent to him later by Alexander Ogilvy.

How it came into that gentleman's doubtful hands does not appear. By a curious oversight, Hill Burton, in his narrative of the case, assumes that all three letters were written by Katharine "to her alleged paramour," and even quotes from the two former as such.

The trial commenced before the High Court of Justiciary at Edinburgh upon the 5th of August 1765. The judges present were the Lord Justice-Clerk (Sir Gilbert Elliot of Minto), Lords Auchinleck (Alexander Boswell, father of the immortal Bozzy), Alemore (Andrew Pringle), Kames (Henry Home), Pitfour (James Ferguson), and Coalston (George Brown). The Lord Advocate (Thomas Miller of Barskimming, the pawky Sheriff Miller of *Catriona*), the Solicitor-General (James Montgomery), Sir David Dalrymple (the future Lord Hailes), and two juniors conducted the prosecution. Alexander Lockhart (afterwards Lord Covington) and the great Henry Dundas appeared for Mrs. Ogilvy; David Rae (later the eccentric Lord Eskgrove) and Andrew Crosbie (Scott's Counsellor Pleydell) represented Lieutenant Patrick Ogilvy. The first day was occupied in the usual debate upon the relevancy of the indictment, which was duly found relevant to infer the pains of law. On the following day there was presented to the Court a petition in the name of the pannels regarding Anne Clark, then in custody in the Castle. The movements of this exemplary female since we left her reinstated at Eastmiln are uncertain. Although in her private capacity of friend and relative of the prisoners she had told extra-judicially everything she could against them, and made a formal statement before the Sheriff, she is said to have shrunk from the painful necessity of swearing to her story in the witness-box. She therefore disappeared from the ken of the Lord Advocate until the eve of the trial, when she communicated with his lordship as follows:—

LORD ADVOCATE,—Upon my coming to town, I am informed that you have been searching for me. It would never bread in my breest to keept out of the way had it not been for terror of imprisonment; but houping you will be more favourable to me I shall weat upon you tomorrow morning at eight of the clock.

ANNE CLARK.

Sunday evening, eight of the clock.

Despite her "houp," Miss Clark was lodged in the Castle, along with the three women servants from Eastmiln who were to be witnesses in the case. The petition stated that "as she was in a combination to ruin the pannels and, as far as she could, to deprive them of their lives as well as their reputations," it was obviously unfair to them that she should have an opportunity of tampering with the other witnesses. It was accordingly craved that she should be separated from them. This was granted by the Court; but it afterwards appeared that Anne was only removed for one night, and was then replaced in the same room with them as before, by order of Lord George Beauclerk, Commander-in-Chief of the forces in Scotland, who considered "that the room in the gunner's house she was by desire put into, was by no means a place to keep a prisoner in safety."

At seven o'clock in the morning of Monday, 12th August, a jury was empanelled, and the examination of witnesses began. It was the practice of those times that after a jury was once charged with a pannel the Court could not be adjourned until the jury was inclosed, i.e. till they withdrew to consider their verdict. The hardships thus entailed upon all concerned where the case was of any length are evident. In the present trial the proceedings up to that stage lasted for forty-three consecutive hours, the jury not being inclosed until two o'clock in the morning of Wednesday, 14th August.

The purport of most of the evidence adduced for the Crown has been given in the foregoing narration, but certain points remain to be considered. With regard to the proof of a criminal intrigue between the pannels, the prosecution relied mainly upon the testimony of Anne Clark—"whose evidence," as Hill Burton well observes, "is always suspicious"—corroborated to

some extent by that of the servants, Katharine Campbell,
Elizabeth Sturrock, and Anne Sampson. No doubt their
memories had been much refreshed by Anne's reminiscences
while in the Castle. To Campbell, the most damaging witness
of the three, it was objected that she had been dismissed
by her mistress for theft, which she practically admitted,
and had sworn revenge. The Court, however, allowed her
to be examined. When Anne Clark was called, Dundas,
for the defence, strongly objected to her admission on the
grounds of her infamous character and lurid past; that, in
confederacy with Alexander Ogilvy, she herself had propagated
the false reports which led to the pannels' arrest; and that she
had expressed deadly malice against them, and threatened to
bereave them of their lives. Sir David Dalrymple, in reply,
did not attempt to whitewash his fair witness, but contended
that general proof of character was incompetent; that the
crimes charged were occult crimes, only provable by witnesses
who lived in the family, "be their character what it will"; that
until the evidence was closed it could not be said whether the
reports spread by Miss Clark were false or not; and that the
pannels must prove the cause of her alleged ill-will. The Court
admitted the witness, reserving the question of malice. Anne
Clark's examination occupied eight hours. We cannot here
discuss the infragrant details of her evidence, though these
present many singular and suggestive features—the case was
heard with closed doors, from which let the gentle reader, like
the stranger admonished by Mrs. Sapsea's epitaph, "with a
blush retire"; but in reference to the proof upon this part of
the case it may be generally remarked that the behaviour of
the prisoners, as described by Anne Clark and her attesting
nymphs, exhibits a reckless disregard of consequences which
well-nigh passes belief, while the corroborative evidence of
undue intimacy is to a large extent discounted by what we
know of the coarseness of speech and manners pervading
Scottish society in those days. The acts of familiarity upon

which the prosecutor relied to support Anne's tale were said to have occurred in public and before third parties, some even in presence of the husband himself. The very limited capacity of the house of Eastmiln has also to be borne in mind. It appears from an unpublished sketch plan, prepared for the use of Crown counsel, that the house consisted of two storeys; upon the ground floor there were but two rooms, kitchen and parlour, one on either side of the entrance hall or passage; on the flat above were two bedrooms corresponding to the rooms below, with a small closet between them over the lobby. A garret in the roof was used as a store-room. We learn from the evidence that the servants slept in the kitchen, beneath the west bed-room occupied by the laird and his wife; that the east bedroom, above the parlour, was assigned to the lieutenant; and that Anne Clark and old Lady Eastmiln shared a " box-bed " in the parlour. So homely and primitive were then the habits of the Scots gentry that a family of five persons and three servants were thus "accommodated " in four small rooms. It is also in evidence that the kitchen ceiling was unplastered, and that the conversation of the laird and his wife in their bed in the room above was clearly audible in the kitchen below. The partition walls, too, were of lath and plaster, which enabled Anne Clark to overhear from the staircase all that went on in the lieu-tenant's room. Verily the house of Eastmiln was ill adapted to purposes of stealthy intrigue. If Anne Clark's astonishing tale be true the guilt of the pannels on this count must be accepted; but one hesitates at which the more to marvel—the baseness of Anne if forsworn, or Katharine's unblushing impudence if guilty.

The proof of the murder is in a different case. The ground of the prosecution was that Eastmiln died of poison. This, strange as it may seem, looking to the subsequent verdict, the medical evidence entirely failed to establish. Dr Meik, who first saw the body, found "the nails and a part of the breast discoloured and his tongue swelled beyond its natural size and cleaving to the roof of his mouth." He was "unacquainted with the effects of poison," but having been told by Alexander Ogilvy that poison had been administered in this case, he "conjectured" it to have caused the death. Dr. Ramsay concurred as to the post-mortem appearances, with this addition, that the lips were "more discoloured than by a natural death," and, upon the same information, agreed with Dr. Meik. Both admitted having seen similar symptoms in cases of death from natural causes. Dr. Ogilvy, who had inspected the corpse at the request of the Sheriff, deponed "That the breast was white and the lips pretty much of a natural colour. . . . That the face, the arms, and several other parts of the body were black and livid, and that the nails were remarkably black." Manifestly the condition of the corpse, which when seen by the surgeons had lain unburied for six summer days, was due to putrefaction. This Dr. Ogilvy practically admitted, by stating that "he could draw no conclusion as to the cause of the defunct's death." The only appearance that struck him as peculiar was the condition of the tongue, which was "such as occurs from convulsions or other strong causes."

In view of the negative testimony of these experts as to the cause of death, the evidence regarding Eastmiln's general health becomes important. Anne Clark and the three servants represent him as a strong man, sound and hearty until the last day of his life. His mother, a valuable witness on this as upon many other points, was called by neither party—which affords matter for reflection. Mr. Spalding, his brother-in-law, swore that for some years past Eastmiln had been in bad health, "complaining often of a heart-cholic or pain in his stomach, attended with a short cough which was not continual but seldom left him." That some years before he had suffered from "an ulcerous fever" (as was otherwise proved to be the fact), and was never the same man again; also that on one occasion, being seized with illness at the house of Glenkilry, Eastmiln "got hot ale and whisky with a scrape of nutmeg in it, and was put to bed without any supper"—a curious remedy for gastric inflammation. Mr. Spalding further stated that in February, the month after the marriage, he wrote to Katharine's mother, Lady Nairn, advising "that infeftment be taken in favor of Mrs. Ogilvy upon her marriage contract," owing to the unsatisfactory state of her husband's health. His brother-in-law, Andrew Stewart, deponed that Eastmiln was "a tender man," whose sister, Martha Ogilvy (Stewart's wife), used to say that he would not be a long liver. He repeated what Eastmiln had told him, as already mentioned, about "swarfing on the hill." James Millam, his friend and neighbour, said that four days before Eastmiln died he complained to him "of a gravel and a cholic, and that he could not live if he got not the better of it." On the Tuesday before his death he became unwell at the deponent's house. He had a fire lit to warm him, though the night was not cold, and got heated chaff applied to ease his suffering. He remarked to the witness "that he was fading as fast as dew off the grass; that he could not get peaceable possession of his house for Anne Clark; that he wished her away; and he got from the deponent a ten-shilling note for the expense of her journey." But that faithful spinster was not so easily disposed of. Five witnesses from Glenisla proved that the day before his death Eastmiln had been attacked by severe internal pain while visiting his tenants; that he had to lie down upon the ground; that he said he had not been so ill for six years; and that "he behoved to get Dr. Ogilvy to give him something to do him good." It should be remembered that at this time there is no suggestion of his having been poisoned by his wife, who, if she had the will, had not then the means to do so, and it is difficult to reconcile the evidence of these relatives and friends with the laird's rude health, as sworn to by Anne and the accusing maids. To poison a person in such a condition seems, to the lay mind, a superfluity of naughtiness.

What told most heavily against the lieutenant undoubtedly

was his deal in arsenic with Dr. Carnegie at Brechin, of the
purchase and disposal of which no satisfactory explanation was
offered.    But, curiously, it was not even proved that the
substance sold was in fact arsenic ; all that Dr. Carnegie could
say was that he had bought it as such long before, and had
" heard from those he sold it to that it had killed rats."
So much for scientific testimony in 1765 ! With regard to
Katharine, Anne Sampson, one of the maids, swore that on the
morning of the day of Eastmiln's death, having followed her
mistress upstairs on some domestic errand, she saw her in a
closet adjoining the bedroom, " stirring about the tea with her
face to the door," but did not see her put anything in the
tea.   Mrs. Ogilvy made no attempt to conceal what she was
doing, and spoke both to the servant and to a lad employed
in the house, who was also present at the time.   Elizabeth
Sturrock deponed that her mistress had tried to induce her to
say she (Sturrock) had drunk the remainder of the tea.   She
admitted that Mrs. Ogilvy brought her tea that morning, when
she was ill in bed, but she denied it was what had been left
by Eastmiln.   That Katharine did take salts—she being then
in a delicate state of health—Anne Clark admits, and is corroborated by Elizabeth Sturrock, who says she " got a part of
them."   The incriminating letter from Katharine to Patrick
produced by Alexander, if genuine, leaves little doubt as to
their intimacy.   One sentence only can be held to refer to the
poison : " You are not minding the thing that I said to you or
[before] you went out here, and what I wrote for."   This might
equally be referable to the salts which she says she had asked
him to send her.   As already pointed out, this letter 'was
without either date or signature, but the indefatigable Anne,
presumably an expert in handwriting, swore that it was written
by Mrs. Ogilvy.   Yet when shown an undoubted letter of
Katharine, addressed to Eastmiln, " she did not know whose
handwriting it was."
      The case for the prosecution was closed at three o'clock on

Tuesday afternoon, and the exculpatory proof and addresses to the jury occupied till two o'clock on Wednesday morning. Of the sixty-four witnesses cited for the Crown twenty-four were examined; a hundred and eight witnesses had been summoned for the defence, but for reasons that will presently appear, only ten of these were called. The contemporary report of the trial unfortunately does not include the speeches of counsel, but we read in the *Scots Magazine* that "the evidence was summed up by the Lord Advocate for the King, by Mr. Rae for Lieutenant Ogilvy, and by Mr. Lockhart for Mrs. Ogilvy." Ramsay of Ochtertyre, who was then at the Scots bar, says of Lockhart's performance on this occasion: "He never failed to shine exceedingly in a very long trial, when defending criminals whose case appeared to be desperate. Mr. Crosbie told me soon after, that in the trial of the Ogilvies, which lasted forty-eight hours, he stood the fatigue better than the youngest of them. He took down every deposition with his own hands, but no short ones, when he went out to take a little air. In answering Lord Advocate Miller, who was perfectly worn out, he displayed such powers of eloquence and ingenuity as astonished everybody. To save the life of his unhappy client he gave up, with great art, her character; but contended there was no legal proof of her guilt, though enough to damn her fame."

At four o'clock on the afternoon of Wednesday, 14th August, the jury, "by a great plurality of voices," found both pannels guilty as libelled. Lockhart at once entered a plea in arrest of judgment in respect of certain irregularities in the proceedings. We cannot here deal fully with this interesting debate, which throws an extraordinary light upon the judicial procedure of the day—how in the course of the trial the jury repeatedly "dispersed into different corners of the house," eating and drinking as they pleased, and talking to the Crown witnesses and the counsel for the prosecution; how between three and five o'clock on the Tuesday morning only one of the judges remained

upon the bench, " the rest retiring and conversing in private
with sundry of the jury and others ; " how, " when the evidence
on the part of the pannels began to be adduced, several of
the jury showed a very great impatience and insisted that that
evidence which the pannels thought material for them should be
cut short, and some of them particularly disputed the relevancy
and propriety of the questions put by the counsel for the
pannels with great heat, insomuch that some of the judges and
other jurymen were obliged to interpose, in order that the
exculpatory proof might go on ; and the counsel for the pannels
were obliged to pass from many witnesses, in order to procure
attention from those assizers.   Hence, though thirty-three hours
were spent in hearing calmly the proof adduced for the prosecutors, yet the proof for the pannels, after being heard by those
jurymen with great impatience, was put an end to in about
three hours."    Finally, how, contrary to an Act of Charles II.,
whereby the prisoner's advocate was to have the last word,
Lord Kames, one of the judges, addressed the jury upon the
whole case after counsel had done so for the defence.    This
is the first recorded instance in Scots criminal practice of
the familiar charge to the jury by the presiding judge.    The
Court, in respect of the " regularity and accuracy " with which
the trial had been conducted, repelled the plea.    But Lockhart
had still another card to play ; he alleged that his client was
pregnant, and in her case judgment was superseded until her
condition should be reported upon by five professional ladies.
Sentence of death was then pronounced against Patrick Ogilvy,
to be executed on 25th September, and the Court rose, doubtless
with much relief.

Next day the jury of matrons, which included Mrs. Shiells, a
local practitioner eminent in her art, of whom we shall hear again,
reported that they could give no positive opinion on the subject of the remit.   The Court therefore delayed pronouncing
sentence against Mrs. Ogilvy till 18th November, to give the
five ladies the opportunity of arriving at a definite conclusion.

Meanwhile the friends of the prisoners were not idle in their interests. Application was made to the King in Council for a respite to Patrick Ogilvy, not of favour but of right, until certain points of law should be determined :—(1) Whether in a capital case an appeal was competent from the High Court of Justiciary to the House of Lords? (2) Whether the proceedings at the trial were fair and legal according to the law of Scotland? and (3) Whether, if the first point were doubtful, the execution of the convict should be respited till that question was judged by Parliament, which was not then sitting? Prior to the determination of these questions, which were remitted to the decision of the Attorney-General for England and the Lord Advocate, Patrick received four reprieves—the first three for fourteen days each, the last for seven days only. He is said to have been a great player on the violin, and the interval between his condemnation and execution was, we are told, " exclusively devoted to his performance on that instrument."

While the young lieutenant's fate yet hung in the balance, the judicial dovecot of the Parliament House was fluttered by the publication in certain Edinburgh journals of an " opinion " by an English counsel, one Mr. M‘Carty, upon the points at issue. This gentleman, writing from London on 14th September, animadverted upon the conduct of the trial, holding that the prisoners were prejudiced by being tried for two entirely different crimes upon one indictment. He was of opinion that if the crimes charged were considered separately and the evidence produced to support one crime taken singly, without the assistance of the other, no jury in England would have found the prisoners guilty. " The intrigue was supposed to be certain, because the husband was supposed to have been poisoned ; and, on the other hand, the man was believed to be poisoned, because there was a supposed proof of intrigue." After criticising the peculiar features of the evidence with some freedom and to excellent purpose, Mr. M‘Carty saw neither law nor reason why the proceedings of the Court of Justiciary

9

might not be subject, as well as those of the Court of Session, to review by the Supreme Court. These views on the subject of criminal appeal gave great offence to the College of Justice. The publication of the opinion was held to be contempt of Court, and, upon the complaint of the Lord Advocate, the publishers of the *Edinburgh Weekly Journal*, where it first appeared, and of the *Courant, Caledonian Mercury*, and *Scots Magazine*, in which it was reprinted, were haled before the Court of Justiciary to answer for their offence. They severally expressed sorrow for the wrong they had done, and the Court, while dwelling on the "high indignity" which it had thereby sustained, dismissed them with a rebuke.

The law officers of the Crown having reported in the negative upon the questions submitted to them, Patrick Ogilvy was executed in the Grassmarket on 13th November, pursuant to his sentence. Chambers states, so popular was the lieutenant with his regiment, which was then quartered in the Castle, that it was judged necessary "to shut them up in that fortress till the execution was over, lest they might attempt a rescue." A letter from his colonel, giving him an excellent character, is printed in the report of the trial. In "An Authentick Copy" of his dying speech, published at the time, we read, "As to the crimes I am accused of, the trial itself will show the propensity of the witnesses, where civility and possibly folly are explained into actual guilt; and of both crimes for which I am now doomed to suffer I declare my innocence, and that no persuasion could ever have made me condescend to them. I freely forgive every person concerned in this melancholy affair, and wherein any of them have been faulty to me I pray God to forgive them." The newspapers of the day record a shocking incident at the execution. After he was "turned over," the noose slipped and he fell to the ground. The wretched man, "making what resistence he could," was again dragged up the ladder by the hangman and others, "who turned him over a second time, and he continued hanging till dead." For assisting the law on this occasion, a member of the Society of Tron-Men (chimney-sweeps) was expelled from that association and banished to Leith for five years—a grievous punishment for an Edinburgh citizen.

On 18th November the professional ladies were at length enabled to report that Mrs. Ogilvy could not in humanity be hanged for several months, and the Court further delayed sentence until 10th March. Upon 21st November Katharine presented a petition to the Court, praying that a judicial factor should be appointed to administer the estates of the deceased laird in the interests of her unborn child. Alexander Ogilvy, his brother's heir-presumptive, did not meantime oppose the application, but in his answers he indicated that if occasion arose he meant to contest the succession. A factor was duly appointed.

On 27th January 1766, in the Tolbooth of Edinburgh, Mrs. Ogilvy gave birth to a daughter. When the Court met on 10th March to pronounce sentence of death, a physician and two nurses deponed that she was not yet strong enough to be brought up for judgment. The diet was therefore continued for a week. At seven o'clock on the night of Saturday the 15th, however, the interesting invalid summoned sufficient energy to burst her bonds. Her escape, which is said not to have been discovered till the Sunday afternoon, was, as we shall see, probably collusive. The contemporary accounts are suspicious. It is said that, being indulged with "the quiet and privacy which the nature of her illness required," she dressed herself in man's clothes, and, the door of her room having been at her request "left open for the benefit of the air," she naturally walked out. Perhaps the turnkeys and sentries were still celebrating the New Year, old style. On Monday the 17th the Lord Justice-Clerk granted a warrant for her arrest, and the magistrates of Edinburgh issued a notice offering a reward of one hundred guineas for her apprehension. She is described as "middle sized and strong made; has a high nose, black eye-brows, and of a pale complexion"—a description

which seems wilfully at variance with the received accounts of
her beauty.   She "went off on Saturday night in a post-chaise
for England by the way of Berwick; and had on an officer's
habit and a hat slouched in the cocks, with a cockade in it."
On the 22nd the Government announced in the *London Gazette*
an additional hundred guineas reward for her recapture.   It is
therein stated that Mrs. Ogilvy, disguised as a young gentleman,
very thin and sickly, muffled up in a greatcoat, and attended
by a servant, had passed through Haddington on Saturday at
midnight, and had pushed on with four horses, day and night,
from stage to stage, towards London.   The *Gentleman's Magazine*
records "that information was received at Mr. Fielding, the
magistrate's, office, that on the Wednesday following she was
at Dover in the dress of an officer, endeavouring to procure a
passage to France"; and in a later report, that having failed to
do so, she "returned from Dover to London, took a hackney
coach to Billingsgate, got on board a Gravesend boat, with a
gentleman to accompany her, agreed with a tilt boat there to
take them over to France for eight guineas and a guinea a day
for waiting for them four days in order to bring them back;
which tilt boat landed them at Calais, but is since returned
without them."   This, of course, was a device to gain time and
baffle her pursuers.

But tradition gives a more probable account of Katharine's
escape from the prison.   Her uncle, Mr. William Nairn, a well-
known and respected member of the Scots bar, was at that
time Commissary Clerk of Edinburgh.   He was raised to the
Bench in 1786 with the judicial title of Lord Dunsinnan, and
in 1790 succeeded to the baronetcy, which, on his death in 1811,
became extinct.   His lordship is said to have contrived his
niece's freedom.   Sir Daniel Wilson, in his *Memorials*, states, upon
the authority of Charles Kirkpatrick Sharpe, that Katharine
walked out of the Tolbooth "disguised in the garments of
Mrs. Shiells, the midwife who had been in attendance on
her and added to her other favours this extra-professional

delivery." James Maidment, in *Kay's Portraits*, tells the same story, with the additional particular that Mrs. Shiells had feigned toothache for some days before, and muffled her head in a shawl. The doorkeeper, according to Chambers's *Traditions*, knowing what was afoot, gave the fictitious nurse a slap on the back as she left the prison, and bade her begone for "a howling old Jezebel." Sharpe owed his own introduction to the world to the good offices of this benevolent dame, who, as Chambers notes, was still practising in Edinburgh so late as 1805.

There are various accounts of Katharine's adventures after she had successfully "broke prison." Sharpe says that in her confusion she "risped" at Lord Alva's door in James's Court, mistaking the house for that of her father's agent, when the footboy who opened the door recognised her, having been present at the trial, and immediately raised an alarm. As the case was heard *in camera*, this lad must have been exceptionally privileged. Her uncle's house was in a tenement at the head of the Parliament Stairs, the site of which is now occupied by the Justiciary Court-room. Thither, says Sharpe, Katharine fled, and was concealed in a cellar by Mr. Nairn till the hue and cry was over, when his clerk, Mr. James Bremner, afterwards Solicitor of Stamps, accompanied her to the Continent. Maidment, on the other hand, states that on the night of her escape a carriage was in waiting at the foot of the Horse Wynd, in which she and Mr. Bremner at once left the city. In view of the contemporary evidence there is little doubt that this is the correct version of her flight. She probably assumed the officer's dress *en route*. Chambers says that the coachman had orders, if the pursuit waxed hot, to drive into the sea so that she might drown herself. The contingency, fortunately for her fellow-traveller, did not arise. Thus Katharine vanished from the ken of her contemporaries, and history knows nothing certain of her fate.

"Was she guilty, was she innocent, and, if innocent, why did Lieutenant Patrick Ogilvy buy arsenic at Brechin?" asks

Mr. Andrew Lang; and indeed these are "puzzling questions," which every reader must answer for himself.

Wilson states that Mrs. Ogilvy went from France to America, married again, "and died at an advanced age, surrounded by a numerous family." Maidment says she was afterwards "very fortunate, having been married to a Dutch gentleman," with satisfactory results, as above. Alternatively, she took the veil, and, surviving the French Revolution, died in England in the nineteenth century. Chambers marries her happily to "a French gentleman," and credits her with the usual large family. Similar vague surmises are still current regarding the aftermath of Madeleine Smith.

The only fresh light which the present writer has been able to discover is derived from the following sources :—a paragraph in the *Westminster Magazine* of 1777—"Mrs. Ogilvie, who escaped out of Edinburgh jail for the murder of her husband, is now in a convent at Lisle, a sincere penitent"; and an unpublished MS. note in a contemporary copy of the trial— "Catherine Ogilvie or Nairn did not marry a French nobleman as was at one time reported. She entered a convent and remained there until the troubles consequent upon the French Revolution compelled herself and the other inmates to fly to England, where she died. My informant, Mr. Irvine, lawyer of Dunse, tells me that a friend of his saw her tomb, with the name 'Catherine Ogilvie' upon it; and that upon enquiry the superior mentioned that of all the females in the convent she was the most exemplary in every respect."

Of the others concerned in the tragedy, the unconscious infant died in the Tolbooth within two months of her birth. She is said to have been "overlaid," but by whom is not recorded. The mother was then in France. It is satisfactory to learn that Alexander Ogilvy took no benefit from the child's death, for on 1st March 1766, the anniversary of Anne Clark's arrival at Eastmiln, that bold spirit was arrested for bigamy, and was in his turn committed to the Tolbooth. One might have expected that Anne would be the redundant bride, but from his indictment it appears that the favoured lady was a Miss Margaret Dow, daughter of an officer of the Royal Highlanders, unlawfully espoused by him so lately as 24th February. Upon his trial on 4th August, Alexander pleaded guilty to the charge, and was banished for seven years. He was allowed, however, to remain two months in Scotland to settle his affairs, which he effectually did in the following manner: while leaning over the window of a house in one of Auld Reekie's towering *lands*, he lost his balance, fell out, and was killed on the spot. Thus only Anne Clark and old Lady Eastmiln withstood the changes of that eventful year. " Their conversation must have been rich in curious reminiscences," like that of Lady Bothwell and her first love, Ogilvy of Boyne, when they came together at the end of the chapter.

The case of Katharine Nairn is one of the most attractive in our criminal annals, and should this imperfect summary be the means of sending a stray reader to the report of the trial itself, he will not go unrewarded.

# KEITH OF NORTHFIELD

SOCIETY in Scotland had a sufficiency of scandal to furnish topics for many tea-tables in the summer of 1766. In March of that year, the beautiful Katharine Nairn, then under sentence of death for the murder of her husband, made her picturesque escape from the Heart of Midlothian, not without suspicion of her uncle's connivance, himself being a senator of the College of Justice, and successfully fled to that *plaisant pays de France*, where they order some matters better, as Mr. Yorick remarked. The Douglas Cause, that huge, unwieldy lawsuit, was at length well under way, and the portentous pleadings began in July their three weeks' course before " the Fifteen " at Edinburgh, amid the intense excitement of a perfervid people, bets to the amount of £100,000 being laid upon the result. That same month provided a fresh sensation: Mrs. Keith of Northfield, in Banffshire, and her son William were, on the information of the laird, her stepson, arrested for the murder of his father ten years before within the house of Northfield.

"The singular circumstances of this case," observes a contemporary pamphleteer, " the atrocious nature of the crime, the great distance of time since that crime is said to have been committed, together with the doubtfulness and uncertainty of the evidence, have excited the curiosity of the public "—and incidentally inspired his pen. And though the world has long since ceased to concern itself as to whether the widow and her son were cold-blooded assassins or the innocent victims of family spite and medical ignorance, their trial may still be read with interest, as affording a quaint picture of the Scottish life of its day, and as an instructive problem in the niceties of presumptive proof.

Alexander Keith, the late laird—old Northfield, as he was termed at the trial, to distinguish him from his son and successor —was born in 1692, and was thus "three score and three years when he died" on 21st November 1756. Some twenty years before his death, Northfield, a widower with a son and daughter, had married a girl named Helen Watt, the daughter of a fisherman at Crovie, a village in Banffshire, who bore him several children, and with whom, as she afterwards alleged, he always lived very happily. Their union, however, had other and less pleasing results, for the marriage was deeply resented by the family of the first wife, whose brother "thought it a most disgraceful one." It led to a complete estrangement between old Northfield and George Keith, his son and heir, who quarrelled with his father on the subject, and left home in consequence, nor were they ever reconciled during the old man's life. The laird's brother and sister, John and Anne Keith, who lived "about three rig-lengths distant," continued upon friendly terms with their relatives at Northfield. The daughter of the first marriage later made her own experiment in matrimony, so that in the month of November 1756 the household consisted, in addition to the servants, of the laird and his second wife and their five children—William, aged 17 ; Henrietta, 15 ; Elizabeth, 13 ; Alexander, 10 ; and Helen, 7. Old Northfield, it was alleged, had early in life contracted a habit of excessive drinking, which gradually impaired his health, and being persisted in for a long course of years, at length ruined a constitution naturally sound. Be that as it may, there is evidence that during the autumn of 1756 the laird's health was in a critical condition. His brother, John Keith, deponed "that he had been long in a valetudenary way," and considered himself "a-dying"; while his medical attendant, Dr. Chap, surgeon in Old Deer, stated that he professionally visited the laird, who was suffering from "an asthma, attended with a high fever," until the week before his death, when he found him so ill that he also "thought him a-dying." The doctor, who seems to have been an easy-going practitioner, added that in these circumstances he desired Mrs. Keith not to send for him again unless her husband "grew better," and took his departure, leaving the patient to the care of Providence.

Old Northfield, having thus had his own belief that his days were numbered fortified by the expert opinion of the faculty, prepared like a prudent man for the inevitable end. In view of the attitude adopted from the first by his eldest son George towards his father's second wife and family, and of the unforgiving temper which that young man had since exhibited towards himself, the laird well knew that he could trust little to his heir's generosity or good feeling in regard to the future of his widow and younger children. In order, therefore, to secure for them some provision after his death, he decided to make a will settling upon them certain small sums of money, by no means beyond what his estate could easily bear. Accordingly, a few days before his death, Northfield sent for his old friend the Reverend James Wilson, minister of Gamrie, who at his request wrote out for him a short document embodying this intention, which was duly signed by the testator in presence of his neighbour, Mr. Garden of Troup, and his own servant, William Taylor, who subscribed the deed as attesting witnesses. It was admitted that the execution of this will was the voluntary act of the laird, and that the provisions therein contained were equitable, and such as his estate could well afford. Nevertheless, as afterwards appeared, the granting of these sums, small though they were, gave great offence to his successor.

In the evidence led at the trial we have glimpses of the old man on what was to be his last day in this world. Mr. Wilson, the minister, called in the afternoon to see the invalid, and found him looking better. Northfield, who appears to have borne his bodily infirmities with a cheerful spirit, talked to his reverend visitor "in his usual jocose manner." The minister thought him "to be past danger." William Taylor, the servant who had witnessed the will, having finished his day's work, went up to ask for his master. The laird, though confined to

his room, apparently did not keep his bed; he was "sitting in
the chair with one leg above the other, and a pinch of snuff
between his finger and thumb," and remarked that he was
feeling better. George Gelly, a friend, afterwards looked in
before dark to inquire for him, and saw him "sitting in the
chair, and not very well." They talked together for a while,
and Northfield laughed several times in the course of the
conversation. The last caller, one James Manson, shoemaker
in Gardenstoun, came that evening as usual to shave the laird,
who "was sitting in his night-gown, not well." That night
Northfield, as seems to have been his custom during his illness,
supped in his bedroom with his wife and their five children.
We are told that he took "a very little supper, either of
aleberry or kail-brose," which, in view of his condition, is not
surprising. What little he did eat seems to have disagreed with
him, for he complained of feeling worse, and asked to be put
to bed. The bed was accordingly made ready, "a blanket was
warmed and put about him," and the old man was helped
into bed by his wife and her eldest son, William. The
supper dishes having been removed by the servant, the laird
"desired his children to go to bed, for that he wanted to be
quiet." The two eldest girls, Henrietta and Elizabeth, then
bade their parents good-night and went to their own room.

As to what afterwards happened we have no information
except the declarations of the widow and her son, emitted later
with reference to the charge of murder brought against them by
George Keith. In considering these, it has to be kept in view
that although they were made ten years after the event, by
two persons, suddenly seized and separately examined upon
the most dreadful of charges, they are nevertheless strikingly
uniform and consistent. The laird having told his wife that
he was afraid he would die in the night, she insisted that the
boy William should remain in the room, to be at hand in case
his father grew worse, and the old man "desired him to lye
down at his back to see if he could gather any heat." Mrs.

Keith then went to bed herself, along with her two youngest
children, Alexander and Helen, "in a bed at the end of the
deceased's bed," and the lad, having "thrown off all his clothes
but his breeches," blew out the solitary candle and lay down
besides his father. He noticed that the old man's breathing
was barely perceptible, and spoke to him twice, but received
no answer. He then jumped out of bed, and "calling out
hastily in surprise to his mother to rise and light the candle, for
his father was either dead or dying," ran to the door to summon
the two elder girls and the maid. They entered the room as
Mrs. Keith was relighting the candle.

Meanwhile, as appears from her evidence, the servant,
Elspeth Bruce, was in the kitchen immediately adjoining
Northfield's bedroom, from which it was divided by "a timber
partition." She said she heard no sound in the bedroom that
night. After supper Henrietta Keith came into the kitchen and
told her that the laird "was sitting ben yonder, and that he had
taken two spoonfuls of brose to his supper"; and "in a little
time after the cry came ben that he was dead." Elspeth then
ran into her master's room, where she was joined by the two
girls. The subsequent events as spoken to by her are, with the
exception presently to be noticed, in accordance with the declarations of Mrs. Keith and her son. Neither Henrietta nor Elizabeth were called as witnesses at the trial, and the children,
Alexander and Helen, were too young to be examined. William
declared, that when the others came in and the candle was
lighted, he looked at his father's face and saw "one eye shut
and another open; his lips quivered a little, and he could just
be observed to breathe." Mrs. Keith said that she herself did
not then look at her husband, as she "expected he would come
alive again," but that Henrietta did so, and told her that "she
saw her father's lips moving." Elspeth says she looked at her
master, "and found him in appearance dead in the bed." William
states that he then sent her for William Spence—apparently one
of old Northfield's men—"who was drying corn at the kiln,"

and that she returned with Spence forthwith, by which time "the deceased's breathing could not be observed, and the eye that was formerly open was partly shut." Elspeth says nothing of this incident, and Spence was not produced as a witness at the trial. Probably he was dead, for the prisoners' counsel afterwards, with justice, complained that the defence had suffered greatly by reason of the ten years' delay in bringing the charge, owing to the death of several witnesses "who would have been of the most material consequence in their exculpation." Elspeth, according to the story of the mother and son, was then dispatched to bring John and Ann Keith, the laird's brother and sister, who lived at hand, which, as she admits, she did. Mrs. Keith declared, that when John Keith came, they both looked at her husband, and John "said he did not think but he was dead." John Keith, though examined at the trial, was asked no question as to this night's doings, which is the more curious as Elspeth had stated that when she returned at once with the Keiths, she found the laird's body already taken out of bed and "streikit upon a deal"—laid out upon a board; whereas both Mrs. Keith and William declare that this was not done until after the arrival of Northfield's brother and sister. Anne Keith had died some years before the trial, and was not amenable to earthly citation, but John could have told what actually occurred. The importance of this point is, that while we have plenty of evidence as to the appearance presented by the body next day, there is none as to its condition on the night of the death.

Northfield breathed his last about ten o'clock on the evening of Monday, 21st November, and that night there was no suspicion whatever that he had not died in the natural course of his disease. It is therefore instructive to see from what quarter the first suggestion of murder came. We do not know where George Keith lived, but it must have been in the neighbourhood, for he had early information of his bereavement, and lost no time in coming to look after the inheritance. He entered the house of Northfield, to which he had been so long a stranger, on the morning after his father's death, and it is probable that not till then did he learn of the provisions of the will.  Now the sole foundation for the charge brought by him ten years later against the mother and son was a certain discoloration of the skin upon the neck and breast of Northfield's body, seen on the Tuesday and Wednesday after his death.  He was buried, as we shall find, on the forenoon of Thursday, and the "chesting" spoken to by some of the witnesses probably did not take place till the night before, as the coffin had to be made and the funeral arranged.  The first we hear of the mysterious mark is in the evidence of Elspeth Bruce, who depones "That when George Keith, young Northfield, came next morning [Tuesday] and took a look at his father's corpse, he expressed some suspicion of foul play because of a blae [livid] mark round his neck."  Elspeth, who obviously had heard no word of this before, then went into the room and examined the body, when she "saw a blae mark round the defunct's neck about the breadth of two fingers, and a blae spot upon his breast," which she thought "were strange circumstances."  The other evidence of those who saw the marks is as follows: William Taylor, the late laird's servant, "saw a blue mark about his neck about the breadth of three fingers, but whether it went round the back part of his neck he cannot say, because he did not see that part."  John Strachan, wright in Gardenstoun, who made old Northfield's coffin, stated that when the body was being placed in it, young Northfield turned down the grave-clothes "and showed the deponent a mark round the fore part of the defunct's neck, but whether it went round he cannot say, because he did not see the back part of his neck; that he also saw a mark upon the defunct's breast that reached down towards the slot of his breast; and that the marks were of a blackish blue, like the neck of a fowl newly strangled."  James King, who assisted Strachan "to make the coffin for the late Northfield, and to put him into it," said that at young

Northfield's request he looked at the body, and saw "a black red mark round the neck, such as the deponent never saw on any corpse before that time." Alexander Hepburn, in Cushnie, deponed that he inspected the body at the "chesting," being desired to do so by young Northfield, "who threw off or laid aside the dead cloaths from the upper part of the body." The first thing that attracted his attention was "some blue spots upon the breast;" the next thing he noticed was "a blue girth that went round his neck, like bruised blood; and on the back part of the neck he saw a mark like what is occasioned by a knot drawn strait."

The observations of Elspeth Bruce and William Taylor were each the result of a private view of the corpse, but the evidence of Strachan, King, and Hepburn has reference to one and the same occasion, namely, the "chesting," at which young North-field, Mrs. Keith, the lad William, and apparently John Keith, were present. This seems to have been the first time that the widow's attention was specially called to the marks. Hepburn states that she appeared unwilling to have the body inspected, saying "that there was nothing unseemly to be seen there." Taylor, however, depones "That no person, so far as he knows, was hindered from looking to the corpse." The same witness adds that he asked Mrs. Keith, in presence of John Keith "and others," what was the meaning of that mark, and that she answered that it was occasioned by a string tied round North-field's neck "for holding on a plaister." John Keith, when in the witness-box, says nothing about this incident. Such was the explanation given by Mrs. Keith at the time, so soon as she was asked about the matter. Ten years afterwards she and her son gave in their declarations a more particular account of the circumstance. Mrs. Keith declared, "That she did not look at the body that night [of the death], but next day she assisted to put on a shirt on the body, and then she observed something blue about the back part of the neck, but cannot tell whether that blueness was round his neck or not; That she heard a plaister had been applied to the deceased's back or his neck; but when she assisted to put on the shirt on the dead body, as above, she cannot tell whether the plaister was on the body or not, or whether there was any mark of a plaister upon the body or not; and that she can tell nothing more of her husband's death than is above mentioned." William is more specific: "Declares, that there had been a blistering plaister applied to the deceased's back; and after it was taken away, kail-blades [cabbage leaves] were applied to the place where the plaister had been; and in order to keep these blades in the proper place, they were tied on with the deceased's own garters, which went below the arm-pits, and round the farther side of the neck; and these kail-blades and garters continued in that situation after the deceased's death, until his grave-linen was made and put upon him. Declares, that he was present when the grave-linen was put upon the body; at which time some of the women who were there loosed the above garters, and took them away; and the declarant then observed a blue spot upon the left breast, about the breadth of three fingers, but did not observe anything about the neck, further then that there was a great swelling over his whole body. Declares, that from the time the deceased was put to bed the evening of his death, no person went near him until the declarant called to light a candle, as above; nor did the deceased make the least noise after he was put to bed."

Now someone must have helped to prepare the body for the grave, and whoever did so would be likely to notice this curious arrangement of the garters, which can hardly have been invented by William. But throughout the trial no other reference is made to these "women who were there," unless it be that one of them was Anne Keith, who had died some years before, and, as was alleged for the defence, would have confirmed the prisoners' explanation as to "the innocent and accidental cause of these discoloured appearances on the dead body, which are the frail and only foundation of this prosecution." That the plasters, at least, were no creation of the young man's fancy is proved by the testimony of Dr. Chap, who depones that when he withdrew from the case as hopeless, he "left two blistering plaisters to put upon his [Northfield's] back." When and by whom the plaster and "kail-blades" were respectively applied, tied on, and taken off, who took away the garters and what became of them, are matters upon which the evidence throws no light.

It appears that there were "words" between the widow and the heir "about naming a day for the late Northfield's burial," Mrs. Keith proposing Thursday and George Keith wishing the interment postponed till Saturday. The widow carried her point. John Mair, a neighbour, who mentions this difference, states that before the funeral "he heard the said George require Elspeth Bruce to acquaint him with the circumstances of his father's death; to which she made no answer, but turned about her back and wept. Upon which George said that as she would not tell then, she behoved to tell afterwards." Elspeth says nothing about this incident. Plainly, she had no suspicions till these were suggested to her by George Keith. William Taylor says in his evidence that George objected to the earlier date being fixed "before he had time to prepare matters for the burial"—not because he suspected foul play. Taylor, whose sympathies were evidently engaged in behalf of the prosecution, adds that on the night following Northfield's death he heard Mrs. Keith ask her son William what his brother George would get for his supper. Upon which William answered, "That a guidfull of the dog's meat was good enough for him; that he had no business there; and that, cursing his brother, he said that little hindered him to take a gun to shoot him." The lad may be excused this outburst of resentment against the new laird, who hitherto had ignored his existence, and now began their fraternal relations by accusing him of parricide. Neither is it surprising that the widow, after the insulting treatment she had received at and since her marriage, should resent the imputation of having murdered her own husband.

For what happened at the funeral, we have the account of the Reverend Mr. Wilson. "Being invited to the burial of the deceased Northfield, he was taken up to a room privately by the present Northfield, who intimated to him his suspicions that his father had not got justice in his death." Here, as in all the other instances, the first suggestion of foul play is made by the heir. It is evident that George Keith sought to involve the minister in the responsibility of openly charging his stepmother and brother with murder, for he desired Mr. Wilson " to look to the dead body and give him his advice how he should behave." The good man perceived the snare thus artfully set for him, and declined to examine the corpse, " excusing himself by his ignorance in these matters "—he was no expert in the science of forensic medicine as applied to post-mortem appearances. He gave, however, the practical and judicious advice that if George thought anything was wrong he ought to consult a physician. " Upon this he was told by young Northfield that he had wrote Mr. Finlay, surgeon in Fraserburgh, and had got for an answer that he could do nothing single, and advising him to take the assistance of the two physicians at Banff." Dr. Finlay, who, by the way, if actually consulted as George alleged, was not produced as a witness at the trial, showed no anxiety to move in the matter; but why did not George, if he honestly believed that his father had been strangled, call in Dr. Chap, the local practitioner in charge of the case until a few days before the death, who does not even appear to have been invited to the funeral ? During this secret conclave, the last arrangements had been going forward, and the minister states that George, at this point of the conversation, having looked out of window, " observed that the corpse was gone, at which both of them were much surprised." They then left the house in pursuit of the funeral cortege, the young laird on foot and the minister on horseback. The following reference to what occurred on this occasion is contained in the evidence of Taylor, who depones, " That the present Northfield and Mr. Wilson, the minister, were in an upper room when the corpse was taken out of the house for the burial without acquainting them; that when they got notice that the corpse was removed, they followed; but it was a considerable time before they overtook the company; that Northfield was at the time in complete mourning; that the corpse was removed in the forenoon; and that the place of interment was at the distance of three or four miles." This incident is treated by the prosecution as affording one of the proofs of the pannels' guilt, but it is difficult to see what is its bearing upon the question whether old Northfield was or was not murdered. If the widow and her son guessed the purpose for which George Keith was then closeted with the minister, it is very natural that they should have allowed the funeral to proceed without them.

The only other evidence we have regarding George's attitude at this time is that of his uncle, James Gordon of Techmuiry, brother of the first Mrs. Keith. This gentleman exhibited a strong animus against the woman who for twenty years had occupied the place left vacant by his sister in the affections of Northfield. He stated that he saw little of the laird after his second marriage, which he considered "a most disgraceful one," and that he was last at the house of Northfield on the occasion of his niece's wedding, solely to witness that ceremony, "but insisted that Helen Watt, Northfield's wife, should not be admitted." The mistress of the house would doubtless appreciate to the full this courteous stipulation, and it need not surprise us that Mr. Gordon received no invitation to the next family function, his brother-in-law's funeral. He added that some time after the laird's death he received from his nephew George a letter, "signifying a strong suspicion that his father was strangled by his wife and his son William, and desiring the deponent's advice how he should behave." Once again young Northfield lacked the courage of his conviction. Mr. Gordon wrote in answer, advising him not to insist in any criminal prosecution unless he had clear evidence, which rather looks as if the uncle had not much faith in his nephew's detective genius.

There for the time this matter of the alleged murder rested; and not the least mysterious circumstance in the case is that George Keith did nothing further till ten years had elapsed, when he lodged the formal information against his relatives which resulted in their arrest. One would naturally expect that he was led to do so by the discovery of some fresh evidence which justified his former suspicions and at length warranted his making a specific charge, but such is not the fact. This point was well put by counsel for the defence in their pleadings at the trial:—" It is hoped the Gentlemen of the Jury will not be inattentive to these disadvantages under which, from the long delay of this prosecution, the prisoners must necessarily labour in making their defence. We hope they will not fail to observe that the present Keith of Northfield neglected to exhibit any information to the public prosecutor while witnesses were alive who had the best access to know the true state of this matter, and has brought it now after their death when, at the same time, he cannot allege that any new evidence has presented itself."

How the widow and her young family fared when they went out into the world, leaving the rightful heir in possession of the house of Northfield, and whether they ever received payment of the sums due to them under the will, we do not know, but uncertain glimpses of the mother and son may be descried in the evidence given at the trial. William, whose conduct as well before as after his father's death is said by his counsel to have been irreproachable, "employed himself in agriculture," and that with sufficient success to enable him at the time of his trial to support "a wife and a little family." He seems to have quarrelled with his mother, as we shall see from various angry scenes between them spoken to by the witnesses, and there is no doubt that Mrs. Keith's affairs, from whatever cause, were much less prosperous than those of her son. It appears from the evidence of James Duncan, in Whitefield, a shearer in William's employment, that in the harvest of 1761, five years after Northfield's death, his widow's circumstances were so far reduced that she "came to her son William and offered herself to him as a shearer, and that he rejected her services." We shall consider later the relations between William and his mother; in any view the picture thus presented is a pathetic one.

George Keith having for some inscrutable reason at last brought himself to denounce his relatives to the authorities, the mother and son were apprehended by warrant of the Sheriff and lodged in the prison of Banff. The prisoners were respectively examined on 7th and 8th July 1766, in presence of Mr. Alexander Dirom, Sheriff-Substitute of Banffshire, when they emitted separate declarations, and were duly committed for trial. They lay in Banff prison until 26th August, when they were removed to Aberdeen, where at a Circuit Court of Justiciary held by the Right Honourable Lord Kames, one of the Lords Commissioners of Justiciary, on Thursday, 4th September, "Helen Watt, widow of the deceased Alexander Keith of Northfield, and William Keith, eldest lawful son procreated betwixt the said deceased Alexander Keith and the said Helen Watt, pannels, were placed at the bar indicted and accused at the instance of James Montgomery, Esq., his Majesty's Advocate, for his Majesty's interest, for the crime of murder committed by them upon the person of the said deceased Alexander Keith, in manner mentioned in the Criminal Letters raised thereanent."

Henry Home, Lord Kames, a man of much learning and a voluminous writer, "who did more to promote the interests of philosophy and *belles lettres* in Scotland then all the men of law had done for a century before," was noted for his severity as a criminal judge. When at the bar he had acted as counsel for the unfortunate Captain Porteous; and he was one of the judges presiding at the trial of Katharine Nairn in the preceding year, on which occasion he introduced the practice of charging the

jury at the conclusion of the speech for the defence, a custom
since universal but till then unknown.   Lord Kames, however,
is now best remembered in legal traditions on account of his
familiar use of that monosyllable which Mr. John Willet so
reprehensibly called up the stairs of the Maypole six distinct
times, to the grave scandal of the cook and housemaid.   The
"Procurators for the Prosecutor" or counsel for the Crown were
Mr. Cosmo Gordon, Advocate-Depute, and Mr. John Douglas,
advocate; the "Procurators in defence" or counsel for the
pannels were Messrs. Alexander Wight, Alexander Elphinston,
and Robert Cullen, advocates.   Wight afterwards assisted
Henry Erskine in the famous but unsuccessful defence of
Deacon Brodie on his trial before the great Braxfield in 1788.

   The indictment set forth that the deceased having executed
the will to which we have referred, the prisoners became "impatient" for his death; that Mrs. Keith "was heard to express
wishes to that purpose"; that she and her son "did treacher-
ously and wickedly conspire to murder" Northfield; and that
"in pursuance of this their wicked intention," they, in the
circumstances already mentioned, "did wickedly murder the
said Alexander Keith by strangling him in his bed either with
their hands or with some cord or rope or napkin or in some
other violent manner," as appeared from certain marks of
discoloration afterwards seen upon his body, "which could not
have proceeded from the effects of any natural disease, if the
said Alexander Keith had died without violence."   It was
further alleged that Mrs. Keith, "conscious of her guilt in the
premises," attempted to conceal the marks from observation,
invented the whole story of the plaster, and "to prevent further
discovery" caused the body to be buried with unseemly haste
"in a most indecent manner."

   Both pannels having pleaded not guilty, counsel for the
defence stated that while it was not proposed to offer any
objections to the relevancy of the indictment, as the prosecutor
did not pretend to bring against the prisoners any direct proof

of this alleged murder, but meant by a train of circumstances to infer their guilt, "it had become necessary for the prisoners, in justice to themselves, to state the facts which had given rise to this prosecution as they truly happened, and as it was expected they would appear from the evidence to be brought. That this, they hoped, would remove the impression created against them by the frame of the Indictment, and would prepare the Gentlemen of the Jury to attend equally to those circumstances which were to be proved in defence." Counsel then gave their clients' own version of the facts, from which we have quoted in the foregoing narrative. It was argued that in order to support the accusation there were two separate facts, of each of which it was necessary there should be clear and distinct evidence: firstly, that a murder had been committed, and secondly, that the prisoners were guilty of that murder. Was it clearly proved that Keith of Northfield died a violent death? To establish his case the prosecutor relied mainly upon the marks seen upon the body some time after the death, but the jury would bear in mind that the appearances of dead bodies are often so various and extraordinary "that physicians of the greatest abilities and most extensive experience have declared themselves unable to account for their causes, or to determine with any degree of certainty whether they proceeded from a natural or a violent death." Besides the general uncertainty of such post-mortem appearances there was in the present case the further circumstance, "which should make us still more cautious to infer from such discoloured marks that Northfield's death had been a violent one," namely, that the body was neither seen nor examined by any surgeon or person of skill, but that these appearances were now to be described ten years after the event by ignorant, inaccurate country folk, "by whom alone they are said to have been perceived." Physicians who admitted their own inability to determine the cause of such marks when seen by themselves would surely be less able to account for them from the description of ignorant and unskilful observers. The jury were cautioned against confounding the proof required regarding each of the two distinct questions before them. "They will reflect on the dangerous consequence of admitting circumstances tending to fix a crime on particular persons to supply the defective evidence of that crime's having itself existed. Circumstances of conduct in themselves the most innocent may, upon the supposition of a crime, assume a very suspicious appearance, which arises entirely from innocence that had rendered the conduct careless and unguarded. From circumstances, therefore, suspicious only upon the supposition of a crime's having been committed, to reason backwards and conclude from these that the crime truly was committed, is contrary to all just and fair reasoning, and surely inconsistent with that regular form of procedure which has been established for the protection and security of innocence." If, however, the jury came to the conclusion that a murder had been committed, they must carefully examine the evidence adduced to prove the prisoners guilty of that shocking crime. Upon this branch of the case counsel dwelt upon the injury their clients had sustained by reason of the ten years' delay in bringing the charge. Many important witnesses necessary to their defence had died, and in particular Anne Keith, Northfield's sister, the loss of whose testimony was a great misfortune for the pannels, "as she was the only person, besides the two prisoners, who was constantly near the bedside of the deceased." The motive alleged in the present case was, counsel maintained, absurd and incredible. Even if the prisoners were wicked enough to be influenced by such a motive, in view of Northfield's age and serious illness the story was still highly improbable. "Can we believe that when they foresaw his death to be so fast approaching, they would thus wantonly inbrue their hands in the blood of a husband and a father merely to attain a few days, perhaps a few hours, sooner the possession of that pittance which he had provided for them?" On the contrary, it was far more to the pannels' interest that Northfield should survive, for

while he continued in possession of his estate they were much
better off than they would be when reduced to live on the
inconsiderable provision which he had secured to them. There
was no suggestion that Northfield wished to alter his will, and
the only person having any interest to induce him to do so was
the heir, who lived at a distance and never approached his
dying father. Counsel then made a powerful appeal to the
jury on behalf of William Keith, pointing out the extreme
improbability of a boy of seventeen, of previous good character,
and "of all his other children the most beloved and favoured
by his father," committing so atrocious and unnatural a crime.
And when it was remembered that there was the greatest
uncertainty whether any crime had been in fact committed at
all, surely little doubt would remain concerning his innocence.
If, however, the jury were satisfied he was innocent, they were
bound to acquit his mother also; the two prisoners were the
only grown persons in the room with the deceased at the time
of his death, and if he were murdered, both of them must have
been equally guilty of that bloody deed.

An interlocutor was pronounced by Lord Kames finding the
libel relevant to infer the pains of law, and allowing the pannels
to prove all facts and circumstances that might tend to exculpate
them or alleviate their guilt. A jury consisting of local land-
owners and Aberdeen merchants was then empanelled, and the
trial proceeded. With most of the evidence adduced we have
already dealt, excepting that which relates to certain incriminating expressions said to have been uttered by the pannels on
various occasions before and after Northfield's death, which we
shall now consider. The first of these is spoken to by Elspeth
Bruce, who says that the laird and his wife did not live com-
fortably together, but were often squabbling, "though she
cannot say who gave occasion to their squabbling." On a certain
day unspecified Mrs. Keith came "butt the house" in a passion
and exclaimed, "God! that he [her husband] had broke his
neck when he broke his horse's neck, and then she would not

have got so much anger by him"—which hardly implies an intention to murder him herself. This is the only instance given by Elspeth, who of all the witnesses was the one most likely to know the facts. William Taylor deponed that a fortnight before his master's death Mrs. Keith said: "If God would not take her husband, might the devil take him!" and that the reason of her saying so was that Northfield "liked a dram too well and was spending too much." The lady plainly had a sharp tongue and an unweeded vocabulary; but how the laird contrived to be extravagant in his sickroom does not appear. Taylor adds that some time afterwards he heard William address his mother in the following enigmatic and unfilial terms:— "That if it had not been her four quarters his father might have been living; that she never would get justice till she was hung up beside William Wast; and that he could be content to pull down her feet." On research I find that the gentleman referred to was executed at Aberdeen in 1752 for the murder of his wife, where his skeleton still hung in chains on the Gallowhill to give point to William's remark. Isobel Robertson stated that five or six years before, she, being a servant with Mrs. Keith, had occasion to know that William, who was then living with his mother and sleeping in the bed in which his father died, "was frightened with ghosts and apparitions," so that he got a lad to lie in the room with him for a night or two, and afterwards changed his bed. James Irvine, the lad in question, said that six or seven years ago his master, William Keith, complained that he could not sleep in his bed "because he was troubled," but did not say what he was troubled about. At his request the witness sat up with him in his room a whole night, after which William changed his bed. In cross-examination, Irvine admitted it was said that William was afraid of his brother George, but that he never heard that William was afraid of his father's ghost. James Boath, tailor in Banff, deponed that several years after old Northfield's death the pannels quarrelled in his house, "provoking one another by abusive language," when the mother said to the son: "Sir, I know as much of you as would get you hanged." Janet Watt, in Crovie, apparently a relative of Mrs. Keith, stated that once, after a quarrel between the pannels "about milking cows," William observed that his mother was a liar, a thief, and a murderer. John Duncan deponed that when William refused to employ his mother as a shearer, as already mentioned, William said that she would not get justice till she was hanged. Here ends this unedifying testimony. If mother and son did in fact share that fatal secret, it seems unlikely that they would thus twit one another in public with their mutual guilt; more probably when they afterwards fell out, they found in the old suspicions a handy form of recrimination. In any view, William's conduct scarcely warrants the encomiums of his counsel.

The medical evidence adduced for the Crown was confined to that of a single witness, Dr. Alexander Irvine, physician in Banff, who dogmatically deponed that he never saw in the course of his practice such marks as those described in the case of Northfield "that he could suspect was occasioned by any sort of disease, without external violence," and that such marks could not be occasioned by any known disease. This evidence would have immense weight with a local jury. Now, in the year of grace 1766, and for many a long year afterwards, the ordinary country practitioner knew as little about the science of medical jurisprudence as he did of wireless telegraphy. Not until 1806, by the efforts of the great Andrew Duncan, was the study of that subject officially recognised by the University of Edinburgh, when the first chair in the country was there founded. To-day, any final year's medical student knows that one of the commonest of all post-mortem appearances is just such hypostatic lividity as was seen upon Northfield's body the day after his death, and that neither plasters nor garters were necessary to produce it. Nay more, that had he been strangled, as was alleged, by the forcible compression of his throat with cord or handkerchief, the resulting mark would have been pale rather than blue, any livid appearance being above and below the line of constriction. Thus no competent medical man would nowadays peril his reputation by endorsing the scientific testimony of Dr. Irvine of Banff.

The Crown proposed to call as their last witness George Keith of Northfield, to whose evidence objection was taken on behalf of the prisoners that not only was he "the private informer and spring of the present prosecution," but he had likewise acted as an agent by assisting in the precognition—examination of witnesses—before the Sheriff, and had suggested questions to be put to the persons examined. The Court sustained the objection on proof of the fact, and refused to receive George Keith as a witness, which is a matter of regret; for while the prisoners took no benefit from his exclusion, his deposition would probably have made plain many points otherwise obscure. Only two witnesses were called for the defence, John Keith and Dr. Chap, whose evidence has been already noticed. The jury was then addressed by the Advocate-Depute for the Crown and by Alexander Wight on behalf of the pannels, after which Lord Kames ordered the jury to be inclosed "in the laigh council-house," and to return their verdict at ten o'clock next morning. No record of the speeches of counsel has been preserved, nor does it appear from the report of the trial whether or not Lord Kames himself addressed the jury, though, as we learn from another source, it seems likely that his lordship did so.

Next day, Friday, 5th September 1766, when the Court met, the jury "by a plurality of voices" found both the prisoners guilty, but in respect of William's youth and the presumed influence of his mother, they earnestly recommended him to the mercy of the Court. It is said that the jury deliberated for five hours before arriving at their verdict, which was by a majority, nine voting for guilty and six for not guilty. Burnett, in his *Criminal Law*, states that Lord Kames is said to have approved of this verdict; yet the case seems one in which even the Scots form of Not Proven would have been inappropriate. After delivery of the verdict, Alexander Elphinston, one of the counsel for the defence, stated a plea in arrest of judgment. In those days when a pannel was once "remitted to the knowledge of an assize," that is, when the jury were sworn and evidence given, the trial could not legally be adjourned until they had delivered their verdict or were "inclosed" to consider it. Thus in a heavy case the Court had to sit continuously until that point was reached, and even our stalwart forefathers must have quailed before so terrible an ordeal. The worst feature of such a system was the injustice done to the prisoner; for after all parties had been occupied with the prosecutor's evidence, it may be for days and nights, there is little wonder that the case for the defence often received but scant justice. At the trial of Katharine Nairn, for instance, which lasted forty-eight con- secutive hours, the jury became frankly bored, and requested the witnesses for the defence to "cut it short." The heavy strain upon the prisoners' counsel must also have unfairly handicapped the defence.

The objections now taken were that several of the jury had from time to time left the Court-room during the trial, and that in particular, one of them, Mr. Forbes of Skellater, actually went outside, "and was seen on the street going in towards the New Inn," doubtless with a view to alleviate the dryness of the proceedings; and that Lord Kames himself had on one occasion quitted the bench. The Advocate-Depute justified these irregularities as regards the jury on humane grounds, and said that the judge had only gone to "the verge of the Court-house" for a breath of fresh air. Lord Kames repelled the objections, and intimated that he would defer sentence till the following day.

On Saturday, 6th September, the prisoners having been placed at the bar, his lordship sentenced them both to death, Mrs. Keith to be hanged at Aberdeen on 17th October, and

William Keith on 14th November next. His lordship gave
effect to the jury's recommendation in William's case by
adjudging his body merely to be hung in chains upon a gallows
on the Gallowhill of Aberdeen, whereas his mother's remains
were to be delivered to Dr. David Skene, physician in
Aberdeen, "to be by him dissected and anatomised." The
Court then rose.

But, after all, the services of Dr. Skene were not required.
At the instance of the prisoners' friends and of a numerous
public, who considered the evidence insufficient to justify the
verdict, their case was laid before the authorities in London,
with the result that sentence on Mrs. Keith was respited
for four weeks, till the day fixed for William's hanging. On
Sunday, 9th November, an express arrived at Edinburgh with
a free pardon for both mother and son. It was announced that
"His Majesty, upon some favourable circumstances having been
represented to him, was most graciously pleased to grant a
pardon to both the convicts." Such a decision was not at that
period uncommon, for the first Georges were rather given to
interfere in the affairs of the High Court, not so much in the
interests of their Scottish subjects, as to show the Lords Commissioners of Justiciary that they were not masters in their
own house. On this occasion, however, Farmer George did
well to be merciful.

The trial was published on 22nd November at Edinburgh,
though bearing to be printed at London. This was done to
avoid the wrath of the judges, as there was prefixed to it an
"Advertisement" in which, in the course of certain observations
upon the value of presumptive evidence, the administration of
the criminal law of Scotland, as exemplified in this particular
case, was criticised with refreshing freedom. It is interesting to
note that the writer takes exception to that dangerous innova-
tion, the judicial charge, from which it would appear that Lord
Kames had followed the precedent created by himself a year
before on the trial of Katharine Nairn. The curious will find

in the *Scots Magazine* for September 1767 a spirited reply to these strictures.

William Keith only survived his pardon a few weeks; he died on 22nd December following.   What became of his mother is not known.

# "THE WIFE O' DENSIDE"

THE Reports of Proceedings in the High Court of Justiciary from 1826 to 1829—the first instalment of that valuable series—contain two cases of note, by reason of the strange circumstances of the crimes charged, the importance of the legal questions involved, and the eminence of the counsel engaged in the defence. The year 1828 is conspicuous in the calendar of crime as that which saw justice done upon William Burke, who with his partner, Hare, had reduced murder, not indeed to a fine art, but to a vulgar trade. His trial is matter of history; but the fame of Mrs. Mary Elder or Smith, which had filled the public mind since the preceding year till it paled before the wider celebrity of the West Port expert, lingers but as a tradition among the braes of her native Angus, in local ballads of "The Wife o' Denside." Sir Walter Scott was interested in her case. He attended the trial, and, as we shall see, has recorded in striking terms his impressions of the prisoner and his opinion of the verdict. It is here proposed to rescue the memory of this "lost lady of old years" from undeserved neglect.

Poisoning has never been popular in Scotland. It is a crime alien to the character and feelings of the people, and its occurrence is relatively rare. The individual gifts of a Locusta or a Brinvilliers, the collective genius of a race of Borgias, find no parallel in Scottish annals. The poisoner commonly appears in our criminal records as the protagonist of some obscure domestic tragedy. Seldom, as in other countries, is he actuated by the larger motives of ambition, the attainment of place or power; and as his ends are petty, so the means which he employs are curiously limited. The absence of scientific data in the reported cases of early days makes it difficult to tell what deadly drugs were used. Such crimes were often libelled as being committed *per intoxicationem*—not in the modern sense—coupled as a rule with sorcery or witchcraft. But in later times the Scottish poisoner has clung with the persistence of a fixed idea to arsenic, fortunately of all poisons the most uniform in its operation and the most difficult to disguise. From its first recorded use in a tentative way in 1649, to its finished application in the case of Madeleine Smith in 1857, arsenic practically held the field, and has since remained the favourite. This is doubtless due to the common knowledge of its properties and the comparative ease with which it can be procured in various forms. Bold spirits like the late Dr. Pritchard and M. Chantrelle, essaying other methods, have paid the penalty of their rashness.

The year 1827, with which we are now concerned, saw an epidemic of poisoning in Scotland, and three of the four persons severally brought to trial during that period were charged with compassing the death of their victims by arsenic. Despite the strongest presumptive proof of their guilt, each of these conservative practitioners in turn escaped through the postern of "not proven"; the fourth, misled by a taste for novelty and tartar emetic, was convicted. The marked reluctance of Scottish juries to return a verdict adverse to the prisoner upon purely circumstantial evidence in such cases, which by their very nature preclude the possibility of direct proof, may be noted in passing.

Mrs. Smith, who was forty-two years of age at the date of her trial, was the wife of a well-to-do farmer at West Denside, in the parish of Monikie and county of Forfar. Her husband, David Smith, was considerably her senior. Their family consisted of two sons and two daughters. The lads helped their father in the work of the farm; one daughter lived with her parents, the other was the wife of the foreman. Two women servants, Margaret Warden and Jean Norrie, lived in the house;

11

a third, Barbara Small, slept at the foreman's.   Other servants
were employed about the farm whose names, excepting those of
two sisters, Agnes and Ann Gruar, do not concern us.   The
farm of Denside is situated some six miles northward from
Broughty Ferry, on the uplands overlooking the estuary of the
Tay, and within sight of the smoke of Dundee.   Here the
Smiths had lived for twenty years, enjoying the reputation of
respectable, thriving folk, whose prosperity was the ripe fruit
of industry and thrift.   Margaret Warden, a girl of twenty-four,
was the daughter of a decent, hard-working widow who lived
at Baldovie, some distance from Denside.   Mrs. Warden had
been left in poor circumstances, with three young children, and,
in her own words, she was "greatly beholden" to a sister of
Mr. Smith for help in bringing up her family "after her man's
death."   No doubt it was due to the good offices of this kind
friend that Margaret was engaged at Denside.   How long she
had been in service there does not appear, but four years before
the time of which we write, when in her twenty-first year, her
condition was such that she had to give up her work and go
home to her mother's house.   There in due course she gave
birth to a child.   However painful such an occurrence must
have been to Mrs. Warden, she fully forgave her daughter and
undertook the charge of the infant, which she kept from that
time in her own home.   Margaret's employers seem to have
dealt leniently with her fault; after an interval she returned
to Denside, and resumed her work as if nothing had happened.
It may be assumed that the father of this child was in no way
concerned with the later tragedy; at the trial his identity was
not disclosed.

About the end of July, 1826, Mrs. Smith made the un-
welcome discovery that her youngest son, George, was "courting"
Margaret Warden with a view to marriage.   The feelings
of a woman who had toiled early and late for her family's
worldly advancement and had raised their fortunes to a position of credit and respectability, may be imagined.   Margaret's

unhappy earlier lapse enabled Mrs. Smith to treat her as the principal offender, and she denounced the unfortunate girl in terms which might have excited the envy of that master of invective, Mr. John Knox. Margaret was of a passionate and impulsive temper; probably she returned George's affection, and hoped by marriage with him to retrieve the painful episode in her past, and the language which her mistress applied to her was more than she could bear. She left Denside forthwith, and went to her mother's house. Mrs. Warden seems to have induced her to go back, or she herself may have thought that she had been too hasty ; anyhow, she returned to Denside. What happened there we do not know, but a fortnight later she again went home. Perhaps Mrs. Smith had bestowed upon her some further epithets from the vocabulary of the great Reformer. This time the mother believed the rupture permanent, and on returning from her work in the fields a week later she was surprised to find Mrs. Smith closeted with her daughter. Mrs. Smith informed her that she had prevailed upon Margaret to go back to Denside. Mrs. Warden accompanied her visitor to the road. When they had left the house Mrs. Smith remarked, " She wished she [Margaret] was not with child." Mrs. Warden discreetly replied that she did not know ; " it was best known to herself." Whereupon Mrs. Smith " spoke of her daughter's ill behaviour "—doubtless in forcible terms ; prophetically observed that if things were as bad as she supposed it would be " a trial " both to herself and Mrs. Warden ; and said she was then on her way to Dundee, and " would get something for Margaret " there. That night Margaret Warden returned to Denside to meet her fate. From the evidence adduced at the trial, it is manifest that Mrs. Smith desired to get the girl into her own hands, in order that she might, by criminal means, rid her family of the threatened disgrace. It is likely that the luckless Margaret yielded to this infamous suggestion.

The kitchen at Denside contained a box-bed, one of those

unwholesome cupboards, now happily obsolete, in which our
sturdy forefathers were nightly wont to enclose themselves,
in defiance of the laws of health. The closet in question
was shared by Margaret Warden with her fellow-servant,
Jean Norrie. Since Margaret's return to the farm her
mistress had kept her constantly employed in the fields,
ordering her to eat little, work hard, "and take what she
had given her." At ten o'clock on the night of Tuesday, 5th
September 1826, the two girls were sitting by the kitchen
fire, resting after the labours of the day before going to bed,
when Mrs. Smith came in with "something in a dram glass"
and a teaspoon in her hand. The glass was nearly full of
a thick white mixture which resembled cream of tartar.
Mrs. Smith made no statement regarding its contents, but
said that she had been taking some of it herself, and would
let the girls taste it. She dipped the teaspoon into the
mixture, and held a little of it to Jean Norrie's lips, and
handed the remainder to Margaret, who swallowed it without
remark. She then gave her a lump of sugar, and left the
kitchen. Jean had sufficient of the stuff in her mouth to
know that, whatever it was, it certainly was not castor oil.
She barely tasted it, and suffered no ill effects. The girls
then went to their box-bed, and silence fell upon the farm.
In the night Margaret Warden was taken seriously ill, but
she did not rouse her bedfellow, who slept till morning.

Jean Norrie says in her evidence that when she awoke
next day (Wednesday the 6th) she found her companion up
and trying to light the fire. Margaret "grew sick," and she
had to help her back to bed. She then went out to her
work in the fields, and on coming in to dinner at mid-day
found Margaret still in bed, "very ill." She returned to her
work, and when she got home again in the evening about
six o'clock, she asked the invalid if her mistress had been
"owning her" (attending to her) during the day, to which
Margaret answered, "Rather too weel!" So ill did the girl

appear, that Jean told her she feared she was dying. "Some folks would be glad o' that," was the significant reply. They slept together that night, and next morning (Thursday, the 7th) Margaret was much worse, her symptoms being those usual in cases of arsenical poisoning—sickness, thirst, internal pain, etc. Her mistress and Jean attended to her throughout the day, and sat up alternately with her during the night. She asked frequently for her mother, saying if she did not see her soon "she never would"; and Mrs. Smith, in Jean's presence, bade her "wheesht and haud her tongue, till she saw how her physic worked." Jean had previously been told by Mrs. Smith that she had given Margaret castor oil that day. On Mrs. Smith prescribing whisky as likely to allay the internal inflammation, Jean plainly told her that she thought Margaret "had got eneuch o' that or some ither thing, she could not tell what, for sik a purgin' an' vomitin' she never saw"; and the patient called to her from the bed that her mistress had already "burnt her inside with whisky." Mrs. Smith then explained that she had exhibited that stimulant because Margaret "had such a wheezle in her breath," but Jean continued sceptical: "she kent ither things hersel'." When alone with the girl, she warned her to take nothing further from her mistress. It is obvious from this episode that Jean Norrie well knew Mrs. Smith had been drugging Margaret for a particular purpose, but she had no worse suspicion of her mistress at the time.

Early in the morning of Friday, the 8th, Mrs. Smith, yielding at length to the girl's repeated request, sent Barbara Small to Baldovie to summon Mrs. Warden to her daughter's deathbed. Barbara told Margaret of her errand; "she seemed pleased-like," and bid Barbara "tell her sister to go to the Ferry for the doctor." This was the first the mother had heard of the illness, but she at once sent a message for Dr. Taylor of Broughty Ferry, and herself hastened to Denside. Cholera morbus and typhus fever were prevalent in the district, and it was a natural assumption that Margaret had been attacked by one or other of those fell diseases. Mrs. Warden found her daughter crying out in great pain, and complaining that she was "burning." She remarked that her hands were cold, and the girl sadly replied "they wad be caulder yet." In her mother's pathetic phrase, "she took hersel' for death." At one o'clock that afternoon Dr. Taylor arrived at Denside. Mrs. Smith met him at the door and took him into the parlour. She told him that her servant had been ill since Tuesday night, and correctly described the symptoms. He asked if she had given her any medicine, and Mrs. Smith replied, nothing but some castor oil. He then asked why a doctor had not been sent for sooner, and she said that she had not thought there was any danger, adding that the girl was "a light-headed cutty," on account of which she had not paid her the attention she might otherwise have done. She also said that she understood the girl was *enceinte*, and asked if he should know if that were the case, and whether the sickness, etc., would not have the effect of inducing a miscarriage. The doctor interrupted her questions by desiring to see the patient. He then went into the kitchen, where he found the girl at the close of a fit of sickness. Dr. Taylor describes her appearance as follows:—"Her countenance was sunken and ghastly; the whole body, and particularly the hands and feet, were covered with a cold perspiration; there was no pulse at the wrists or temples, and very indistinct pulsations over the heart—about 150 in a minute. I tried to rouse her a little by speaking to her, and asked when she was taken ill. After the question was twice put, she replied that she was taken ill on Tuesday night with vomiting, purging, and pain in the bowels, particularly in the side; I understood her to mean that there were the first symptoms." Her mother was at the bedside during the interview. Having otherwise satisfied himself of the correctness of Mrs. Smith's diagnosis of the girl's condition, Dr. Taylor continues : " I found her in such a state of exhaustion, her replies so difficult, and her case altogether so hopeless, that I did not think it right to put any more questions." He therefore returned to the parlour and told Mrs. Smith that the girl was dying. She received the information without any expression of feeling, and remarked that she had sent for a medical man to take the responsibility off her own shoulders. She resumed her former inquiries regarding the probable effect of the continued sickness, observing that "if the gudeman kent it [Margaret's condition], he would be like to tear down the house about them." Evidently, for her son's sake, she had concealed the girl's situation from her husband. Dr. Taylor then left the house, having formed the impression that Margaret Warden was dying of cholera. He had at the time no reason to suspect that she had been poisoned.

The last words of the dying girl, uttered in presence of Mrs. Warden, Jean Norrie, and Ann Gruar, are highly important. She called Norrie to the bedside, and holding her hand, said, "Jean, ye ken wha is the occasion o' me lyin' here?" "Ay," replied the other, "will you forgie them?" "Yes," answered Margaret, "but they'll get their reward." When left alone with her daughter the mother asked if anybody had hurt her or given her anything, to which she replied, "Jean Norrie will tell you all about it," and being further pressed, she said, "My mistress gave me ——," but was unable to complete the sentence. At nine o'clock that night Margaret Warden died. The mother remained at Denside till the following morning to prepare the body of her daughter for the grave. Nothing further was said by anyone at that time regarding the cause of death. Mrs. Warden seems to have been afraid to ask; Norrie was afraid to speak. On her return home on Saturday, the 9th, however, the widow told her other daughter what Margaret had said, bidding her keep it a secret, but

did not then tell her son—"because it could not bring her
[Margaret] back, and would bring disgrace upon the Denside
family." She afterwards explained her silence as due to
consideration for Mr. Smith's sister, who had befriended
her, as already mentioned.

Mrs. Margaret Smith, the farmer's sister-in-law, calling
at Denside on the Saturday, was told by Mrs. Smith that
Margaret had died of "the fever," that the reports as to the
girl's condition were unfounded, and with reference to some
discoloration of the corpse, that the doctor had said all who
died of "the fever" were of that colour. The same day
Mrs. Smith informed Barbara Small that Margaret had died
of water in the chest, and that Dr. Taylor had told her so.
These statements were all equally false.

On Sunday, the 10th, the second day after the death,
the body was buried in the parish churchyard of Murroes,
in a plain coffin, with the inscription, "M. W. aged 25."
But the secret of Margaret Warden's death was not to lie
hid in her humble grave. Within a week, from some
unknown source, there arose and quickly spread throughout
the countryside a rumour that the dead girl had been poisoned
by her mistress to avert the consequences of a liaison with
her son. Information was lodged with the authorities, and
on Saturday, 30th September, twenty-two days after death,
the body was exhumed by warrant of the Sheriff, and a
post-mortem examination was made by Drs. Johnston and
Ramsay of Dundee, assisted by Dr. Taylor. The internal
organs, which were found to be remarkably well preserved,
bore obvious traces of acute inflammation, and certain portions
were removed for further examination and chemical analysis.
Meanwhile the Procurator-Fiscal continued his inquiries into
the case, and as the result of these Mrs. Smith was summoned
for judicial examination before the Sheriff at Dundee. It
being alleged on her behalf that she was too unwell to be
brought so far, Dr. Johnston was requested by the Sheriff to

visit her and ascertain if she was in a fit state to be examined. He reported in the affirmative, and the examination accordingly took place on 2nd October at Four Mile House, a wayside inn situated between Denside and Dundee. She went, unwillingly enough, in a coach, the doctor, her husband, and one of her sons accompanying her. On the way, Dr. Johnston told them, in reply to a question, that arsenic had been found in the body, whereupon Mrs. Smith remarked that "the girl had vomited so much that she wouldn't have thought anything could have remained in her stomach." At the trial objections were taken to this examination on the ground that Mrs. Smith was then in an hysterical condition, and unfit to be examined. How the evidence stands with regard to this point we shall see later.

The more important statements in Mrs. Smith's declaration are as follows:—Margaret Warden took ill on the night between Tuesday and Wednesday, 5th and 6th September, and on the Wednesday, Thursday, and Friday "vomited and purged much." She denied that she had put to Dr. Taylor on his visit any questions such as he described, or that she was aware of the girl's condition until she heard it reported after the death. A fortnight before Margaret's illness she had given her a dose of castor oil. On the Monday or Tuesday before the death, in presence of Jean Norrie, she gave her, in some "lozenger wine" in a dram glass, another dose of castor oil, which she had bought on the previous Friday from one Mrs. Jolly at Dundee. She "never had any poisonous article about her house." If such were used by persons employed to destroy rats there, they furnished it themselves, and she had nothing to do with it. The last time anyone was so employed at Denside was about two years before. In reply to the Sheriff's final question she stated, " *That the declarant got no drug or other such article from any other person than Mrs. Jolly on the Friday preceding the death of the girl.*" The Sheriff, in whose presence the declaration was emitted, afterwards deponed that no objection was made to her examination either by herself or by her husband, who was present the whole time, nor was anything said as to her mental condition. "During her examination," says the Sheriff, "she was perfectly calm and collected till she came to the last question, when, after it was thrice put by me and thrice answered, she became agitated, gasped, and fell back. I immediately started up, thinking she was unwell, when she suddenly started up too, and said nothing ailed her." The significance of this incident will afterwards appear. As the result of the examination, Mrs. Smith was committed to the prison of Dundee.

A night in the cells may have stimulated the prisoner's memory, or the line which the fiscal's inquiries had taken may have been communicated to her by her friends; be that as it may, next morning she sent to the Sheriff a request that she might be re-examined, "as she wished to tell the truth," and had certain corrections to make in her former statement. In her second declaration, dated 3rd October, the prisoner said she now remembered that on the Friday before Margaret Warden's death "she got from Mr. William Dick, surgeon in Dundee, something to put away rats." A fortnight earlier she had sent to Mr. Dick by one of his daughters a message, asking him to give her "something" for that purpose. When she got the article she was not told that it was poison—"there was some writing on it, but she does not know what it was." As instructed by Dr. Dick, having mixed the article with meal in presence of Margaret Warden in the kitchen, she put it on the Monday following into "the holes and craps of the walls in a loft above the bothy." She did not tell anyone that she had done so. Denside was then infested with rats; in the byre they were "like a drove of cattle." The farm servants complained of the noise they made. In spite of her laudable desire for accuracy it afterwards appeared that the prisoner's recollection of the facts was still imperfect.

On 12th October Mrs. Smith was fully committed for trial,

and on 12th December she was served with an indictment, the
diet being fixed for the 28th of that month before the High
Court of Justiciary at Edinburgh.  The prisoner, availing herself of the provisions of the Act 1701, had elected to " run her
letters," whereby the prosecutor was bound to proceed against
her within a limited time.  The best possible legal advice had
been obtained for her, Francis Jeffrey and Henry Cockburn,
since equally famous in law and letters, and then the twin
ornaments of the Scots bar, being retained in her defence.
When the diet was called on 28th December the Lord
Advocate, Sir William Rae, who appeared for the Crown, at
once moved for a postponement.  He had only learned, he said,
the day before the nature of the defence to be made, viz. that
the deceased had committed suicide.  He understood that forty-
eight witnesses were to be adduced in support of that defence,
which was so contradictory of the evidence laid before him that,
notwithstanding the trouble caused thereby to all concerned, he
felt it his duty not to proceed with the case until he had an
opportunity to investigate the grounds upon which that defence
rested.  The Court accordingly continued the diet against the
prisoner until 12th January 1827.  The length of the pannel's
list of witnesses was such the Crown had not completed their
precognition by that date, and a further postponement was
necessary, the trial being finally fixed for 5th February.  All
this delay was the result of the tactics of the prisoner's advisers
in springing upon the Crown at the last moment the defence
of suicide.

On Monday, 5th February, after two false starts, the trial
began in earnest.  The Lord Justice-Clerk (Boyle) and Lords
Gillies, Pitmilly, Meadowbank, Mackenzie, and Alloway, being
the whole Lords Commissioners of Justiciary, occupied the
bench ; the Lord Advocate, assisted by two Advocates-Depute,
Robert Dundas, and Archibald Alison (the future historian of
Europe), represented the Crown ; while Jeffrey and Cockburn,
with a junior, Menzies, appeared for the defence.  As the case

had excited intense public interest, particularly in medical and
legal circles, the court was crowded to the doors when the
proceedings began at nine o'clock.   The indictment charged the
prisoner with administering to Margaret Warden on Tuesday,
5th, and Thursday, 7th, September 1826, within the house of
Denside, arsenic mixed with water or some other substance,
which she was induced to swallow as medicine intended for her
benefit, and was thus wilfully murdered by the prisoner.   An
objection taken to the relevancy was repelled, the libel was
found relevant, a jury was balloted and sworn, and the following
special defences were lodged :—

1. The pannel does not admit, but on the contrary denies,
that the deceased died by poison.

2. If, contrary to her belief, it is established that poison
was the cause of her death, then the pannel maintains that in
all probability it was taken by the deceased herself, who had
recently before threatened to destroy herself, or her unborn
child, and was of a temper, and in a situation, which made the
execution of this threat not unlikely.

3. At any rate the pannel solemnly denies that any poison was
administered by her.   She was under no conceivable temptation
to commit such a crime, and it can be proved by unexception-
able witnesses that her general character renders its commission
incredible.

4. The pannel gave the deceased no drug or substance under
any false pretence whatever.

5. The pannel pleads Not Guilty.

The examination of witnesses for the Crown commenced and
had proceeded until half-past five in the afternoon, when one of
the jury was seized with convulsions and was carried out of
Court insensible.   Professor (afterwards Sir Robert) Christison,
then the "unacknowledged standing medical counsel for his
Majesty's interest," as he elsewhere describes himself, happened
to be in the witness-box at the moment.   Along with Dr.
Mackintosh, who was also in Court, he attended the juryman

in another room. After the lapse of an hour Dr. Christison returned to Court, and, having been already sworn and under examination when the accident occurred, was examined as to the juryman's condition. Dr. Christison stated that the fit was epileptic, and that the man's memory was affected. In his opinion it was unlikely that the juryman would be able to return to court that night and go through the rest of the trial. Dr. Mackintosh corroborated. The Court held that in these circumstances it would be improper to insist on the juryman's return to the box, and the Lord Advocate moved that the diet be continued and the pannel recommitted to take her trial before a new jury. In view of the novelty and importance of the point, Jeffrey objected to this course being taken without full argument, and wished the matter kept open in the meantime to allow of consideration and discussion. The Lord Advocate replied that if this course were adopted he would not consent to the discharge of the present jury; the criminal letters were nearly run, and he acted under great responsibility. The Court, without prejudice to any objections on the part of the pannel to the further proceedings in the case, discharged the jury, continued the diet till the following Monday at ten o'clock, and warned the reporters of the press to abstain from printing any of the evidence already heard.

When the Court met on 12th February all the Lords of Justiciary were present, and the Lord Advocate, in view of the importance of the matter in hand, was accompanied by the Solicitor-General (Hope), this being the first occasion on which the Court had to determine the legality of resuming a trial interrupted by the illness of a juryman. As the debate upon this point occupied no less than seven hours, considerations of space forbid even a summary of that interesting discussion. The professional reader will find it set forth at length in Syme's *Justiciary Reports*. The Lord Advocate having moved that a new jury be empanelled, Cockburn objected to the competency of continuing the trial upon the same indictment. Dundas, who replied for the Crown, maintained that the prosecutor was entitled to proceed with the case. Jeffrey supported the objection; the Solicitor-General said he had nothing to add to what had been so ably stated by Mr. Dundas. Each of the six judges delivered a separate opinion in favour of the Lord Advocate's contention, and the Court pronounced an interlocutor finding the whole of the former proceedings after the interlocutor on the relevancy null and void, the pannel still subject to trial upon the present libel and by a jury to be balloted for of new, and continuing the diet against her till the following Monday at nine o'clock

As a relief from these technicalities the following extract from Sir Walter Scott's *Journal* will be welcome to the general reader. Under date 6th February, Sir Walter writes: "Dined at Sir John Hay's, where met the Advocate and a pleasant party. There had been a Justiciary trial yesterday, in which something curious had occurred. A woman of rather the better class, a farmer's wife, had been tried on the 5th for poisoning her maid-servant. There seems to have been little doubt of her guilt, but the motive was peculiar. The unfortunate girl had an intrigue with her son, which this Mrs. Smith was desirous to conceal, from some ill-advised puritanic notions, and also for fear of her husband. She could find no better way of hiding the shame than giving the girl (with her own knowledge and consent, I believe) potions to cause abortion, which she afterwards changed for arsenic, as the more effectual silencing medicine. In the course of the trial one of the jury fell down in an epileptic fit, and on his recovery was far too much disordered to permit the trial to proceed. With only fourteen jurymen it was impossible to go on. But the advocate, Sir William Rae, says she shall be tried anew, since she has not tholed an assize. *Sic Paulus ait—et recte quidem.* But, having been half-tried, I think she should have some benefit of it, as far as saving her life, if convicted on the second indictment.

The advocate declares, however, she shall be hanged, as
certainly she deserves. But it looks something like hanging
up a man who has been recovered by the surgeons, which
has always been accounted harsh justice." This contingency,
fortunately or otherwise, did not arise. Rae was the son
of Lord Eskgrove, the eccentric judge whose peculiarities
of voice and manner, as Lord Cockburn relates, Scott
was wont to mimic, to the delight of the Parliament
House.

When the Court met again on 19th February, a new
jury was empanelled, and the Lord Advocate adduced his
evidence. The first two witnesses called for the Crown
were Mr. Kerr, the Sheriff, and Mr. Baxter, the Procurator-
Fiscal, who proved the prisoner's declarations, which the
Lord Advocate then proposed should be read. Jeffrey,
however, objected, and offered proof that the prisoner was
unfit to be examined at the time they were emitted, so the
matter was reserved till the close of the Crown case. The
next witness was Jean Norrie, upon whose evidence we
have already drawn freely in narrating the history of the
case. Jean deponed that when Margaret Warden returned
from her mother's house for the last time, she told witness
that her mistress had called at Baldovie and insisted on
her going back to Denside, saying, "She [Mrs. Smith] had
warran' she was with child; but she would have something
for her, be the cost what it would." Margaret added that
her mistress might as well have told her at once that it
was to do her harm. She spoke frequently of things she
was getting from her mistress. A fortnight before her
death, "on the preparation Saturday, the day before the
Monikie Sacrament," she told witness that her mistress had
just given her a drink, alleged by Mrs. Smith to be "whisky
that the laddies had left," adding that "if it was something
to do her harm, it was an awfu' thing for her [Mrs. Smith]
to gang where she gaed the morn," *i.e.* to Communion. When

Mrs. Smith heard "the clash of the country" regarding
Margaret's mysterious illness and death, she told Jean that
"she did not know she [Margaret] was with child, and did
not know there was any poison in the house, except some
king's yellow that she had hained [kept] to poison the flies."
King's yellow, it may be explained, is sulphuret of arsenic.
This was probably some of the "stuff" left with Mrs. Smith
by a professional rat-catcher, as after-mentioned. Jean stated
that Mrs. Smith had repeatedly asserted after the death that
the dose she gave Margaret on the Tuesday night was merely
castor oil to relieve her breathing. It appeared that the
deceased did suffer, not unaccountably, from shortness of
breath. Jean, who had been at Denside since Martinmas
1825, and milked the cows in the byre, saw no rats there,
except one after the prisoner's arrest, nor did she ever hear
of poison being laid for them. The deceased never said
anything of having taken poison, and witness found nothing
of that kind about her bed after her death. The cross-
examination by Jeffrey was mainly directed to establish
the fact that Margaret Warden had threatened to take her
own life. Jean Norrie remembered that the deceased, some
time before her death, while they were lifting potatoes in
the fields together after the general harvest, had said she
was unfit for her work, "and wad surely do some ill to
hersel'." She had also said on another occasion that she
would be obliged to go away somewhere before the term,
but did not know where, "as her mother would not let her
come within the door." Jean maintained that she did not
think the girl serious, "for she was always a rash creature
of her words." She did not actually see her sick on the
Wednesday, but found traces of sickness on her clothes on
the Thursday morning. In reply to the Court, Jean stated
that she never heard of Margaret buying or having any
drugs except some pills which she said she got from her
mistress after her last return to Denside. Mrs. Smith

seemed "very good friends" with the deceased while attending to her and giving her drinks.

Barbara Small and Mrs. Warden repeated what they knew of the girl's illness and death. Barbara deponed that so far as her knowledge went Margaret was neither melancholy nor low-spirited, and never expressed any intention of doing herself harm. On the Thursday she was so ill that she could not even retain a drink of water, and said that "her inside was burning." That afternoon Mrs. Smith told her, in witness's hearing, "she would be better when the castor oil had wrought." Barbara had been at Denside since Whitsunday 1826, but never saw any rats, nor was she ever told that poison had been laid for them. A hen and chickens were kept in the loft above the bothy. In cross-examination, Jeffrey elicited that she had seen no sickness on the Wednesday, that Margaret took "a flour cake and a mutchkin of milk" for her dinner that day, and that Mrs. Smith treated the girl kindly during her illness. Mrs. Warden corroborated Jean Norrie's account of her daughter's dying words. She said that she and Margaret were quite reconciled after the birth of the child, and denied she had ever said anything to indicate that she would not have taken her daughter in, had she returned home. The reader will remember that the girl had in fact been living with her mother, who was aware of her condition, until Mrs. Smith induced her to go back to Denside. In cross-examination, Mrs. Warden gave her reasons for remaining all night at Denside, as before related.

Ann Gruar or Brown, wife of one of the farm servants, also spoke to Margaret's last conversation with her mother. In reply to Jeffrey, she said that she was shearing in the fields with the girl on the Monday before her death. Margaret remarked that she must leave Denside, as she was not able for her work. She did not know where to go, but could not go to her mother; she "wad put an ill end to hersel'." The witness

12

was so shocked by this remark that, ejaculating "God help me!" she went to another rig. She spoke of the matter at the time to a woman in the field (who was not called as a witness), but was unable ever to refer to the subject again, though she often wished to do so—"The Almighty had taken the power from her." Mrs. Smith was always very kind to Margaret. In re-examination, the witness said she had never mentioned this conversation in the field to anyone but the invisible woman. Margaret gave no details of how she proposed to execute her purpose of self-destruction.

Dr. Dick of Dundee, a most important witness for the Crown, deponed that he was an old friend of the Smith family, and had attended them professionally for many years. On Friday, 1st September 1826, Mrs. Smith called at his house. "You have forgot my poison for rats!" said she. "What poison?" he asked. "The poison I sent the message about, I was so annoyed with rats," replied his visitor. The doctor said he had received no such message, and did not keep poison; but if it would oblige her, he would procure some for her. He then went out and got an ounce and a half of arsenic from a neighbouring chemist. The quantity was not weighed. "Arsenic" was written on one side of the packet and "Poison" on the other. He handed it to Mrs. Smith, *told her it was arsenic—poison,* and warned her to be very careful in using it. In reply to Cockburn, Dr. Dick said he had known the prisoner for forty years. She was of a humane character. She had suffered from hysteria twelve years before. Mr. Russell, chemist, Dundee, spoke to selling an ounce of oxide of arsenic, marked as above, to Dr. Dick on the date mentioned. Mrs. Jolly, referred to by the prisoner in her declaration, deponed that Mrs. Smith, shortly before her arrest, consulted witness about her health, and bought an ounce of castor oil for her own use. Several other witnesses spoke to points of minor importance, and two of the farm servants who slept in the bothy said they had neither heard rats in the loft, nor did they ever complain to Mrs. Smith of being disturbed by them.

The medical evidence, though lengthy and elaborate, must be mentioned briefly. A verbatim report thereof, with notes and commentaries, was communicated by Professor Christison to the *Edinburgh Medical and Surgical Journal*, No. 91, where it may be studied with profit by the professional reader. " It embraces," writes Dr. Christison, " two very different questions ; *First*, the soundness of the prisoner's mind when she underwent her examination and prevaricated so much; and *Secondly*, the cause of Margaret Warden's death—whether she died of poison ? —whether she took poison on Tuesday ?—whether what she took on Tuesday was the fatal dose ?—whether the poison she took was the same with that procured a few days before by the prisoner ? etc." With regard to the first question Jeffrey, as already said, had objected to the admissibility of the pannel's declarations, and was allowed to adduce evidence in support of his contention that she was at the time unfit to be examined. Upon this point Dr. Alexander, surgeon in Dundee, stated that he had attended the Smith family for five or six years. He was called in to see Mrs. Smith on 1st October 1826, the day before her arrest. She was suffering from a violent nervous attack which he treated as such with antispasmodics. When he left her at five o'clock she was not in a fit state to be examined as a person accused of a crime. Temporary loss of memory was a common consequence of such an attack. He saw her next day in jail after her examination, and found her not thoroughly collected even then. Between these two occasions it was impossible she could have been perfectly recovered. He never saw her in a similar state before. Mr. Crichton, surgeon in Dundee, deponed that some time in December, 1826, he visited the prisoner in jail, and found her in convulsions and foaming at the mouth. He had no suspicion at the time that she was feigning illness, so did not apply any test to settle that point. It is difficult to see the bearing of this gentleman's

testimony upon the prisoner's state of health in the preceding
October.   Rebutting evidence was given by Dr. Johnston, to
whose account of the circumstances in which the examination
took place we are already indebted.   At Four Mile House he
asked his patient if she was any worse for the journey, and she
replied that she was not.   She was in a perfectly fit state
to be examined at that time.   He saw her after the examination; there was no change in her appearance.   Jeffrey
was then heard in support of his objection, after which
the Court, without requiring the Lord Advocate to reply,
found that the declarations were admissible and that it was
for the jury to judge what weight should be attached to
them.

   With regard to the cause of death and the several questions
connected with the administration and effects of arsenic, the
result of the medical evidence was generally as follows :—As to
the cause of death, Dr. Taylor, who when he saw the deceased
on her death-bed had formed the opinion that she was dying of
cholera, stated that from the symptoms, the examination of the
body, and the analysis of the contents of the  stomach he had
now no doubt that she died of poison, and that the poison
was arsenic.   Drs. Ramsay and Johnston, who along with Dr.
Taylor had conducted the autopsy and the subsequent chemical
tests, deponed that arsenic was detected in various parts of the
alimentary canal, but particularly in certain yellow particles
found in the stomach, and that the result of the inspection and
analysis led them to infer that the deceased died of poisoning
with arsenic.   Jeffrey's cross-examination was directed to showing that the doctors' diagnosis was wrong, and to casting doubt
upon the reliability of the tests employed; but as their validity
was endorsed by Professor Christison, and the results confirmed
by that gentleman's independent analysis of other portions of
the viscera, the evidence for the prosecution remained unshaken
upon this point.   As to the administration and effect of the
arsenic, however, there was some difference of opinion among

the Crown doctors. There was no direct evidence of the deceased's symptoms on the Wednesday being so violent as those which commonly follow the taking of arsenic, and she was proved to have had a pint of milk and a scone for dinner that day. Dr. Ramsay held that the fatal dose was the "castor oil" given by Mrs. Smith on the Tuesday night, and that the suspension of symptoms, though remarkable, was not unprecedented. In Dr. Christison's opinion death was occasioned by a dose taken later than Tuesday and more than a day before death, probably thirty-six or forty-eight hours. It will be remembered that on the Thursday Mrs. Smith spoke of having given the deceased "castor oil" again that morning, and bade her wait "till she saw how her physic worked." With regard to the nature of the poison found in the body, both oxide and sulphuret of arsenic were detected by Dr. Christison, who considered that the oxide might either have been converted into the sulphuret in the stomach by a chemical process after death, or administered during life in the form of king's yellow. Drs. Fyfe and Mackintosh of Edinburgh gave expert evidence for the defence. Dr. Fyfe thought Dr. Christison's explanation of the generation of the sulphuret of arsenic found in the stomach scarcely admissible ; he rather thought it had been swallowed in that state. The prisoner, however, had king's yellow in her possession, as we know from her own admission to Jean Norrie. Dr. Mackintosh maintained that the symptoms of cholera and poisoning with arsenic were the same, but on cross-examination he admitted that he believed the deceased had died of arsenic.

Nine other witnesses were called for the defence. Two daughters of Dr. Dick spoke to receiving from the prisoner a message for their father, which they forgot to deliver, asking him "to make up some powder for the rats." They were on a visit to Denside at the time, and the request was made in presence of Mrs. Smith's two daughters, Jean Norrie, and Margaret Warden. Andrew Murray, rat-catcher, said he had been employed to destroy rats at Denside some three years before. He left " medicine," arsenic, in case they should return. He was there again professionally in 1825 at the Mill of Affleck, occupied by Mr. Smith, a mile and a half from Denside. Mrs. Smith complained of rats, and he left some more of " the same stuff" with her. He had recently visited Denside by request of the prisoner's agents. He then saw no rats, but found traces of " the small black Scots rat, and mice." James Millar, foreman at Denside, son-in-law of the prisoner, said he had seen rats at Denside, but none since the preceding Whitsunday, except one which he killed after Margaret Warden's death. William Stoddart, a local elder, said he dined at Denside on 3rd June ; Mrs. Smith then complained of rats, and said she must get some " medicine " for them ; " what the man had left was spoilt." Thus the " droves " of rats so graphically described in the prisoner's declaration were reduced to one dead specimen of the species. With reference to the alleged threats of suicide by Margaret Warden, Agnes Gruar, sister of Ann Gruar, a Crown witness, deponed to overhearing what passed between Margaret and her sister in the field on the Monday before the girl's death. It is remarkable that sister Ann in her evidence did not refer to the presence of Agnes at the time. Ann Lees, formerly servant at Denside, spoke to a conversation which she had with Margaret Warden in January, 1826. Margaret, referring to her past experience, remarked that rather than face another such misfortune " she would put away wi' hersel'," whereupon witness philosophically pointed out that " the best o' folks might get into a scrape o' that kind." Mrs. M'Haffie, an itinerant vendor of " little things about the country," said she slept in the barn at Denside two or three weeks before Margaret's death. This lady gave a highly-coloured version of a scene in which the girl disclosed her condition, saying that she (Margaret) had got " gross usage " from her mother on a former occasion, rather than submit to which again she would put an end to herself. The witness having exhorted her to repentance in moving terms, Margaret replied that if she (the hawker) disclosed her state to anyone "she would put an end to herself before to-morrow morning." The weight attaching to the testimony of these two witnesses is lessened by the fact that the one spoke to a date some five months before the situation contemplated by Margaret arose, and that about the time referred to by the other the girl, whose condition was well known at Denside, actually lived with her mother for eight days, and only left her home at the urgent solicitation of the prisoner. Robert Esson, merchant, Broughty Ferry, deponed that on the Monday or Tuesday before Warden's death a small boy came to his shop and asked for twopenceworth of arsenic, which he did not supply. This closed the evidence for the defence.

The *Edinburgh Evening Courant* (22nd February 1827), in commenting on the trial, gives us a wonderfully vivid glimpse of the prisoner's calm and thrifty mind: "After the lights were brought, one of the candles placed near Mrs. Smith was exposed to a cross-draught and ran down on one side, on observing which she very coolly at different times lifted the candle and turned it to the other side."

At eleven o'clock at night the Lord Advocate rose to address the jury. His speech was a closely-reasoned and, one would have thought, convincing argument on behalf of the Crown. With reference to the unprecedented situation which had arisen during the former trial, he remarked that what had happened was an advantage to the pannel, as nearly the whole of his proof had been disclosed. The first question was: Did Margaret Warden die of poison? Of that there could be no doubt. The second question was: By whom was it administered? From the whole tenor of the defence they must come to one conclusion, either that she poisoned herself or was poisoned by the prisoner. Norrie was his leading witness: her means of knowledge and the manner in which she gave her evidence entitled her to belief. It was an answer to one part of the defence that the girl, throughout her illness, cried constantly for her mother.

The conversation between mother and daughter, as proved by the mother and two other witnesses, went to the very root of the case. These words used on death-bed, by a person who knew she was dying, excluded all idea of suicide. Dr. Christison had said that the non-appearance of early symptoms did not absolutely preclude the possibility of poison on Tuesday night; but even if it did, poison was given subsequently, and given by the pannel, for the girl was in bed, and there was no poison in the house except in the pannel's possession. It was proved that Mrs. Smith did give Warden something on Thursday, but from the evidence of Dr. Taylor and her own declaration it appeared that the symptoms dated from Tuesday night. Dr. Christison admitted that if that were so, it would alter his view. With regard to the motive for the crime, they would see from the whole evidence that the pannel, in spite of her most suspicious denials, knew of Warden's condition and looked upon it as likely to bring disgrace on the family and to excite her husband's indignation. She plainly wanted to procure abortion, and probably she was led on step by step to the commission of this crime. She had the means of death in her possession, and the fact that she obtained it openly was immaterial, if her alleged reason for doing so was false. After examining the evidence as to the presence of rats at Denside, the Lord Advocate said he had been informed that the species of which the rat-catcher alleged he saw traces was extremely rare in Scotland. All the evidence contradicted the pannel's statement that rats were there in droves and were complained of by the servants. He next dealt with the prisoner's declarations, and said that her denial of having had poison and her retraction next day carried conviction of her guilt to his mind. Her conduct and conversation with Dr. Taylor, her misstatements and denial of facts, her whole behaviour throughout, led to the same conclusion. On the question of suicide, he pointed out that it was not the first time this unfortunate girl had found herself in such a condition, so it was necessary to allege cruelty

on the part of her mother to account for her determination to
take her own life. The jury would judge from the appearance
and proved conduct of the mother whether such a state of
things had existed between them as would drive the daughter
to that fatal extremity. The two Gruars never mentioned the
alleged conversation in the field to anyone, even when the girl
became seriously ill. If it were argued that the pannel was only
guilty of an attempt to procure abortion, the word "arsenic"
alone was a sufficient answer; no one could use that without
a deadly purpose.

Jeffrey began his speech for the defence at one o'clock
in the morning. We may marvel in passing at the endurance
of our mighty forefathers; the case had been in progress
since 9 A.M. the day before. The great resources of that
famous reviewer and judge must have been taxed to the
uttermost to save his client's life, and we may assume that
he left nothing unsaid which could be urged in her behalf.
If she was guilty, said he, she deserved death as a most
foul and detestable murderess. Yet they were asked to believe
that she, having neither motive nor provocation, committed
a crime altogether incredible from its extreme atrocity.
The symptoms of the deceased were, he contended, those of
cholera, and there was nothing except the result of the
analysis to exclude the belief that she perished under that
disease. He suggested that the tests employed were unsatisfactory, and that the Crown experts might be mistaken.
"He had a great respect for science; but there were
uncertainties, blunders; and it was the pride of one age to
rear up theories to be trampled down and triumphed over by
the next." But assuming arsenic was the cause of death, he
submitted that there was no proof of administration on either
Tuesday or Thursday, and therefore, as the prosecutor had
failed to prove the specific guilt charged, the pannel was
entitled to acquittal. Dr. Christison had said that the dose
of Tuesday could not have been the cause of death, no human

being could lay his hand on anything like poison being given
on Thursday, and it was not enough for the prosecutor to
say, "Oh, I have proved a poisoning somewhere about that
time, and I am entitled to a verdict." The previous
character of the deceased, her sense of the forlorn situation
in which she was, acting on a violent and hasty temper, and
the repeated expression of a settled purpose to deprive
herself of life, were an answer to the alleged improbabilities
of her committing suicide. There was no evidence that the
pannel had assurance of the girl's condition, and an immense
interval lay between a purpose to procure abortion and the
destruction of a human being by a process of slow and
deliberate torture. He maintained that the circumstances in
which the pannel acquired arsenic inferred her innocent
intention, and he argued that there was proof of the presence
of rats at Denside. Had Margaret Warden believed that
her mistress had poisoned her, she would have cried aloud
for vengeance on the head of her inhuman destroyer. Her
words, "You know who is the occasion of me lying here?"
probably had reference to George Smith or to her mother, of
whose harsh conduct she had complained. It was natural
that the unhappy girl should not wish to go down into the
grave with the additional stain upon her memory of having
perpetrated her own destruction. They could not believe the
mother; it was incredible that she would have remained in
that house all night if she really thought her daughter had
met her death at the hands of that woman. In estimating
the credit to be given to the pannel's declarations the jury
would not deal so lightly as his learned friend had done with
the proof of her incapacity from illness, and if they thought
she should not have been examined they would throw the
declarations aside. In view of the character and conduct of
both parties, and bearing in mind the testimony to the
kindness and benevolence of the pannel, was suicide or
murder the more probable explanation of Margaret Warden's

death? In a case so involved in mystery, he would not ask
for a triumphant acquittal; they would be warranted in
finding the pannel not guilty, but he demanded a verdict of
not proven.

The Lord Justice-Clerk commenced his charge at three
o'clock in the morning, and did not finish until half-past five.
It is said that the jury, having risen when his lordship began,
were not told, as was usual, to sit down again, and so remained
on their feet during the two and a half hours to which the
judicial comments extended. As they had been already
engaged upon the trial for eighteen consecutive hours their
case was grievous, and one need hardly be astonished at any
verdict at which, in such trying circumstances, they might
arrive. His lordship observed that this was a case of
circumstantial evidence in which there were only two points
of law—(1) The objection to the mode in which the charge
was drawn. The prosecutor having charged two acts, he
could not prove a greater number; but as to the time, he
was not confined by the terms of the indictment to Tuesday
and Thursday. (2) The objection to the declarations. These,
by the unanimous judgment of the Court, were held to be
admissible, but their credibility was left to the jury. He
could not concur with what had been said upon this point
by the pannel's counsel. It was impossible that a declaration could have been taken with greater caution. The first
question for their consideration was the proof of the *corpus
delicti*—Did the deceased die of poison, and was that poison
arsenic? After reviewing the medical evidence, his lordship
thought there could be no doubt of that. The next question
was of the pannel's guilt. His lordship, having gone over
all the leading facts of the evidence on both sides, observed
that they would consider whether the evidence, upon a full,
fair, and enlarged view of the whole of it, satisfied their minds
that arsenic was administered by the prisoner at the bar.
They would not strain it against her, and if it did not carry

conviction to their minds, they would give her the benefit of
any doubt. But if they could not reconcile the accounts,
and thought there was no sufficient motive for the deceased
poisoning herself, it was their duty to act accordingly.
They would also consider if it had been sufficiently proved
that Margaret Warden was her own murderess. The evidence
of what she said was before them, and they would particularly
attend to the conversation between her mother and herself on
the day of her death. Keeping that in view, he thought the
probability of her having committed suicide a very strong
proposition to press upon them in the manner in which it
had been pressed. If they believed arsenic to be the cause
of death, everything turned upon the question—By which of
the two was it administered? They would decide. On the
conclusion of his lordship's address the Court adjourned till
two o'clock that afternoon.

"The trial of Mrs. Smith," says the *Courant*, "from the
nature of the case and the repeated delays which took place,
excited from the beginning the deepest interest, which increased
with the progress of the proceedings. During the whole of
Monday and Tuesday till two o'clock, when the verdict was
given in, the crowd was excessive. Not only the Court-room,
but the Outer House, the Lobbies, and the Parliament
Square were filled with crowds of persons anxious to hear
the result; and though the weather was intensely cold, yet
they remained on the streets during the whole night, and at
two and three o'clock in the morning every door was as
closely besieged as at ten o'clock on the preceding morning
of Monday."

On Tuesday, 20th February, when the Court met, the jury
returned the following verdict:—"Unanimously find the
libel Not Proven." The Lord Justice-Clerk, in discharging
the jury, remarked that it was their verdict, and he had no
observations to make. The prisoner was then assoilzied, and
dismissed from the bar, and the Court rose. We learn from

the *Courant* that, " to avoid any insult or violence from the
crowds assembled in the Parliament Square, Cowgate, head of
Libberton's Wynd, and other places, whose aspect was rather
threatening, Mrs. Smith was conveyed by her friends to the
Lock-up House, as a temporary asylum," from which it may
be gathered that the verdict was unpopular. On that date
Sir Walter Scott records in his *Journal*: " At Court, and
waited to see the poisoning woman. She is clearly guilty,
but as one or two witnesses said the poor wench hinted an
intention to poison herself, the jury gave that bastard verdict,
Not Proven. I hate that Caledonian *medium quid*. One who is
not proven guilty is innocent in the eye of the law. It was a face
to do or die, or perhaps to do to die. Thin features, which had
been handsome, a flashing eye, an acute and aquiline nose, lips
much marked, as arguing decision and, I think, bad temper—
they were thin and habitually compressed, rather turned down
at the corners, as one of a rather melancholy disposition.
There was an awful crowd; but sitting within the bar, I had
the pleasure of seeing much at my ease; the constables
knocking the other folks about, which was of course very
entertaining."

Lord Cockburn, in his *Circuit Journeys*, writes: " Lockhart
mentions Scott as having gone to see my old client, Mrs. Smith,
who was guilty, but acquitted, of murder by poison. The case
made a great noise. Scott's description of the woman is very
correct. She was like a vindictive masculine witch. I remember
him sitting within the bar, looking at her. Lockhart should have
been told that as we were moving out, Sir Walter's remark
upon the acquittal was: 'Well, sirs, all I can say is, that if
that woman was my wife, I should take good care to be my
own cook!'" This was written by Cockburn in 1838, when
he was reading the last volume of the famous *Life*, in which
Lockhart had incorporated the passage from the *Journal* quoted
above.

Thus it will be seen that the reader who ventures to doubt

the soundness of the verdict does so in good company.    If
every prisoner's counsel kept a diary, and published it in
the cause of truth, the labours of the historian would be
agreeably lightened, and Pilate's eternal question might sometimes find an answer.

# CONCERNING CHRISTINA GILMOUR

THIRTEEN years before Madeleine Smith, "with the air of a belle entering a ballroom or a box at the opera," stepped gracefully into the dock of the High Court of Justiciary, and, having arranged with her little lavender-gloved hand the elegant brown silk gown to the best advantage, and made ready the silver-topped smelling-bottle which she never used, composed herself to witness the nine days' wonder of her trial, another girl prisoner had occupied her place. Charged with a similar crime committed by the same deadly means, that prisoner was also recalled to life by the dubious verdict peculiar to her country's laws. But there the likeness ends, for the earlier case, though notable in its day and generation, was totally eclipsed by the lurid fame of the greater *cause célèbre*, and long since has ceased to be remembered. Yet the trial of Mrs. Gilmour in 1844, for the murder of her husband in the previous year, deserves the attention of those who pursue the study either of psychological anomalies or of the principles of circumstantial evidence, and for such a brief narrative of the forgotten facts may prove of interest.

Christian or Christina Cochran was the eldest daughter of Mr. Alexander Cochran, the proprietor of certain farms at South and West Grange, in the Ayrshire parish of Dunlop—where the cheeses come from. He and his father before him had dealt largely in the local produce, by which they made a considerable fortune. Christina is said to have been born at South Grange on 25th November 1818, and was thus twenty-five at the time of her trial, but in her declaration she gives her age as twenty-three. Mr. Cochran appears to have been an austere man of rigid Presbyterian mould, a type familiar in the home country of Robert Burns.  Though her father was a land-owner and a man of substance, Christina's upbringing was practical and homely.  After receiving a good education at a Glasgow boarding-school she had, on leaving it, to take her share in the ordinary work of the farm, and later, in accordance with the thrifty custom of her class, she was sent to learn dressmaking, which she did at Paisley under a professional exponent of the art.  Thence she returned home fully equipped with the accomplishments requisite for a young woman of her time and station, and as she was a good-looking and amiable girl with an assured portion, she found plenty of suitors for her hand.  The offers she received were from men socially her superiors, any one of which her parents would gladly have seen her accept, but she refused them all, having avowedly set her affections upon a young man, ten years her senior, named John Anderson, the son of a neighbouring farmer.  They had known each other from childhood, and although there was no engage-ment between them, it seems to have been understood that Anderson would marry her so soon as his circumstances per-mitted.  But another Richmond entered the field, in the person of Mr. John Gilmour, a well-to-do farmer in Renfrewshire, whose father was a neighbour of the Cochrans.  He was an educated and agreeable man, much esteemed in the district for his upright, sterling character, and was several years younger than Anderson.  His overtures were well received by the girl's parents, who being plain, unambitious folk, considered him an excellent match.  John Gilmour was an ardent wooer; his attachment, we are told, was "passionate and irrepressible," and Christina accepted his attentions with apparent equanimity, giving him no reason to think that her heart was already bestowed.  He proposed, was refused, and, in Ercles' vein, threatened suicide.  The lady appeared impressed, and yielded. Meanwhile, Anderson had continued his visits to South Grange as usual, and on one of these Christina suddenly announced to him her engagement to another.  By what motive she was actuated in behaving as she did we can only conjecture. Perhaps she thought that Anderson was, as the phrase goes, rather backward in coming forward, and hoped that the fact of an accepted rival would bring matters to a head. If this be so, she was woefully mistaken; Anderson expressed suitable surprise at the news, but "conjured her to abide by her promise," and resigned all pretension to her hand.

From that moment Christina was a changed girl. Her disposition had been notably bright and cheerful; she became moody and abstracted. She who hitherto had been afraid of the dark now roamed the fields alone of nights, and had to be sought for and brought home by her wondering sisters. Curiously enough, her appetite, which by all accepted canons ought to have been lost with her heart, increased enormously, and is described as insatiable; her family strove to regulate it in vain. Plainly all was not well with Christina, and the happy day, twice named, was as often postponed. It is a remarkable fact that the girl is said to have been most like her old self during the visits of her fiancé. She continued, however, to correspond with Anderson, and her parents, although aware of the whole circumstances, were anxious to hasten on the marriage. Their action in this matter is variously represented by the two contemporary pamphlets on the case, published respectively at Edinburgh and Glasgow. The former describes Christina as being entirely a free agent, her parents merely indicating that they thought the marriage desirable, but putting no restraint upon her wishes; the latter states that the step was forced on her by her father, not only against her will but in spite of her urgent and repeated appeals to be allowed to remain single. However the fact stands, Mr. Gilmour, who does not seem to have suspected the real cause of his betrothed's unsatisfactory condition, was naturally impatient of further delay. Christina bowed to her fate. She went with him to Glasgow, where they bought the necessary wedding "braws," and for the third time the marriage day was fixed. On 29th

13

November 1842 the ceremony was performed by the Reverend
Mr. Dickie, minister of the parish, who noticed nothing amiss in
the bride's demeanour, and the newly-wedded pair, accompanied
by one of her sisters, left for the bridegroom's farm, Town of
Inchinnan, Renfrewshire.   The house is near Inchinnan Bridge,
where, in 1685, the unfortunate Argyll was captured at the
ford by the servants of Sir John Shaw of Greenock.

The unusual attitude adopted by Mrs. Gilmour towards her
husband from the outset of their married life must be indicated,
as it has an important bearing on the subsequent events.   The
bride sat up by the fireside the whole of the first night in her
new home.   The bridegroom, we are told, generously ascribed
her conduct to the novelty of her situation, but as day after
day passed without any modification of her attitude towards
him that explanation became no longer tenable.   Christina displayed no enmity to the man she had so inexplicably married ;
she said that she respected him, but would never live with him
as his wife.   In this difficult situation her husband seems to
have behaved with the utmost tact and delicacy, trusting that
time would bring about a better understanding between them.
But John Gilmour's time, little though he knew it, was terribly
short; within six weeks of his ill-omened wedding-day he was
a dead man.

The evidence taken at the subsequent trial is rendered
somewhat confusing by reason that many of the witnesses
speak to a variety of disconnected facts applicable to different
branches of the case; it will therefore conduce to clearness if
we consider the events in the order in which they successively
occurred.   The *ménage* at Town of Inchinnan was simple and
primitive, recalling the homely ways of some west country
household as preserved for us by the admirable art of Galt.
The laird busied himself in the affairs of his farm, while as
there was but one woman servant within-doors, the house
required all his wife's attention.   Several men were employed
about the farm.   During the whole period in question one or

other of Mrs. Gilmour's sisters resided at Inchinnan, though, curiously, the guest took her meals in the kitchen by herself, the host and hostess having theirs together in the parlour. It is remarkable that neither of these ladies was called as a witness at the trial. The bride from the first made no secret of the unusual footing upon which she and her husband lived. She early informed the maid, Mary Paterson, who was an old family servant of the Gilmours, that she had married the laird un-willingly, because her father wished her to do so, and that she had "intended to take John Anderson."

The first important date in the case is Monday, 26th December 1842, a month after the marriage. On that day Mary Paterson went to visit a relative in Dunlop parish. Before she left, her mistress told her to purchase twopence worth of arsenic in Paisley, which was on her way, and gave her the money for that purpose. Mrs. Gilmour instructed her not to buy the poison personally, but to go to a certain house and send a "callant" (boy) to get it for her. She said she wanted it to poison rats. We may pause here for a moment to deplore the curious lack of originality shown by our criminals in attempting to give a legitimate excuse for the acquisition of arsenic. In almost every Scottish trial for poisoning, from that of the Lady Fowlis in 1590 to Madeleine Smith's in 1857, these equivocal rodents have figured with such wearisome persistence that the formula seems to be accepted as classic. In England, one must in fairness admit, the amateur toxicologist has dis-played upon occasion less poverty of fancy. Mary forgot the address, and on her return through Paisley on the following day, Tuesday, 27th December, she went herself for the arsenic to a chemist's shop kept by one Dr. Vessey. He asked her for whom it was required, and she answered, Mrs. Gilmour of Inchinnan. The chemist, having taken her own name, gave her a packet labelled "Arsenic—Poison," which Mary duly delivered to her mistress, telling her what had happened. Next day, Wednesday, 28th, when Mary was in "the boiling-

house " in the afternoon, Mrs. Gilmour produced a packet
similar in appearance to that containing the arsenic, which she
threw into the boiler fire in Mary's presence, with the remark
that "it would be of no use to her, and she was frightened she
could not use it right."

When Mary Paterson left for her brief holiday Mr. Gilmour,
a hale man of thirty, was in his ordinary health and spirits, but
on Thursday, 29th, he suddenly became unwell and suffered
from violent sickness.    His disorder continued during the
week-end, but, as it had been arranged that on Monday, 2nd
January, "the happy pair" should pay a New Year's visit to
the bridegroom's family in Ayrshire, Mr. Gilmour, though still
very unwell, left Inchinnan that morning with his wife in a
gig for Dunlop.   At South Grange he complained of internal
pain to his father, who says that John Gilmour's face was
swelled, and that he had several attacks of sickness during
the visit.   On Tuesday, 3rd January, he and his wife drove
home, arriving at Inchinnan in the afternoon.   That night the
laird had a recurrence of his mysterious ailment, the symptoms
of which continued with increasing severity until his death a
week later.   Throughout the illness his wife was his assiduous
and sole attendant, preparing his food and drink, and administering the medicines which, as we shall see, were afterwards prescribed for him.   In the earlier stages of his malady Mr.
Gilmour, as one witness says, "was whiles in bed and whiles
out of it."   John Muir, one of the men on the farm, saw him at
the stables on Wednesday, the 4th.   His face was then swollen
and his eyes were watering.   He said he had been sick.   Next
day he was confined to his room, which he was never to leave
again alive.

Friday, 6th January, is a red-letter day in the case.   John
Gilmour was on his death-bed.   Early that morning his wife
left the house.   She informed Mary Paterson that she was going
on an errand to Renfrew, as "she wanted something, to see if
it would do her husband any good," and asked Mary not to tell

the other servants that she had gone. Renfrew is some two
miles from Inchinnan, Paisley about four. She returned "shortly
after breakfast." Between eight and nine o'clock that morning
John Muir, "going out from his breakfast," found at the corner
of "the boiling-house," which adjoined the dwelling-house, a black
silk bag. He had passed the place as he went in for his breakfast, and the bag was not then there. He opened it, and found
that it contained a small phial full of liquid and a paper packet
tied with thread, marked with the single word "Poison." The
smell of the phial suggested scent to him; it was not the smell
of turpentine, which he knew. He handed the bag to Mary
Paterson, who also examined the packet and the "wee phial."
She carried the bag with its contents to her mistress, asking if
it was hers, and Mrs. Gilmour took it from her, remarking that
"she had got turpentine to rub John with." The packet in
appearance was similar to the one which Mary had bought
previously in Paisley. That same night, "after the horses had
been suppered," Mrs. Gilmour again left home, taking with her
Sandy Muir, another of the farm hands. She told him that,
as the master refused to see a doctor, she was going to consult
her uncle, Robert Robertson, at Paisley. When they arrived
at that gentleman's house Sandy waited for her in the kitchen,
and Christina was announced to her uncle. Mr. Robertson was
surprised by his niece's visit, as he had not seen her for four
years; he scarcely recognised her. He remarked that they
were almost neighbours now, and she said that it was against
her will that she was at Inchinnan—"she would rather have
preferred one Anderson." Whereupon her uncle delivered a
little homily on the duties of marriage, winding up with the
consoling reflection "that many persons had not got the one
they liked best," which, he says, she received "quite pleasantly
and reasonably." She then informed him of her husband's
illness and alleged aversion from professional treatment.
Mr. Robertson at once proposed to send his own medical man,
Dr. M'Kechnie, but Christina said she would rather her uncle

came down first, "to see what Mr. Gilmour would say."
Having arranged to go to Inchinnan next day, he bade his
niece good-night.

Meantime, John Muir, the other servant, had been thinking
about the strange contents of the bag found by him that morning, with the result that after his mistress left home in the
evening he went "ben" to see his master about half-past eight.
The sick man was alone and in great pain. Without disclosing
the discovery which had prompted the suggestion, Muir asked if
he would like to see a doctor, and Mr. Gilmour replied that he
would do so in the morning if he were no better. Muir proposed to fetch one there and then, to which his master agreed,
mentioning Dr. M'Laws of Renfrew. Christina, with wifely
anxiety, would seem to have unduly magnified her husband's
repugnance to the faculty. When Muir was leaving the bedroom, his master, making use of a significant but untranslatable
Scots idiom, said, "Jock, this is an unco thing!" which suggests
that he was uneasy in his own mind as to the nature of his
illness. Accompanied by one of the other farm lads, John then
set out for Renfrew and Dr. M'Laws. They were saved their
journey by meeting fortuitously at Inchinnan Toll-house the
doctor in person, who readily agreed to go with them, though
it was then near midnight. It is in every way regrettable that
Dr. M'Laws, as unfortunately appears from the evidence to be
the fact, was at the time of his visit "under drink taken." He
afterwards stated that he found Mr. Gilmour in bed, complaining of pain, fever, and thirst, but was not told about the sickness. In his opinion the complaint was an inflammatory one,
so he bled the patient, and ordered him to be rubbed with
turpentine. His horse was yet at the door when Mrs. Gilmour
returned from Paisley. She went straight to her husband's
room, but we have no account of her interview with the festive
physician, whose further services were dispensed with. If, as
Christina alleged, the "wee phial" found that morning did,
despite its smell, contain turpentine "to rub John with," that

she should have procured it before it was prescribed was a happy coincidence.

About eight o'clock next morning, Saturday, 7th January, a respectably-dressed young woman entered the shop of Mr. Wylie, chemist in Renfrew, and asked for arsenic—of course for killing rats, but with this realistic touch, "in the field." In reply to the usual questions, the lady stated that her name was Robertson, and that the arsenic was required for one John Ferguson, a local farmer, but as "it was not long since she came to the place," she could not give the name of the farm. Mr. Wylie then ran over to her a list of such farms as he remembered in the neighbourhood, but the customer hesitated to select one. The chemist was not satisfied; he summoned James Smith, the oldest inhabitant, who was conveniently at hand. That veteran named every farm in the district, but knew none associated with the name of Ferguson. The lady then said it was "up by Paisley," which seems to have been deemed sufficiently specific. Twopence worth of arsenic was put up in paper, marked "Poison—Arsenic," and sold to her. Mr. Wylie entered the transaction in a book kept by him for the purpose, the veteran signing as a witness, and "Miss Robertson" left the shop with her purchase. Mrs. Wylie, who was also present, noticed that she did not go in the direction of Paisley. At the trial Wylie, his wife, and the oldest inhabitant all positively swore to the identity of "Miss Robertson" and Christina Gilmour, then at the bar. Mary Paterson said that her mistress went from home upon a second early morning errand about that time, but could not tell the exact date. Thus, within ten days, three packets of arsenic had found their way into Mrs. Gilmour's possession, and the rats at Inchinnan were still unslain.

Between ten and eleven o'clock that Saturday morning old Mathew Gilmour, who had heard that his son was worse, came from Dunlop to see him. John Gilmour complained of sickness, pain, and persistent thirst; his wife was in constant attendance.

He asked his father to stay with him, but Mathew had to go home again in the afternoon. Before he left, Mr. Robertson arrived about four o'clock, and remained an hour with the sufferer, who was continually sick and in great pain. He told Mr. Robertson about Dr. M'Laws' visit the night before, and Mrs. Gilmour said she would send for Dr. M'Kechnie if her husband got worse. Christina, when alone with her uncle, recurred to the subject of her marriage, saying "it had been against her mind in taking Gilmour."

Next morning, Sunday, 8th January, Mr. Robertson received a message from Inchinnan at nine o'clock, asking him to send a doctor and to come himself. Who sent this message we do not know. At his request Dr. M'Kechnie went down and saw the patient, whom he found very feverish—his pulse was 112—"with a very great thirst." The doctor heard of the sickness. He asked to see the vomited matter and also the *excreta*, but was told by Mrs. Gilmour that none had been preserved. He then gave her particular orders that these were to be kept for his inspection on the following day. He considered the case a bilious one, and prescribed calomel, tartaric acid and soda powders, and a blister. Mr. Robertson arrived before the doctor left, and stayed all night to relieve Mrs. Gilmour in the nursing, and John Muir was dispatched forthwith to Renfrew to get the medicines made up at Wylie's shop. On the Sunday evening, Christina again reverted to the vexed question of her marriage, which, as her uncle thought, "appeared to be brooding on her mind." On Monday, the 9th, Dr. M'Kechnie paid his second visit. He found the patient, who said he had been less frequently sick, much relieved by the application of the blister, and his pulse down to 94. The doctor ordered the treatment to be continued, and asked Mrs. Gilmour for the matters which she had been told to preserve. She replied that "there was so little she did not think it worth while keeping them." Unfortunately, on neither of these two occasions was the patient sick in Dr. M'Kechnie's presence. The doctor did not see him again alive. It is a remarkable fact that throughout the case no mention is made of purging, one of the leading symptoms of arsenical poisoning. On Tuesday, the 10th, old Mathew Gilmour returned to Inchinnan, and remained till the death of his son, which took place on the following day. He found him much worse, complaining of pain and thirst, and frequently sick. The father assisted the wife in nursing him. One or other of them was always in the room, and regularly administered the effervescing powders prescribed by Dr. M'Kechnie. In the afternoon of Wednesday, the 11th, Dr. M'Kechnie's son, who assisted his father, called, and found the patient " very low "; he considered him in a dangerous state. The young surgeon promptly bled him, and departed. This, probably, was the last straw, for shortly afterwards the end came. There were present in the death-chamber the wife, the father, a cousin named Andrew Gilmour (a boy of fourteen who was staying in the house), and Sandy Muir. Sandy deponed that Mr. Gilmour, shortly before he died, " expressed a wish to be opened," and that he heard him say, " Oh, that woman! If you have given me anything!" The boy stated that he heard the dying man say " he wished to be opened," and also, " Oh, if you have given me anything, tell me before I die!" He remembered the words distinctly, and had mentioned immediately after the death that he heard them spoken. Old Mathew Gilmour, who was deaf, heard nothing. On Monday, 16th January, the body of John Gilmour was buried in the churchyard of Dunlop, Ayrshire; by whom the certificate of his death was granted does not appear. After the funeral, the widow returned to her old home at South Grange, where she lived with her parents as before her marriage. She wrote a letter, which was not preserved, to her former lover, John Anderson, with whom she had held no correspondence during her brief wedded life.

The mysterious illness and sudden death of John Gilmour were much discussed in the neighbourhood. The servants at

Inchinnan told what they knew, and soon the report spread that he had died from the effects of arsenic, administered to him by his young wife. In the month of April, according to the evidence, the authorities first heard the rumours which led them to investigate the circumstances of the death, and Superintendent M'Kay of the Renfrewshire rural police went to Inchinnan to make inquiries. As the result of these, upon the application of the procurator-fiscal, a warrant was granted by the Sheriff on 21st April for the apprehension of Mrs. Gilmour and exhumation of the body. Meanwhile, Alexander Cochran, Christina's father, aware of the reports that his son-in-law had been poisoned, and hearing that the body would probably be raised, "advised" his daughter to leave home. He admits that she was most unwilling to go, and that she had no idea she was being sent to America. All that the father says about the matter is that he employed his brother Robert (who was not called as a witness) to make the necessary arrangements for her compulsory flight. According to Christina's own account, given later in her declaration, her family did not inform her why she was to go away until she asked if it was because of her husband's death "being blamed on her," when they told her that such was the reason. She pointed out that her disappearance would be construed as an acknowledgment of her guilt, but was assured that "she would be back in a few days." Her father would not even allow her to say good-bye to her mother before she went. She left home on foot, in charge of a man she did not know, and at a certain place was handed over to another stranger, who drove her in a gig to a house, where she was delivered to a third man, with whom she travelled by rail to Liverpool. This third cavalier is stated to have been one Simpson, a Renfrewshire gardener, alternatively, an Ayrshire shoemaker, who was going to America, and at Robert Cochran's request undertook to see Christina safely to the New World. She was to pass on board ship as his wife, and to baffle possible pursuit they adopted the names of "Mr.

and Mrs. John Spiers." On arriving at Liverpool the couple took their passage to New York in the packet *Excel*, and before sailing Christina wrote to John Anderson a letter, dated 28th April, to which we shall afterwards refer. It appears from the account given by Christina in America that "Mr. Spiers" was no Bayard; he sought to take advantage of their nominal relations, and she had to appeal to the captain for protection. In the care of that officer she may be left for the present, while we see what was taking place at home.

On 22nd April the body of John Gilmour was exhumed, and was duly inspected by Drs. Wylie and M'Kinlay of Paisley, who prepared a report of the examination then made by them. The intestines exhibited a blush all over the external surfaces, and were found to be stained throughout with spots and streaks of a bright yellow colour. The internal surface of the stomach was thickly sprinkled with small yellow particles. As the result of their observations, the doctors reported that in their opinion John Gilmour had died from the effects of an acrid poison, which produced the inflammation of the stomach and bowels above mentioned, and that from the appearances referred to they suspected that acrid poison to have been arsenic. Certain parts of the viscera were therefore removed for future chemical examination.

When the police arrived at South Grange on 24th April, to execute the warrant for Christina's arrest, they found the bird flown. None of her relatives would give any information as to her whereabouts, so after making some inquiries in the neighbourhood Superintendent M'Kay went home for the time empty-handed. Satisfied that she had but recently left the district, he continued his investigation, and finally lit upon the fugitive's trail, with the result that he traced her to Carlisle, and thence to Liverpool. As it was found that she had left the country for America, a new warrant had to be obtained on 18th May. Armed with this, M'Kay started in pursuit on board the Cunard steamer *Acadia*, and arrived at New York three

weeks before the *Excel*, which had made a bad passage.  In
co-operation with the New York authorities M'Kay, so soon as
the packet was signalled, went down to Staten Island to inter-
cept her, in order to prevent anyone from the shore communi-
cating with those on board.  The knowledge of what was afoot
had created much interest and excitement in America, as this
was the first case of extradition under the new Treaty of Washington, concluded between Great Britain and the United States
on 9th August 1842, and the New York papers had handled
the subject with the moderation and restraint for which the
press of that city is still so justly famed.  M'Kay, accompanied
by an official of the New York police, on 21st June boarded the
*Excel* in a Custom-House boat, and, much to the astonishment
of the captain and passengers, took the amiable " Mrs. Spiers "
into custody.  At first she attempted to deny her identity, but
by a fortunate chance M'Kay, who had known John Gilmour,
once actually met Christina at Inchinnan, and knew her by
sight; so seeing that the game was up she made no further
resistance, and was forthwith taken away on the police boat.
In the hurry of the moment M'Kay did not then learn of the
existence of " Mr. Spiers," who modestly kept out of view.
That gentleman proceeded in the *Excel* to New York, where,
unobserved by the police, he disembarked and vanished.  The
flight of the " wanted " person, the pursuit across the Atlantic,
and the subsequent dramatic arrest at sea curiously anticipate
the modern instances of Oscar Slater and Dr. Crippen.

The extradition proceedings were duly opened before Mr.
Sylvanus Rapalyea, the United States Commissioner.  Application for delivery of the fugitive was made under Article X of
the recent Treaty, whereby persons charged with murder and
certain other crimes, committed within the jurisdiction of either
of the respective countries, seeking asylum in the other, should,
upon evidence of criminality, be surrendered to the proper
authorities.  Mr. Warner of the New York bar, who appeared
for the prisoner, represented that his client was insane; he

therefore moved for and obtained a postponement of the hearing of her case until she could be examined by medical men. This examination having been made, the case again came before the Commissioner on 12th July. Eight New York physicians had minutely studied and tested the prisoner's mental capacity; five of these were examined and cross-examined at vast length, two did not appear when called, and the evidence of a third was disallowed. The united testimony of these gentlemen was to the effect that although the behaviour and conversation of the prisoner was suggestive of imbecility—she sat on the floor, lacerated her hands, and talked nonsense, *e.g.* that as she had been sick on the voyage out, she would " rather go home in a coach "—they could discover no sign of mental disease, and were of opinion that her insanity was feigned. The necessary evidence of her alleged criminality was then given by Superintendent M'Kay, despite the vigorous protests of her counsel. Mr. Warner, thus defeated in the first round, now moved that the proceedings were incompetent upon a variety of technical grounds, all of which being repelled he appealed unto Cæsar in the person of His Excellency John Tyler, President of the United States of America. The decision was unfavourable, and on 9th August the Secretary of State issued an order for the surrender and delivery of Christina Gilmour to George M'Kay, an officer of the Government of Her Britannic Majesty. Mr. Warner made a last effort; he presented a petition for a writ of *habeas corpus* to the judges of the Second Circuit of the Southern District of New York, setting forth that all the proceedings hitherto had against his client were illegal, as no legislative action had been taken by Congress to make the Treaty of Washington effectual in law, and further, that no sufficient evidence was produced before the Commissioner to sustain the charge of murder. On 12th August the judges refused to allow the writ, and Christina's fate, so far as American law was concerned, was sealed. She was to fare better in the old country, as we shall presently

see.  On 16th August Superintendent M'Kay and his fair
charge sailed in the packet-ship *Liverpool* for the port of that
name, the services of " a trustworthy elderly female belonging
to Paisley, who was anxious to return to her native country,"
being retained to attend her on the voyage, which, owing
to continuous gales, occupied twenty-six days.  How Christina
must have sighed for that coach!  On reaching Liverpool she
was transferred to the steamer *Achilles,* in which she was
conveyed to Greenock, and thence by rail to Paisley.  There
on Wednesday, 14th September, Mrs. Gilmour was judicially
examined before the Sheriff, and, having emitted a lengthy
declaration, was committed for trial.

In this document she set forth the circumstances of her
flight, and admitted that before she left home she had heard
that her husband's body was likely to be raised.  Her statement
regarding the charge made against her was to the following
effect :—Before the New-Year visit to Dunlop John Gilmour
had complained of a severe headache and pain in his breast,
" and said he thought it was his heart"; he was not sick until
after their return home.  Shortly before his death he told her
that she had broken his heart, to which she replied that he had
already broken hers.  One morning during his illness she
walked to Renfrew, and there bought from Wylie some arsenic,
in the name of Robertson.  It was in a packet marked " Arsenic
—Poison," which she took home in a black silk bag.  She
" rather thought" she dropped the bag before entering the
house, and that it was brought to her by one of the servants.
She afterwards kept the poison in her pocket till the string
came off the paper and some of the contents were spilt.  This
she only discovered when she returned to her parent's home
after the death.  The packet was then taken possession of by
her mother, who questioned her about the matter, and she told
that lady she had got it " because they were all tired of her and
would not let her have peace."  The truth, as she now declared,
was that, being made unhappy both before and after her marriage,

she bought the arsenic "thinking that she would put an end to herself with it." Before making the above purchase she had procured another packet of arsenic, which Mary Paterson bought for her in Paisley. This supply "was intended for rats," but after hearing from Mary "what the druggist had said about the danger of it" she burnt it "before her face" in the furnace fire of the boiling-house, upon the same morning on which Mary brought it to her. The packet was never opened. She administered no arsenic to her husband at any time, either before or during his illness. She frequently proposed to send for a doctor, but her husband as often refused to see one. She then described her interview with her uncle Robertson, Dr. M'Laws' visit, and the calling in of Dr. M'Kechnie, all as before related. If arsenic was found in her husband's body she could not account for it: "He got none from me, and I am not aware that he got any from anybody else." It is noteworthy that she made no suggestion of her husband having taken his own life.

For four months Mrs. Gilmour remained in Paisley prison until she was removed to Edinburgh for her trial, which began before the High Court of Justiciary on Friday, 12th January 1844, the day after the anniversary of her husband's death. The judges were the Lord Justice-Clerk (Hope) and Lords Moncreiff and Wood; the counsel for the Crown, the Lord Advocate (Duncan M'Neill, afterwards Lord Colonsay), assisted by Messrs. Charles Neaves and David Milne, Advocate-Deputes; and the counsel for the pannel, Messrs. Thomas Maitland (later Lord Dundrennan) and Alexander M'Neill. A contemporary account remarks, "From the circumstances of this being the first case that has occurred in this country under the Ashburton Treaty, and from the interest which it had already excited in the public mind by the proceedings in the American Courts, independently altogether of the importance of the charge itself, the greatest anxiety was manifested as to the issue. At a very early hour the doors of the Court were beset by a dense crowd of persons of both sexes desirous of admittance, and long before the proceedings commenced, the Court was crowded in every part." Christina, becomingly dressed in widow's weeds, and looking younger than her years, was placed at the bar; the indictment was read, and the prisoner, "in a low but firm voice," pleaded not guilty to the charge. This, briefly, was that on repeated occasions between 26th December 1842 and 12th January 1843, at Town of Inchinnan, and on 2nd and 3rd January 1843, at South Grange, she did wickedly, maliciously, and feloniously administer to John Gilmour in some articles of food or drink certain quantities of arsenic, in consequence of which he became ill and died on 11th January 1843, and was thus murdered by her; and that she, being conscious of her guilt in the premises, did abscond and flee from justice. The Lord Advocate moved that the medical witnesses be allowed to remain in Court to hear the evidence, which practice, he said, was not unusual; but the Lord Justice-Clerk considered such a course "inconvenient," and the motion was refused. A jury was then empanelled, and the Lord Advocate adduced his proof.

The foregoing narrative of the case having been derived from the evidence led for the Crown, we have only to notice such of it as has not been already mentioned. The shopman who had seen the late Dr. Vessey sell the arsenic to Mary Paterson corroborated her account of that purchase, and Wylie, the chemist, produced his books, containing the entry of a similar sale on 7th January to " Miss Robertson," with whom, as has been said, Christina, apart from her own admission, was clearly identified. The contention of the defence was that John Gilmour either poisoned himself accidentally, or committed suicide owing to the unhappy issue of his matrimonial venture, and certain of the witnesses were cross-examined to that effect. Mary Paterson said she had seen her master use arsenic for killing rats about the stable. He kept it in a " kist" (chest) in the kitchen at that time, and the " kist " was afterwards removed to his bedroom before the marriage. Sandy Muir stated that he had helped his master to kill rats with arsenic in the offices. He only knew of him getting poison once for that purpose, from Mr. Paton, a neighbour. It was not used again after the marriage. This is the whole evidence relating to John Gilmour's possession and use of arsenic. Several witnesses were cross-examined with regard to the prisoner's demeanour during the illness. Mr. Robertson, her uncle, said that when she spoke to him of her marriage she did not do so bitterly, but seemed to be grieved. Her tone was one of depression and regret. He thought her kind and attentive to her husband— "she held his head when he was vomiting." There was no excitement in her manner, and he saw nothing to indicate any alienation between them. John Gilmour made no complaint to him of Mrs. Gilmour's behaviour when he (witness) was at Inchinnan. Dr. M'Kechnie stated that on the occasion of his two visits Mrs. Gilmour behaved in all respects most properly. She was very cool and collected, and showed no sign of excitement.

The interest of the audience must have quickened when the Lord Advocate called Christina's old love, John Anderson. He said he had known the prisoner before her marriage. He received from her in January 1843, after her husband's death, a letter which he had not preserved. After she left home, she wrote to him again from Liverpool on 28th April. Her brother asked him for that letter, and kept it. The letter having been destroyed, the Lord Advocate proposed to ask the witness—"Was there anything in that letter on the subject of her husband's death?" The witness was removed while the point was discussed whether or not the question was admissible. Mr. Maitland, however, withdrew his objection, in respect of which the Court allowed it to be put. "She said," replied Anderson, "she would confess she had bought arsenic to take herself, but she did not admit she had administered it to John Gilmour." She also complained of having been sent away, as she would rather have "stopped till all was settled."

14

In cross-examination, Anderson said he had known the prisoner from infancy; "she was of a very gentle, mild, fine disposition." Thomas Cochran, the prisoner's brother, stated that he got the letter from Anderson and gave it to his father. Before doing so he read it; there was nothing in it about arsenic. Alexander Cochran, her father, upon this point said that after reading the letter he destroyed it. He recollected no mention of arsenic.

There only remain the medical witnesses, who need not detain us, as their evidence was not disputed by the defence. Dr. M'Kechnie stated that, having been present at the post-mortem examination and seen the results of the analysis of certain portions of the body, he was satisfied that the deceased died from arsenic. The symptoms observed by him during life were consistent with that opinion. While other doses might have been administered before he saw the patient, he believed that the fatal dose was not given till shortly before death. Dr. Wylie, who, along with Dr. M'Kinlay, made the post-mortem examination, proved their joint report. The suspicion therein expressed regarding the cause of death became a conviction after they had completed their analytical tests, the results of which plainly indicated the presence of arsenic in the contents and substance of the stomach and bowels. Dr. M'Kinlay corroborated. An independent analysis of other portions of the internal organs had been made by Professor Christison. That eminent authority, having tested the various articles submitted to him by the processes of Reinsch and Marsh, detected arsenic unequivocally in the contents of the stomach, in the stomach itself, and in the liver. Dr. Christison stated in the witness-box that this was the second instance in this country in which arsenic had been found in the liver. The symptoms of the deceased and the post-mortem appearances, as described, were, in his opinion, consistent with death from arsenic. One single dose might produce such protracted illness, but not so probably as repeated doses.

The Crown case closed with the reading of the prisoner's declaration, and her counsel intimated that they did not propose to lead any evidence for the defence. The Court then adjourned till the following day.

On Saturday, 13th January 1844, on the resumption of the diet, the Lord Advocate addressed the jury for the prosecution. The first question, he said, which they had to determine was, Did John Gilmour's death result from the administration of arsenic ?  He submitted that upon this point the medical evidence was conclusive.  The symptoms of vomiting, thirst, and internal pain were consistent with that view, the appearances observed at the post-mortem examination indicated it, and arsenic was found in the stomach and its contents and in the liver by three medical men, one of whom was known to all the world as a most skilful and accurate analytical chemist.  If ever there was a case where arsenic was found in the body of a deceased person they had it there.  In the opinion of those experts, death had been caused rather by repeated doses than by one administration.  The illness began on 29th December 1842, and ended fatally on 11th January 1843, and the continued symptoms indicated such repetition. The second question was, How was this arsenic administered ? In all cases of criminal poisoning the administration was secret, and evidence of it must be sought in the circumstances of the case.   There was no ground even for suspecting that John Gilmour had committed suicide, which was, moreover, entirely out of the question in view of the prolonged character of his illness.  He would not voluntarily have taken poison in small doses, perseveringly repeated so as to cause a lingering and painful death.  For the same reason there was as little ground for the theory of accidental administration.  The poison with which he was said to have once killed rats on the farm was not proved to have been in his possession since his marriage or at the time of his illness.   No jury could expect direct evidence of administration in any case of poisoning, particularly where, as in that case, the accused had charge of everything, prepared the food, and was constantly about the person of her victim. As the proof must necessarily be circumstantial, let them examine the circumstances on which reliance could be placed as establishing the guilt or innocence of the accused. Had she possession of poison of the kind which was used, at the time when it must have been administered ? It was proved that she had obtained no fewer than three several packets of arsenic during that period—(1) the packet marked "Arsenic—Poison," procured for her by Mary Paterson in Paisley on Tuesday, 27th December 1842; (2) the packet marked "Poison," found in her bag by Muir and Paterson on Friday, 6th January ; and (3) the packet marked "Poison— Arsenic," bought by the pannel herself in Renfrew on Saturday, 7th January 1843. All these acquisitions were made in a secret and mysterious manner. The first was obtained upon a false pretence, and by indirect and most suspicious means; how she got the second did not appear, further than that she did not do so openly and avowedly ; the third was bought by her under a false name and upon statements equally false. Was her account of the disposal of the poison thus acquired satisfactory ? She said that she threw the first packet into the fire before the girl Paterson on the morning she obtained it, but Paterson stated that it was not until the following after- noon that her mistress burnt a packet which was "like" the one she had bought for her. Had that arsenic been intended for poisoning rats, there was no need to destroy it merely because the chemist knew the purchaser's name and address. But if it were not so intended, then, in view of the chemist's information, she had either to destroy or pretend to destroy it in the presence of the person who procured it. As to the second supply traced to her possession, there was no account whatever of what became of it. Then as to the third packet, which she now endeavoured to confound with the second, discovered the day before, but which was plainly a different parcel obtained

the next day, she said that she carried it about in her pocket
until after her husband's death, when it was found by her
mother, who destroyed it, and that she told her mother that the
purpose for which she acquired it was suicide.   No attempt
had been made to support that statement, and the mother was
not called as a witness.   That this third packet obtained by her
from Wylie on the Saturday was not the packet found in her
bag by Muir on the Friday, was clearly proved by the evidence
of Muir and Paterson, who were positive that the incident
occurred on the morning of the day (Friday) when Dr. M'Laws
was summoned.   Muir stated, in reply to the Court, that it was
the finding of this bag which led him to urge his master to see
the doctor that night.   He was also certain that only the single
word "Poison" was written upon the packet he found, whereas
the third packet was proved to have borne the two words,
"Poison—Arsenic."   Further, along with the packet in the
bag was found a small phial, also acquired by herself, containing
some fluid alleged by her to be turpentine, which, as Muir
proved, it was not.   There was no evidence that she got that
phial at Dr. Wylie's or anywhere else on the Saturday.   Paterson
stated that her mistress left home early in the Friday morning
"to get something for her husband," telling her not to mention the matter to the other servants, and there was no trace
of anything brought home by her for her husband except the
contents of that bag.      Friday, therefore, was the day on which
she had both a parcel and a phial, Saturday that on which she
had a parcel but no phial.   How, then, did the prisoner account
for the acquisition of arsenic at all ?   She said at first that it
was for killing rats ; in her declaration she alleged self-destruction as the reason, which rested entirely on her unsupported
statement.   Her husband was dying; was that a likely time
for her to be contemplating suicide ?   And was it credible that
for such a purpose she required those repeated quantities of
arsenic, successively procured at short intervals, more especially
as she made no attempt whatever to use it ?   The next element

in the case was the question of the opportunity of secret administration, upon which the Lord Advocate remarked he need say little; the prisoner had every opportunity that could possibly exist. She was the sole attendant of the deceased, and all that he took was taken from her hand without the observation of others. Then they came to the question of motive. Of course, no motive could be adequate to so terrible a crime, but there they had such a motive as in other cases had been found to lead to similar lamentable results. There was the evidence of the prisoner herself and of various witnesses that she was dissatisfied and grieved with her condition as John Gilmour's wife, on account of her previous attachment to another person. She was constantly complaining to servants and others that she had been compelled to marry her husband against her will. Her distress was so extreme that, according to her own account, she actually meditated suicide, and acquired poison for the purpose of putting an end to the unbearable union. " Gentlemen," said the learned advocate, " there are two ways in which arsenic might be used by her to attain that end; she might have poisoned herself, or she might have poisoned her husband. Her husband is poisoned—she is not. By a most extraordinary chance, the cup which she mixed for herself has not been quaffed by her, but by some unknown and mysterious hand was conveyed to the lips of her husband. Can you, then, doubt the purpose for which that poison was obtained or the purpose to which it was applied ? " No sooner was the union dissolved by his death than she was found in correspondence with the person who had never been absent from her mind during the whole progress of those disastrous events. In short, all the circumstances of that melancholy case concurred in establishing the prisoner's guilt. Besides the general view, there were certain minor circumstances, all pointing also to the same conclusion, which called for attention. The first supply of arsenic was obtained on Tuesday, 27th December; the husband's illness began on Thursday the 29th, and, though he continued seriously ill, no doctor was sent for till Friday of the following week.    She went, however, on that Friday to her uncle, Mr. Robertson, and stated to him the condition of her husband.    That interview was very remarkable, and whether she expected her husband to be alive or not, she put off the visit of a doctor till after the Saturday.    When Dr. M'Kechnie came the first time, he gave the prisoner special instructions to preserve certain matters for his inspection. Those instructions were not obeyed, and the excuse she gave was that there was so little that she had thrown it away. Then, so soon as suspicions arose and it was known that the body was to be exhumed, she fled the country secretly and under a false name.    Though she now alleged that she went unwillingly, still she did go, which was a strong circumstance against her innocence.    With regard to the letter which she wrote to Anderson from Liverpool, that was destroyed by her father, under whose advice she was acting.    Anderson swore that it contained a reference to the purchase of arsenic, and " that she would admit " it was for her herself, but not for Gilmour ; yet neither the father nor the brother, who read it, had any recollection of such a passage in the letter.    They did remember that it expressed her unwillingness to go away, and still, in these circumstances, the father said he destroyed it. In conclusion, the Lord Advocate submitted that the jury had all the elements required in a case of murder by poisoning, and it was his painful but imperative duty to ask them to find that case established.

Mr. Maitland then addressed the jury for the defence.    He contended that unless the case on the part of the Crown had made guilt certain and innocence impossible, the jury could not convict his client.    The question was, not whether the prisoner was covered by a very dark shadow of suspicion, not whether they had strong doubts of her innocence, but whether there was legal evidence which entitled them to hold her guilty. With regard to the medical evidence, he admitted that arsenic was found in the body, and that John Gilmour died from the effects of that poison ; but he argued that the Crown had not established that death had been caused by repeated doses. Dr. Christison himself admitted that a single dose might have produced the illness.   The evidence adduced in support of the charge was purely circumstantial, yet the crime was of no ordinary kind, and was one which could with difficulty even be imagined.   After referring to the innocent and blameless character of the prisoner before her marriage, and narrating the history of her home life prior to that event, counsel submitted that apart from the improbability of a young girl so brought up committing such a revolting crime, there was no motive sufficiently strong to induce her to do so.   Before they could convict her they must be satisfied that she hated her husband, of which there was not the slightest proof.   She was shown to be in some degree dissatisfied with her marriage, and had spoken to her uncle on the subject, but she took kindly his advice to make the best of it, and exhibited no ill-feeling whatever towards her husband.   The general conduct and deportment of the prisoner during the deceased's illness was of great importance.   If they were to believe the Crown case, this young and gentle girl was for thirteen days constantly and continuously employed in perpetrating by slow degrees the murder of her own husband.   In such circumstances human nature must have exhibited some remarkable symptoms, either of excitement or confusion.   But in the whole history of this domestic tragedy her conduct betrayed no consciousness of guilt. Dr. M'Kechnie declared that so far as he saw she behaved quite collectedly and properly, and Mr. Robertson stated that she complained of no unkindness on the part of her husband, that she seemed grieved, and that she wept when she spoke of her marriage.   "Nothing could exceed her attention and kindness," said counsel ; "she did all that an affectionate wife could do for a husband on his death-bed."   She sought medical aid when he took ill, she allowed the servants and others free access

to his sickroom, and, in short, everything she did was inconsistent with the conduct of a guilty woman. Upon the important
question of her possession of poison, counsel maintained that
there were only two parcels of arsenic traced to her, and denied
it was proved that the prisoner had arsenic on Friday, 6th
January. The witnesses who spoke to finding it in her bag on
that day had, he argued, forgotten the exact date, and made
the mistake of ascribing to Friday the 6th the occurrences which
took place on Saturday the 7th. If that was so, and there were
in fact but two packets of arsenic, they had both of these
accounted for; the first was burnt, as declared by Paterson,
while the second remained in the prisoner's pocket until it
was found by her mother some weeks after her husband's
death. Except the possession of these two packets of arsenic,
the prosecutor had failed to prove a single fact warranting a
suspicion against the pannel's innocence. Her own explanation sufficiently accounted for their possession. A broken heart
might lead to suicide but not to murder, and it was less
extravagant to suppose that the deceased had destroyed himself than that in such circumstances he was murdered by his
wife. If the union was unfortunate he had as good reason as
she to wish it terminated. But apart from the possibility of
suicide, was it not probable that he was poisoned accidentally,
either by his own or by some unknown hand? He was proved
to have had arsenic in his possession, and other white powders
were administered to him medicinally. Who, then, could say
that in this case of circumstantial evidence the proof was so
strong as to exclude a reasonable possibility of accident? In
conclusion, the learned counsel made a lengthy quotation from
the speech of Francis Jeffrey in defence of Mary Elder or
Smith, "The Wife o' Denside," on her remarkable trial for
poisoning in 1827, after which he said: "You may not be
satisfied that this unhappy lady is guiltless of her husband's
blood—nay, you may suspect or even be inclined to believe
that she is guilty. But that is not the question at issue. You

are sworn to say upon your oaths whether guilt has been
brought home to her by legal and conclusive evidence, and,
applying this test, I feel confident you can arrive at no other
verdict than that of Not Proven."

The Lord Justice-Clerk then proceeded to charge the jury.
His lordship's observations on the case occupied four and a half
hours, but neither the official report nor the contemporary
accounts detail his review of the evidence.  After commenting
on the peculiarly atrocious character of the crime charged and
the youth and previous respectability of the prisoner, his
lordship said if the jury were satisfied that the death of John
Gilmour was caused by poison, that poison must have been
administered either accidentally or voluntarily.   The deceased
was proved to have been using arsenic, some of which might
still have been in the chest removed into his room after the
marriage.   If it was administered accidentally no one else was
affected by it.    But even if they were not satisfied of the
probability of accident, much remained to be proved before
they could fasten on the pannel the horrid charge of intentional
administration.   They must consider also the possibility that
he took it voluntarily.  Those two views must be dismissed
before they could convict her.   His lordship cautioned them
against accepting it as proved that she was forced into the
marriage against her will.   [Apparently, the jury were to dis-
believe her own repeated statements to that effect.]  He was
glad for her sake that this material fact was awanting, which
otherwise might have weighed against her, as supplying a
motive for the crime.   There was no proof that John Gilmour
knew of the attachment entertained by his wife for another,
and no one in the house observed any unkindness between
them.   But even if he did know, was he a man of such nice
sensibility that the knowledge would drive him to suicide ?  He
made no complaint against her to that respectable person,
Mr. Robertson.  Would anyone committing suicide choose such
a slow and lingering death ?  But it was not enough to find

the prisoner in possession of arsenic and with the opportunity to use it; they must consider the circumstances in which it was obtained, the purpose for which it was procured, and the manner in which it was disposed of. The prisoner was not suspected during her husband's life, and she so conducted herself as to avoid all suspicion. [What of John Muir and the action taken by him upon finding poison in her bag?] After commenting on the medical evidence and the purchases of arsenic by the pannel, his lordship observed, " You see, therefore, that with all the improbabilities which the charge rears up, there are strong and weighty facts proved; and it will be for you to say what result you can arrive at, taking the whole evidence into view. It is a sad and fearful alternative that is presented to you by the prisoner's own statement in her declaration, that she bought the poison for the purpose of dissolving her marriage by committing suicide, especially considering the mysterious result that her husband dies of the same kind of poison, and that she lives. Still that statement *may* be true, and the pannel be innocent, and you, who are the only judges of the facts in this case, may say that without any proved act of administration on her part, your minds revolt from the notion that she committed the crime charged against her." Finally, if they entertained a serious doubt of her guilt, and considered her conduct during her husband's illness inconsistent with the charge, if, in short, they thought there were mysteries unexplained, which ought to have been explained in order to clear up the truth, his lordship need not tell them that they should give the full benefit of that doubt or obscurity to the individual charged with such a dreadful crime.

It is unfortunate that we have no report of how the learned judge dealt with the " strong and weighty facts proved." The jury then retired, and after an absence of an hour returned unanimously a verdict of Not Proven, and the prisoner was dismissed from the bar. The verdict, we are told, was received in Court " with loud, but not very general applause."

In two other celebrated trials at which his lordship afterwards presided, namely those of Dr. Smith in 1854 and
Madeleine Smith in 1857, similar verdicts were returned. Lord
Justice-Clerk Hope is said to have enjoyed no great popularity
with members of the bar by reason of the intolerance of the
judicial temper, but even the sorest of juniors could not have
called his lordship a hanging judge. Apropos of the Justice-
Clerk's alleged susceptibility to feminine charms, the irreverent
tale is told that Madeleine, who had a pretty foot and a well-
turned ankle, did, by counsel's advice, make effective display
of those assets for behoof of the bench. In the prosecution of
attractive young ladies the Crown is unduly handicapped. The
gentle Christina, in common with her more brilliant rival of
the 'fifties, doubtless owed not a little to her beauty, her circumstances and her youth.

# THE ST. FERGUS AFFAIR

In the year 1853 there occurred in Scotland a case which in its salient features curiously foreshadows by forty years the great Ardlamont mystery of 1893. Each was one of purely circumstantial evidence, resulting in the failure of either side to obtain a decisive verdict. The manner of death, the alleged motive, the means, the opportunity, and the inferences of guilt sought to be drawn from the accused's conduct, together with the character of the defence, present many points in common. Both arose from the death of a young man, unquestionably caused by a shot-wound in the head, the prosecution alleging that he was killed by the hand of a trusted friend, the defence contending that he died by his own act. In each case the accused had effected certain insurances upon the life of the deceased shortly before his death, while the position of the body when first found was equally important in determining the question at issue. Both prisoners were defended by the leading counsel of their day; at each trial the judge plainly indicated to the jury that in his opinion the Crown had failed to prove its case; and, finally, the respective juries delivered that ambiguous and indefensible verdict, peculiar to Scottish practice— "Not Proven."

The scene of the tragedy was the village of St. Fergus, situated in a remote corner of Aberdeenshire, five miles north-west of Peterhead, and the protagonists were William Smith, the local doctor, and a young farmer named William M'Donald. The latter lived with his widowed mother, his brother, and his sister at their farm of Burnside, about two miles from Kirk-town of St. Fergus. Dr. Smith, a married man, resided in the village and owned certain fields in its neighbourhood. Despite the differences in their social position, the two had been for long upon terms of intimacy, and M'Donald, who held the highest opinion of the doctor's ability, appears to have been completely under his influence. Dr. Smith had attended the family professionally for about eight years. M'Donald, for one of his class, was in comfortable circumstances. He farmed his mother's land, and was engaged to a girl named Mary Slessor, who lived at Hill of Mintlaw. They were to marry so soon as he could get a suitable farm, for which he was on the outlook, and they were willing to wait—"waiting cheerfully," as she herself declared. He was of steady and sober habits, kindly, cheerful, and industrious, a regular reader of his Bible. He had no cares or worries whatever, his health was sound, and he was on the best of terms with his family and neighbours.

In these circumstances, on Saturday, 19th November 1853, having been at work all day upon the farm, William M'Donald left home in the "gloamin'," between four and five o'clock, for St. Fergus. He had three trysts before him, two of which he did not live to keep. He was to see his betrothed at Mintlaw market in a few days' time, and on the following Tuesday he and his brother Charles, who had left home that morning to go to service, were to meet at Peterhead. The third tryst was with Dr. Smith on the evening in question, at his stable door in the village, at six o'clock.

Kirktown of St. Fergus consisted of a short street running east and west, with small houses on either side. Behind those on the north ran a parallel road called the Back-dyke-road, from the west end of which a footpath went out over the fields in the direction of Burnside. At the east end of the street were the church and manse, near which, at the junction of a road leading from the main street across the back road to Netherhill on the north, stood the house and offices of Dr. Smith. On the south side of the street, at the opposite corner, between the doctor's house and the church, was the shop of James Smith, the village cartwright. On this Saturday night the shop was lighted, and the windows were unshuttered. About seven o'clock William M'Donald came in and gave the wright an order for some "hames" (harness) to be made, also for a grub-harrow for turnip land, and said he would be needing some palings for the farm. He was in his usual health and spirits, and was quite sober. He remained in the shop talking to some friends for about half an hour, and remarked that he was then on his way home. "It's getting late," said he; "I have need to be away"; and he left shortly before half-past seven. Thereafter, but for the disputable testimony of one witness, he was seen no more alive.

All night long the family at Burnside anxiously awaited his return, and next morning, Sunday, the 20th, his young brother Robert went out to look for him. He took the byway through the fields to St. Fergus. Near the village the path crossed a six-acre field belonging to Dr. Smith. It was bounded on the west by a ditch, having a bank on the east and a hedge on the west side, through a "slap" (opening) in which the pathway lay. On arriving at this point, the lad was horrified to find the dead body of his brother lying in about an inch of water at the bottom of the ditch. There was a bullet-wound in the right cheek, and the face was blackened with gunpowder. The boy lifted the head clear of the water on to the bank, and, looking about, saw a pistol on the east side of the ditch, four feet from where the head had lain. He then ran to the village for the doctor. Dr. Smith was out, so the boy left a message for him and returned at once to the spot. While he was standing there, "greetin'," beside his dead brother, he saw the doctor and James Pirie, the farrier, approaching from the main road. Dr. Smith came first. On seeing the body he held up his hands and exclaimed, "God preserve us!" He stood looking down at it, but made no further examination, and, picking up the pistol, remarked,

"That's the thing that's done it." He expressed the opinion that the deceased "was partly shot and partly drowned," and that the wound had been caused by a wad only, not by a bullet. The body was then carried to the nearest house, that of James Fordyce, at the corner of the field, on the main road, whence it was taken in a cart to Burnside. M'Donald, when he met his death, was wearing a kind of jacket known as a "polka," the pockets of which, as was afterwards proved, were too small to contain the pistol. At Fordyce's house his pockets were searched for powder and shot, without result; nothing but his watch and snuff-box was found. He never carried money.

Dr. Smith proceeded to Burnside to break the news to the bereaved mother. On the way he met Mr. Moir, the Free Church minister, who, being informed by Smith that M'Donald "had shot himself last night," accompanied him on his sad errand. The doctor told Mrs. M'Donald that her son " had done it himself," and that he was " suffocated or drowned." The mother refused to believe that he had shot himself, either accidentally or by design, as to her knowledge her son never had a pistol. She asked the doctor if he had seen William, according to their tryst, on the previous evening, but he denied that he had done so, or that there was any arrangement between them to meet that night.

Dr. Smith certified the death as follows:—

St. Fergus, 20*th November* 1853.

I do hereby certify, on soul and conscience, that I was called upon this morning about half-past 9 o'clock, by Robert M'Donald, to see his brother William, who was found in a field near St. Fergus, and who had received a shot from a pistol in the right cheek, taking an upward and backward direction. There was a small quantity of blood coming from the ear and nostrils, the face completely covered with powder, so that the pistol must have been close to him, and from the direction it takes, I infer it is not likely to have been done by any other than deceased.

W. Smith, M.R.C.S.L.

The doctor took entire charge of the funeral arrangements, first suggesting Tuesday, which was afterwards changed to Wednesday. He remarked to the mother, "If Boyd heard what had happened, he would be out"—*i.e.* Mr. Boyd, the procurator-fiscal, would come from Peterhead to make inquiries into the circumstances of the death. The fiscal did in fact arrive in the forenoon of Monday, the 21st, and commenced his investigation, and at his request two medical men examined the *locus*, made a post-mortem examination of the body, and prepared a report. As the result of these proceedings Dr. Smith was arrested next day for the murder of William M'Donald, and was taken to Peterhead. There he emitted, in presence of the Sheriff, three several declarations, dated respectively 23rd and 24th November and 1st December 1853, and was committed to prison to await his trial.

The accused was originally indicted for 13th March 1854, upon which date the trial began before the High Court of Justiciary at Edinburgh; but on the second day of the proceedings a juryman, who had been overcome by mental excitement, was certified by Dr. Douglas Maclagan as unfit to continue his duties. The jury was therefore discharged, and the diet continued, the accused being taken back to prison. He was then cited upon criminal letters for his second trial, the proceedings in which occupied the 12th, 13th, and 14th of April 1854. The judges present were the Lord Justice-Clerk (Hope), who three years later presided at the trial of Madeleine Smith, and Lords Cowan and Handyside. On this occasion the Lord Advocate (Moncreiff), who had personally represented the Crown at the first trial, did not attend, and the prosecution was conducted by the Solicitor-General (Crawfurd), afterwards Lord Ardmillan, with Messrs. Thomas Cleghorn and Andrew (later Lord) Rutherfurd Clark, Advocates-Depute. The Dean of Faculty (Inglis), afterwards the great Lord President, and Mr. George Young, later the eminent and witty judge, appeared

15

for the defence. The same distinguished counsel also success-fully defended Madeleine Smith in 1857.

It was, of course, essential to the charge against the prisoner that there should be proof of what, in Scots law, is termed the *corpus delicti*, that this was a case of murder and not of accident or of suicide. The ditch was eighteen inches deep, three feet broad at the top, and from one and a half to two feet at the bottom. There was longish grass and decayed matter at the bottom of the ditch, and also about an inch of stagnant water. The hedge on the west side was five feet above the bottom of the ditch. The surrounding ground was hard and dry, and presented no appearance of any struggle having taken place. When first discovered by the boy, Robert M'Donald, the body was lying below the hedge, extended to its full length in the water at the bottom of the ditch. It lay with the head to the south, and slightly on its left side by reason of the narrowness of the ditch. The left arm was bent underneath the body, the right was partly across it. The face was turned towards the hedge, with the wound uppermost. The body was fully clothed except for the hat, which lay in the ditch. Dr. Comrie, Peterhead, and Dr. Gordon, a retired naval surgeon from the neighbouring hamlet of New St. Fergus, who conducted the post-mortem examination and prepared a joint report, on visit-ing the spot on the Tuesday after the death saw the impression of the body quite distinctly in the bottom of the ditch. It corresponded with the description given by Robert M'Donald. Outside the ditch, on the west bank, to the left of the body, they observed a mark of blood.

The medical report stated that the doctors found on the right cheek of the deceased a circular, blackened, ragged wound with inverted edges, as if produced by a pistol ball, situated below the promontory of the cheek, midway between the tip of the nose and the ear. The skin around it, the eyelids, and the side of the nose were scorched and blackened by gunpowder. On tracing the course of the wound, the direction of which was obliquely upwards and backwards towards the left side, they found a pistol bullet lodged in one of the convolutions in the middle lobe of the left hemisphere of the brain. They were of opinion that the death was caused by the injuries discovered in the brain, and that the same had been inflicted by a pistol-shot discharged at a very short distance from the cheek.

Dr. Comrie in his evidence stated that the deceased was not suffocated or drowned. Death must have been instantaneous, and the man could not have moved. The pistol must have been fired only a few inches from the head—three to twelve. If shot by another, that other must have been at his side. The position in which the body lay was a very remarkable one. If he fell dead and no one touched the body, it could not take the position of the impression. The witness could not account for it, whether the man shot himself or was shot by another, if he were shot outside the ditch. If he shot himself he must have been sitting in the ditch, if he did not his body must have been placed in that position by another; he could not have moved into it himself. All the probabilities were against his assuming that position if he were shot outside the ditch. If he fell outside the ditch it would be a matter of a few seconds for anyone to put him into it in that position. It was, said witness, inconceivable that the wound could be caused by accident. He was unable to form an opinion whether the shot was fired by the deceased or by another; he had no materials satisfactory to his mind upon which to arrive at a conclusion.

Dr. Gordon concurred with Dr. Comrie as to the medical report. He thought the pistol must have been close to the face—twelve to thirteen inches. He had made experiments upon which he based that opinion. In a case of suicide he would expect the distance to be less, and he considered it remarkable that the pistol should have been pointed a little above the gums instead of at the ear or temple. If the deceased shot himself he must have lain down in the ditch to do so; if shot by another his body must have been afterwards placed in position. He could not so fall if shot standing. If he shot himself in the ditch witness could not account for the blood on the bank beyond. From the appearances witness could form no opinion as to whether deceased was shot by himself or by another, but from his personal knowledge of M'Donald, with whom in life he was well acquainted, he could not believe that it was a case of suicide.

Such being the only medical testimony bearing upon the question of the death, we shall now notice the evidence as to the motive by which, according to the theory of the Crown, Dr. Smith was actuated in shooting his friend. The life of this young man, William M'Donald, was insured with three separate insurance companies for no less a sum than £2000, in each case in favour of Dr. Smith. The policies in force at the time of the death were as follows :—£500 with the Scottish Union Insurance Company for five years, commencing 9th January 1852; £500 with the Northern Insurance Company for five years, the last premium on which was paid by Dr. Smith on 18th November 1853, the day before the death ; and £1000 with the Caledonian Insurance Company for one year only, the risk on which began on 24th November 1852, and ended on 24th November 1853, five days after the death of M'Donald. All the proposals were made by Dr. Smith himself, who stated his insurable interest in M'Donald's life as "dependent on the life of a third party from whom he [Smith] expected double the amount proposed to be insured." Each policy contained a condition that it would not be vitiated in the event of suicide if assigned to a third party for onerous causes, or where the life insured was that of another person. At the request of the companies Dr. Smith sent M'Donald to their agents at Peterhead to be medically examined. The agents stated that the young man understood nothing as to the insurances, and appeared to take no interest in the matter. On one of them expressing astonishment at this ignorance and indifference,

M'Donald replied, "The doctor's a fine chiel', and I have always done as he bade me." The life was accepted, and the policies were duly issued to Dr. Smith, who paid the premiums. It appeared from the evidence of Mary Slessor, the girl to whom M'Donald was engaged, that he had told her he expected to "get something off the insurance" from Dr. Smith, but that he did not seem to understand the nature of the transaction.

The mystery attending this matter of the insurances was not dispelled by the defence. William Milne, a brother of Mrs. M'Donald, had died on 20th December 1852. There was some evidence that M'Donald had expected to succeed to his uncle's farm, and was disappointed at its being left to his cousin Charles. The latter, who, along with Dr. Smith, was one of Milne's executors, had never heard of the insurances. The prisoner at his first examination before the Sheriff declared that he had not effected any insurance on the life of M'Donald, but that Milne had done so, and had given him the money to pay the premiums. He was not sure if he had the policies, was unaware of their terms, and did not know they were payable to him in the event of M'Donald's death. He expected nothing would be recovered from them, as M'Donald had committed suicide. He had no writing from Milne about these insurances, nor could he say what interest Milne had in effecting them. He had an account against Milne for £46 for professional attendance, and the money for the premiums was a present from Milne (apparently a set-off against this account). The defence produced no evidence in support of this remarkable statement, and no attempt was made to prove that Milne even knew anything about the existence of the policies. With reference to the doctor's ignorance thereof, as alleged in his declaration, James Greig, a friend of his and a local farmer, had been examined by the procurator-fiscal at the inquiry after the death. He told Dr. Smith that the fiscal had asked about insurances, and Smith then admitted that these existed and were in his own favour, adding that he expected to get £1500 or £1000 from them. Whereupon Greig, with untimely humour, remarked: "They'll blame you for pistolling M'Donald!" and Smith said that he had no doubt he would be made a prisoner. This conversation took place on the day of his arrest.

The only other point of importance in connection with this matter is the fact that Dr. Smith, aware from the conditions of the policies that if he could show no pecuniary interest in M'Donald's life, his claim might be resisted as being of the nature of a wager or gambling transaction, had prepared so lately as 14th November a declaration, signed by M'Donald and himself, to the effect that there was no wager of any kind between them. This document, together with the three life policies, was found in the doctor's repositories after his apprehension.

The evidence regarding the weapon with which the fatal shot was fired has next to be considered. It was proved that the bullet lodged in the brain fitted the pistol found beside the body. The relatives of William M'Donald all positively swore that to their knowledge he never had a pistol in his life, and certainly no ammunition was found in his possession, nor was there any evidence that he had ever bought any. In his first declaration of 23rd November the prisoner denied that he had seen the pistol until the Sunday morning after the death, and stated that he had only the remains of an old pistol at home, which he had broken four months before, also that he had neither gunpowder, moulds, nor bullets in his possession. That day, however, the police had found in his house a pistol with a broken trigger, a pistol key, and a packet of gunpowder. They also ascertained that in the end of the previous August he had bought a second pistol in a shop in Peterhead, paying 4s. 6d., which price included a mould and key; that about the same time he purchased two dozen percussion-caps, and that two ounces of gunpowder had been bought by him at M'Leod's shop in the kirktown, "a little before dark" on the very day of the death.

Questioned as to these matters on 24th November, the prisoner
in his second declaration stated that he had bought a pistol
two years before at Peterhead, and that it had been repaired
by Murison, the village blacksmith.    He also admitted the
purchase of the gunpowder, which he had meant to use for
ointment for a patient, Margaret Reid, for whom he had made
up some a fortnight before.    He denied, however, that he had
opened the packet.

Now all these statements were directly contradicted by the
evidence.    The Peterhead pistol was *not* the pistol repaired
by Murison, who identified the one with the broken trigger,
found by the police, as that repaired by him in July.    The
doctor was seen, a few weeks before M'Donald's death, practising with a pistol in a park to the west of the village, and again,
by a different witness, on 29th October, firing a pistol near his
own stable door.    It was therefore proved that the prisoner
had possessed another pistol for which he did not account, and
the defence made no attempt to show what had become of it.
The Crown, on the other hand, alleged that this pistol was the
fatal weapon, and a second pistol key, found on the prisoner
when arrested, fitted it better than the broken pistol.    The
man who sold the pistol to the prisoner, however, could not
say more than that it was one of the same class and of similar
make, but he swore he did not sell the broken one.    It was
proved that the day before the death, the prisoner, in a shop
at New St. Fergus, had made an unsuccessful attempt to
purchase gunpowder, stating that he required it " to shoot
crows."    It was also proved that the ointment made up
by the prisoner for Margaret Reid did not contain gunpowder, that the packet which he procured on the Saturday
had been opened and the string of it cut, and whereas
it contained two ounces when sold to him, the contents, when
found, only weighed one ounce and three-quarters.    The
defence maintained that the packet had been burst by the
procurator-fiscal during the search of the premises, and a small

quantity of the powder—" not half a teaspoonful "—was proved
to have been spilt at that time, but "the fiscal made a pinch
of it, and put it back." Joseph Harkom, gunmaker, Edinburgh,
deponed that the quantity required to fire the ball in question
(which weighed a quarter of an ounce) from the pistol produced
would only be about eight grains. It would not take more
than the eighth part of a quarter of an ounce.

All this looked bad for the doctor, but the surprise of the
trial was the appearance in the box of the last witness in the
case, Adam Gray, designed as "brother to the Provost of
Peterhead," who told the following remarkable tale:—He was
at one time an auctioneer in Peterhead, and knew the late
William Milne intimately. On Friday, 15th September 1848,
in Peterhead, William M'Donald introduced himself to him as
Milne's nephew, and made an appointment to meet his uncle.
M'Donald then said: "You pick up things at roups [auctions];
have you no gun that you could sell me?" Gray asked, "Are
you going to poach?" and M'Donald replied that "it was to
frighten rooks from the crops." Gray then sold him a " useless "
pistol for 4s. 6d., which he now identified by a notch on the
stock as the pistol found beside the body—" I believe it to be
the same pistol which I sold to M'Donald." In support of this
statement he produced a small memorandum book, containing
an entry of the transaction.

Gray was rigorously cross-examined by the Solicitor-
General. He admitted that on his examination regarding
this matter before the Sheriff, he had stated that there was
no mark by which he could identify the pistol alleged by
him to have been sold to M'Donald, and that he had no note
of the time of the sale. The book, witness said, was kept as
he pleased. The first page bore entries of the dates 1843 and
1831, the second 1843 and 1827, and so forth. The pencil
entry as to the pistol was made at the time in his office.
Another entry, dated "September 1848," was, he admitted,
written by him in Edinburgh that week. "Everyone keeps

a jotter as he likes," explained the witness; "it may be a queer book, but it is true." The sale of the pistol was not recorded in his regular books, nor was an entry, which appeared in the jotter, relating to the purchase of a case of pistols by him in 1831. He had been convicted and fined five pounds a year or two ago, for firing a gun at a man who was trespassing upon his property. He had known Milne's nephews by sight from infancy, but "could not point them out now." He had not seen the deceased for two years. He was not related to the prisoner, but had known him for several years, and believed him to be an excellent man.

Whatever weight may attach to the uncorroborated testimony even of a provost's brother, the crucial point of the case was the question of opportunity. The defence was virtually an *alibi*. M'Donald was last seen alive when he left the wright's shop shortly before half-past seven. The time when the shot which killed him had been fired was fixed within a minute by no less than five witnesses, who severally heard the report at twenty-five or six minutes to eight. Saturday was a busy night, and many of the villagers were out of doors. The church clock at the east end of the street was the criterion by which were regulated the individual timepieces of the inhabitants. They had the further advantage of a local bellman, who nightly performed the ceremony of curfew at eight o'clock. William Fraser, the celebrant in question, left his house, situated on the Netherhill road, a quarter of a mile north of the village, at two or three minutes after half-past seven. When forty or fifty yards from his own door, he saw a flash to the south-west and heard the report of a shot. After visiting the shops of M'Leod and of Smith, the wright, he went to the church and rang the bell. Alexander Forman, at his farm at Netherhill, half a mile off, was waiting, watch in hand, "to supper his horses." At twenty-six minutes to eight he heard a shot from the direction of James Fordyce's house. The three other witnesses heard the report at five minutes after the half-hour.

How Dr. Smith spent certain momentous minutes between seven and eight o'clock that night was the matter of greatest contention between the prosecutor and the defence. It was admitted that about six o'clock the prisoner visited the manse, where he was not expected, although he had been professionally attending one of the servants, and that he remained there till five minutes to seven. Two Crown witnesses, Mr. and Mrs. M'Pherson, swore that they met him between the manse gate and his own house at ten or fifteen minutes past the hour, and recognised him by the light from the unshuttered windows of the wright's shop at the street corner, in which, as will be remembered, M'Donald then was talking to his friends, and could be seen by anyone outside. In his declaration the prisoner said that he went home from the manse at seven, that five or ten minutes afterwards he went into his garden and brought in some flower roots which had been previously dug up, that he next walked about at the back of the house for some minutes, and then left ·to visit a patient, Isabella Anderson, at whose house he arrived at twenty-five minutes to eight, having observed the hour on her clock. We shall see later what Miss Anderson had to say to this.

For the defence, Martha Cadger, the doctor's servant, said she let her master in between twenty-five minutes and half-past seven, that ten minutes after he went out by the backdoor to the offices, that she followed him there "to meat her pig," and saw him in the garden with a spade, that she did not see him again till he came home at nine, and that next morning (Sunday) she saw in the house some dahlia roots which she had not observed there on the Saturday. Eliza Park, his other servant, said that the doctor came in at half-past seven and went out again in ten minutes. The house clock, she admitted, was five or ten minutes fast. Some dahlias were brought in on the Sunday; she saw none on the Saturday. Alexander Duguid, who was in the kitchen that evening, said he left to go home at a quarter to eight. He heard the doctor's step in the passage about half-past seven.

The evidence adduced by the Crown upon this point was as follows:—John Aden, labourer, Moss of Rora, who lived near the M'Donalds and knew William well, stated that he walked home from Peterhead on the night in question. He was passing through St. Fergus when, at eighteen or twenty minutes past seven, west of Widow Robertson's inn, he met M'Donald and Dr. Smith, whom he knew by sight, walking side by side and speaking to each other. He said that he recognised M'Donald's voice, and he accurately described his dress. The doctor was wearing a white hat (as was otherwise proved he did that night). In the course of a lengthy and searching cross-examination by the Dean of Faculty it appeared that Aden, east of Robertson's inn, a few yards from where he met M'Donald and the prisoner, had asked a man the time. The latter struck a light and showed him that it was seven on his watch, which he said was half an hour fast. It was, therefore, in fact then half-past six. Aden could give no explanation of how he had come to say that he met the others a few yards further on at "eighteen or twenty minutes past seven." Although in hopeless confusion as to the hour, he stuck sturdily to his statement that he had seen M'Donald and Dr. Smith together that night. After being sharply interrogated by the Justice-Clerk, Aden was committed to prison for prevarication.

In considering the evidence regarding the movements of the prisoner on the Saturday evening, the following facts should be kept in view:—According to the evidence of a land surveyor the distance from the doctor's house at the east end to the field at the west end of St. Fergus where the body was found was only five hundred yards, which the witness said he walked easily in three minutes and forty-five seconds; the houses of the several witnesses now to be mentioned were all situated in the main street between those two points; and it was in evidence that rain began to fall that evening at five minutes to eight, and continued heavily for some time.

Isabella Anderson sent out her servant, Christina Gavin, shortly before eight on a message to M'Leod's shop, practically next door. The girl was five or six minutes in the shop, and met the bellman at the door as she went out. She returned home before the eight o'clock bell began to ring. During her absence Dr. Smith called on her mistress. When he came in he took up a candle to look at the clock, and drew Miss Anderson's attention to the time by it—twenty-five minutes to eight. He said he was going to Pirie's and to Manson's. He only remained for about five minutes, and did not sit down. She saw nothing particular in his appearance. Now Miss Anderson swore that her clock was then a quarter of an hour slow, and that the actual time of his visit was ten minutes to eight.

Mrs. Pirie deponed that the doctor came to her door about five minutes to eight. He only stayed two minutes, saying he had to see Mrs. Manson, who lived over the way, and would shortly return. He did so in about ten minutes. She heard the bell ring in the interval. It was beginning to rain when he was at the door the first time; it was very heavy before he came back. Her husband offered him his chair by the fire, but after taking it the doctor rose and took one " far back at a side." He remained a quarter of an hour and then left.

Mrs. Manson said that the doctor paid her a visit about eight o'clock. She had been confined that day, but was not expecting to see him then. He remarked when he came in that it was raining. He moved his chair behind her, and sat down without taking off his hat; she thought he did not wish her to look at him. He did not stay long. That evening she said to her husband that she did not know what was the matter with Dr. Smith; he was wiping his face frequently; she thought his nose was bleeding.

The arguments of counsel for and against the prisoner upon

these facts will be noticed when we consider the addresses to the jury.

The only evidence as yet unexamined is that whereby the Crown sought to infer the prisoner's guilt from his conduct at and about the time of the death. It was disputed whether the message given by the boy Robert to the prisoner's wife after the discovery of the body, was such as to indicate precisely the locality of the accident. However that may be, Dr. Smith was proved to have been seen about eight o'clock that Sunday morning going up the Netherhill road and standing for some time looking westward, at the point nearest to his house from which was visible the field where the body lay. The evidence of Pirie, the farrier, who at his request went with him at half-past nine to find the body, showed that the doctor certainly knew where to look for it; yet in his declaration the prisoner expressly stated, "I had no information where the body was," and when questioned on the point by Mr. Moir, the Free Church minister, he said, "We did not know where to go." He stated to several persons that M'Donald's snuff-box had contained gunpowder, but none of the witnesses who examined it saw anything of the kind. On the Monday after the death Dr. Smith told Mr. Moir that M'Donald had shot himself "by design," because "there were quarrels in the family," the existence of which was afterwards denied on oath by Mrs. M'Donald, her daughter, and her sons. Mr. Moir said it was a great mystery, which he would like to see better investigated, and remarked that it was a strange thing that anyone should have looked for the lad at a place so little frequented; if some-one else had done it, he must have been dogged from the village. "I looked into his [Smith's] face," said the minister, "and asked, 'And where were you on Saturday night, doctor?'" It is due to the prisoner to say that without hesitation he mentioned the manse, Anderson's, Pirie's, and Manson's, and that the minister, who possibly had his own suspicions, saw nothing peculiar in his manner. Charles M'Donald, hearing

of his brother's death, returned home on the Sunday and had
a conversation with Dr. Smith. The latter said that William
had been in low spirits of late, and that he had seen him at
Burnside sit "with his head hanging among his feet, and not
speaking." Charles from his own knowledge denied this, as
also did the other relatives; and indeed all the evidence proves
that William M'Donald was hale and hearty to the last day
of his life.

Both Mrs. M'Donald and Robert saw Dr. Smith talking to
William at the farm about two o'clock on the Saturday, and
thereafter William told them that he had promised the doctor
to meet him at his (Smith's) stable door that evening about six,
"to see a large printed paper he had never seen before." Mrs.
M'Donald also swore that on the previous Monday she and
William, being at Peterhead, met the doctor, who gave William
a document resembling "the wager paper," which he was to
sign and return to Smith the following night. The prisoner
in his third declaration denied that this incident occurred, but
the document itself bore to be signed by him and M'Donald
that very day. From the first Mrs. M'Donald naturally refused
to believe that her son had shot himself, and did not conceal
her belief that he had met with foul play, but Dr. Smith
"warned her that she would get into trouble for the way she
was speaking." She also swore that William told her he was
in the habit of meeting the doctor at his stable door of an
evening "at bell-ringing"—"a mark was on the door to show
whether he was to meet him"—and that William said he ought
not to have mentioned the fact, as Dr. Smith had forbidden him
to tell anyone of their meetings.

It was proved that on the Sunday Dr. Smith accompanied
Hunter, the constable, who was making inquiries about the
accident, to the house of Fraser, the bellman. The latter told
them how he had heard the shot fired the night before. The
doctor made no comment at that time, but returned later alone,
and asked Fraser, "If it would not be a quarter from eight that

he had heard the report?" When under arrest at Robertson's inn on the following Tuesday, the prisoner privately gave the landlady's daughter letters to deliver to his wife and James Greig, and asked her, in a whisper, to go and see if Miss Anderson could remember that he was in her house at twenty-five minutes to eight, "and all would be right." Miss Anderson, however, "would not depart from the truth." The prisoner in his letter to Greig wrote as follows:—" As I said—I would be a prisoner. Would you oblige me by asking, privately, at Mrs. M'Donald what she said to Mr. Boyd [the procurator-fiscal] to-day about me and William M'Donald, and about any insurances? But this must be very private, as the whole thing may be revealed."

We can only glance at the long and eloquent addresses of counsel to the jury. The speech of the Solicitor-General, while marked by strict fairness, marshalled with excellent effect the facts and circumstances which appeared upon the proof inconsistent with the prisoner's innocence. His argument, as reported, is more cogent and convincing than that of his great opponent, the learned Dean, who was stronger upon the moral improbabilities of the case than upon the proven facts.

The Solicitor-General at the outset referred to the difficulties which had attended the investigation, owing to the isolated and rustic nature of the place and the ignorant and simple character of the local witnesses. He then gave an admirable exposition of the nature and importance of circumstantial evidence. "It is impossible," said he, "that there can be direct evidence of secret crime, but circumstances in such a case may be viewed as the links scattered over a field of inquiry which, when gathered and put together, form a coherent and consistent chain by which you can be led up to the very door of Truth." He maintained that here there could be no question of accident, and that suicide, while possible, was in the circumstances of the case highly improbable. The doctors could only account for the position of the body if M'Donald had shot himself sitting or lying in the ditch, or had been placed in it by another.  Now, if he shot himself in the ditch, he was below the level of the surrounding ground; but Fraser, the bellman, actually saw the flash from a spot several hundred yards off, with more than one fence and some rising ground between, and at a point where he could not have seen a flash within the ditch.  If M'Donald did not shoot himself it was done to look like it, both as to the manner of the shot, the line of fire, and the placing of the pistol beside the body, by " a deliberate, knowing, skilful, I was almost going to say surgical, hand." In dealing with the insurances the Solicitor-General said that the effecting of these by the prisoner was not merely a motive, it was an important step in the perpetration of the crime, and could not be separated from the other facts.  He pointed out the absence of any evidence of Milne's knowledge of the insurances, and characterised as " monstrous and incredible " the prisoner's story that Milne embarked in these transactions because he was unable to pay his doctor's bill.  The prisoner had denied that he knew the terms of the policies or that they were in his own favour, yet he told Greig he expected to get £1500 or £1000 out of them, and the £1000 policy was within five days of expiry on the day of M'Donald's death.  With regard to the weapon, the Solicitor-General referred to the fact that the prisoner was proved to have purchased a second pistol of which no account had even to that day been given, that he had bought gunpowder upon a false pretence of making it up into ointment, and that the quantity missing from the packet was sufficient to have charged the pistol eight times.  It was proved that M'Donald was never known by any of the family to possess either a pistol or gunpowder.  Upon this point he criticised severely the evidence of Gray, whose allegation of having sold the pistol to M'Donald he attributed to his zeal to serve a friend, and said that he (counsel) did not value his evidence a single rush, and he was satisfied that the jury would not believe it.  On the question of opportunity the Solicitor-

General observed that the shot was proved by five witnesses to
have been fired at twenty-five or six minutes to eight. Till seven
the prisoner was in the manse, till past seven M'Donald was
in the wright's shop. Mrs. M'Pherson saw the prisoner near that
shop (those within being visible from the outside) at ten or
fifteen minutes past seven, but up to ten minutes to eight,
when he visited Miss Anderson, the prisoner was unaccounted
for. The jury must judge of the evidence of Aden that the
two were seen by him together that night, which could not be
true unless the time he named—eighteen or twenty minutes past
seven—were nearly correct. It was proved that it would take
less than five minutes to walk from the prisoner's house to
where the body was found, so that he had ample time to
commit the deed. Even upon the evidence of the witnesses for
the defence, fourteen minutes elapsed between the prisoner
leaving his house and the hearing of the shot, which was about
three times as much as was required to reach the place. He
contended that the evidence for the defence on this point had
not shaken that given for the Crown. Then there was the visit
of the prisoner to the bellman and the message he sent to Miss
Anderson, whereby, "finding himself under the necessity of
proving an *alibi*, he endeavoured to adjust the evidence as to
time; to get the man forward and the woman back, so that
the time of Fraser's hearing the shot and the time of the
prisoner's visit to her might be brought as near as possible."
They also had the prisoner's conversation with Greig and the
letter which he wrote to him. All these acts were inconsistent
with his innocence. The Solicitor-General concluded by saying
he had satisfied the jury that M'Donald's death was not the
result of accident or of suicide; that the prisoner had the most
tremendous motive to wish him dead, and had shown that by
that motive he was actuated; that he possessed the means;
that he had the opportunity; and that the indications he gave
of his mind all led to the conclusion that he was the guilty man.
On the whole matter he believed he had good grounds for

16

asking and expecting from the jury a verdict of guilty against the prisoner.

The Dean of Faculty, in his address, expressed the greatest astonishment at the confidence displayed by his learned friend, as he had never seen a case in which a prosecutor was less entitled to adopt such a tone. It was a remarkable feature of the case that there did exist upon the part of the prisoner an interest or motive to commit this crime; but if there was no evidence of the commission of the crime, separately and independently of the motive, on which they could come to a sound and rational conclusion, the motive alone was by itself perfectly insufficient. The learned Dean then proceeded to walk delicately over the thorny ground of the insurances. He contended that if M'Donald understood very little about the matter it was his (counsel's) belief that the prisoner did not understand much more. However the insurances came to be effected, whether by Milne himself or by the prisoner at the instigation of canvassers, they began in 1852. The crime must therefore have been projected and prepared in the mind of the prisoner from the very beginning of the insurance business. If so he must have been a wonderful man, continuing as he did in daily, friendly intercourse with his family and acquaintances, while "meditating one of the most fearful offences that had ever been brought under the cognizance of a court of justice." After drawing a graphic picture of the mental state of such a miscreant, "he ventured to say that such a thing never occurred before—it was beyond the dream of a romance writer." Eleven years later, however, the Dean of Faculty himself presided, as Lord Justice-Clerk, at the trial of Dr. Pritchard, whose character and conduct afforded a complete refutation of this argument. The first essential step in the prosecutor's case was the truth of the *corpus delicti*, which, the Dean submitted, it had failed to establish. He admitted that the circumstances of M'Donald rendered suicide exceedingly unlikely, but it was vain to say that antecedents were conclusive in such a case. Both the medical men said that there were no materials on which they could form an opinion. Was murder, then, proved? It was impossible to say so. It was a very remarkable thing that, while the death of M'Donald was caused by a pistol bullet, neither bullets nor mould were found in the prisoner's house. If he had put them out of the way "it was a very odd thing that he should not have disposed of the powder also." The learned Dean did not point out that it was at least equally remarkable that M'Donald had no ammunition whatever in his possession, while the prisoner had been seen practising with the missing pistol on two occasions shortly before the death. Why, continued the Dean, should the prisoner, who had been maturing this crime for two years, have resorted to the noisy violence of shooting? "There were subtle and secret agents by which human life might be destroyed, of which any man in the medical profession had the most secure and perfect command." It must have been within the Dean's recollection that in 1849 Dr. Webster, Professor of Chemistry in Harvard University, a man of noted scientific attainments, decoyed his benefactor, Dr. Parkman, into his own laboratory in Boston Medical College, and there, "surrounded," like Mr. Venus, "by the trophies of his art," this chemical adept set upon and slew his unsuspecting visitor with a bludgeon. In regard to the purchase by the prisoner of a second pistol at Peterhead, the Dean complained that, when examined, he had not been asked what had become of it. It was all very well to say that he might have brought witnesses to speak to this, but there were some things incapable of proof. It was true that he had bought caps and gunpowder; these were just the scraps of which the case was made up. What did it matter whether the powder was bought on the Friday or the Saturday? It was as likely to have been bought on the former as on the

latter day, if a murder were contemplated. He contended
that the packet was burst by the fiscal when engaged in the
search of the prisoner's house, and that it was by no means
certain the box of ointment produced was that given to the
girl Reid by Dr. Smith.   The Dean maintained the credibility of Gray, and said that, on the assumption that he was
worthy of belief, there was no proof that the pistol ever
belonged to the prisoner, while they had direct evidence
that it belonged to M'Donald.   On the question of opportunity
the Dean asked the jury to trust to something better than
the time of clocks, namely the sequence of events.  He said
that if there was in fact a tryst between M'Donald and the
prisoner for six o'clock, which he thought highly improbable,
it was very certain that the doctor did not intend to keep
it, for he visited the manse at six, and remained an hour.
The Dean then exhaustively reviewed the evidence of the
witnesses who spoke to the movements of the prisoner, and
argued that he could not have committed the murder between
his leaving home and his going to Miss Anderson, and that
it was impossible that he could have been elsewhere than in
her house when the shot was fired.   With the exception
of an absurd observation of Mrs. Manson, the prisoner when
seen that night had none of the *indicia* of a murderer about
him.   As to the various instances of the prisoner's actions
subsequent to the death, from which the Crown sought to
infer his guilt, " these were not in the least wonderful points
in the conduct of an innocent man, anxious to prove his
innocence."   The learned Dean concluded by saying that he
had never seen a prosecution fail as that one had done and
the Crown still ask for a verdict, and that on coming into
Court that morning he had not expected to have been
obliged to address the jury.  He confidently asked a verdict
which would completely clear the prisoner's character.

It is interesting to note in passing the marked difference
in tone between this speech and that delivered three years

later by the same great advocate in defence of Madeleine
Smith. The latter, an acknowledged model of forensic
eloquence, contains passages so powerful in. argument, so
impassioned in rhetoric, as to take captive alike the reason
and the imagination. The former, from whatever cause,
presents no such attractive features.

The Lord Justice-Clerk, in charging the jury, said if this
were a case of murder, it was certainly the most atrocious
one that was ever brought before that Court. At an early
period of the trial, however, he had formed the impression
that, unless there was more evidence brought than appeared
likely, there was not enough to infer the guilt of the prisoner
or to substantiate the fact that a murder had been committed.
Since hearing the whole case that impression had been
strengthened and confirmed. After the evidence of Gray,
he thought it was necessary to call their attention to the
question whether a murder had been committed at all? The
doctors could not say whether the death was caused by
violence or by suicide. The pistol purchased by Dr. Smith
at Peterhead was only proved to be "like" that found
beside the body, and there was not a single circumstance
tending to prove that it was a murder and not suicide,
except that pistol. If that pistol, therefore, was not proved
to be the prisoner's, what single act had they in the case
bringing him into contact with M'Donald at all in the matter
of his death? The motive might have existed, but
from that they could not infer the commission of such an
act. The opportunity he might have had, but so had many
other persons in the kirktown. The prisoner ought to have
been asked as to the pistol bought by him at Peterhead;
that point was of ten times more importance than many
of the circumstances on which he was examined. After the
evidence of Gray, unless they believed that he had committed
deliberate perjury, it was impossible any longer to hold
that the pistol found near the body was the pistol of the

prisoner. Unquestionably, in view of M'Donald's character and position, the moral evidence was all against the supposition of suicide; but looking to all these facts, assuming that they did not think it was a case of suicide, it still remained a murder wholly unexplained, and not proven against the prisoner. As to Dr. Smith's false statements in his declaration about the insurances, these might be accounted for by those mistaken acts by which accused persons, whether innocent or guilty, sometimes endeavour to clear themselves. The whole case might be surrounded with suspicion and difficulties, but in the view he took of the case it came to be an unexplained murder, the evidence having failed to connect the crime with the prisoner at the bar.

His lordship then asked the jury whether they wished him to go over the evidence; and the jury, having intimated that they did not, then retired to consider their verdict.

During their deliberations the unfortunate Aden, who had been committed for prevarication as already mentioned, was brought to the bar. The Justice-Clerk was of opinion that he had wilfully stated what he knew to be false, either from a desire to make himself of importance or to bring himself into the case. His lordship said his intention had been to pass sentence of six months' imprisonment, but as the other two judges thought Aden's behaviour was only due to stupidity, the Court would not inflict any punishment. He was accordingly discharged. With reference to this matter the *Edinburgh Courant* (18th April 1854) contained a paragraph to the effect that they had been requested to state that the Solicitor-General had seen and precognosced (examined) this witness himself before the trial, and that Aden had then told the story as to meeting Smith and M'Donald together about twenty minutes past seven substantially as he had repeated it in the witness-box. The conduct of Aden was probably due to confusion arising from the novelty of his position.

The jury, after an absence of ten minutes, returned into Court with a verdict of "Not Proven, by a majority." The Justice-Clerk then put the somewhat unusual question whether their difference of opinion was between "Not Proven" and "Not Guilty," and received the unexpected reply that it was between "Guilty" and "Not Proven." The prisoner was accordingly dismissed from the bar.

The failure of the prosecution to obtain a verdict was, like the acquittal of Madeleine Smith, largely due to the fact that the Crown did not prove to the satisfaction of the jury that the prisoner was in company with the deceased on the night in question. It was stated in the *Scotsman* (19th April 1854) that the division among the jury was eleven for "Not Proven" and four for "Guilty"; and that the prisoner, on being liberated, was not, as currently rumoured, re-arrested upon another charge. The verdict would not appear to have been popular. It was received with hisses by a crowded court, and although the prisoner, for his own protection, was detained within the building for some time, when at length he was allowed to go he met with a hostile reception. He left the city that night, and so passes from the public view.

We have the authority of the late Lord Moncreiff for the fact that, notwithstanding his acquittal by the jury, Dr. Smith did not succeed in obtaining payment of the policies of insurance. Actions were raised, but on the insurance companies defending them they were abandoned, and the policies lapsed.

# THE DUNECHT MYSTERY

THE body-snatcher is a type of felon happily obsolete in our criminal practice, save for one signal instance, since the passing of the Anatomy Act in 1832. Prior to the introduction of Warburton's Bill, Scotland had paid a high price for the pre-eminence of her medical schools in the outraged feelings of the living and the violated sepulchres of the dead. The revelation of the hideous traffic driven by Burke and Hare, that hellish partnership whose transactions horrified mankind, at length roused the nation from its apathy. Science, wilfully blind or culpably incompetent, had seen nothing amiss, and as the doctors either would or could give no aid in securing the conviction of the murderers, Justice was forced to loose her hold on the more fiendish of the pair, lest both miscreants should escape unpunished. Legislation followed, to render needless and unremunerative for the future a form of sacrilege which had made possible the perpetration of such fearful crimes. The methods of the professional resurrectionist became but an unclean memory, and only the ugly iron mortsafes in our older graveyards served as reminders of his power in the past.

When, therefore, on 3rd December 1881, the readers of the daily journals learned, some twelve months after the death and burial of the late Earl of Crawford and Balcarres, that his remains had been stolen from the family vault at Dunecht House, near Aberdeen, in circumstances inexplicable and mysterious, the excitement throughout the country was intense.

A similar outrage had startled the civilised world in 1878, when the body of Mr. Stewart, an American millionaire, was carried off and held to ransom, and, notwithstanding a reward of 25,000 dollars offered by his widow, was never recovered; but with this exception such a crime had been unheard of for over half a century.

The dead earl had been in his day a notable nobleman. Born in 1812, he succeeded to the title in 1869 as eighth Earl of Balcarres and twenty-fifth Earl of Crawford. He was a man of many tastes and talents; much of his time and money was devoted to astronomical research, and he was a capable theologian as well as an erudite antiquarian and genealogist. He published much, and in his *Lives of the Lindsays* has left an exhaustive history of his ancient house, while the great library at Haigh Hall, near Wigan, his Lancashire seat, is a monument to his industry and learning. The outrage offered to the mortal remains of a man of such illustrious lineage and of a personality so distinguished was calculated to shock the least susceptible of his fellow countrymen.

In the winter of 1879 the Earl of Crawford, whose health had begun to fail, visited Egypt and afterwards Italy, where he died at Florence on 13th December 1880. His body, which for removal to his native land was embalmed by a Florentine chemist skilled in the art, was placed within three coffins, the inner one being of soft Italian wood, the middle one of lead, and the outer one of polished oak, elaborately carved and mounted with fittings of chased silver. These three coffins were deposited within a huge walnut shell, on the top of which was a cross carved in high relief, the weight of the whole amounting to nearly half a ton. The conveyance of the remains across the Alps was attended with great difficulty, but under the care of a trusted family servant they reached France in safety. A special steamer was chartered to convey the body to London, and in crossing the Channel she encountered so heavy a gale that the coffin had to be lashed to the deck. The removal to Aberdeen on 24th December was more easily effected, but there an unexpected obstacle arose. No hearse large enough to contain the coffin was procurable, and the outer shell had to be removed. It was afterwards deposited in the crypt beside the three coffins in which the body was encased. The last stage of its long journey, that from Aberdeen to Dunecht, was undertaken in one of the most violent snow-storms ever experienced in Scotland, and it is recorded that the hearse, when returning to Aberdeen, was snowed up by the wayside for several days. These inauspicious happenings, however, were but the prelude to a misadventure yet more remarkable.

The house of Dunecht, one of the finest mansions in Aber-deenshire, had been for some years undergoing a complete restoration. The alterations included the erection of a private chapel attached to the house, with a mortuary chapel of white marble in connection, beneath which was a mausoleum intended to supersede the old family vault of the Lindsays at Wigan. But recently completed, the mortuary chapel had not been con-secrated at the time of the earl's death, so that rite was duly performed by the Bishop of Aberdeen before the interment, and on 29th December 1880 the first tenant of the new mausoleum solemnly entered into possession. The crypt, which is built throughout of massive granite blocks, is about twenty-one feet long by eleven feet wide, in the centre an octagonal pillar supports the groined roof, and the walls on each side are occupied by catacombs arranged in tiers capable of containing twenty-five coffins. Access to the vault is obtained solely by means of a short flight of eight steps descending from the level of the ground outside the mortuary chapel. When the remains of the earl had been laid in what was believed to be their last resting-place the steps and stairway were covered by four immense slabs of Caithness granite, the interstices of which were filled with lime. Five months later earth was spread over the flags to a considerable depth, in which grass was sown and shrubs

and flowers were planted, and the whole was enclosed with an
iron railing. In such circumstances the dead might well have
been expected to rest in peace.

On Sunday, 29th May 1881, exactly five months after
the interment of Lord Crawford's body, the housekeeper at
Dunecht, coming home from church through the grounds,
perceived a pleasant aromatic smell issuing from the vault.
Next day the gardener also noticed the odour, which he attributed to the *arbor vitæ* used as a background to the flowers of
the numerous wreaths left upon the coffin. He thought that
it came through the ventilator, but though he had been in
the habit of passing the vault daily, he had never observed
the smell before. It was afterwards remarked by several
other persons about the estate, and masons were accordingly
employed to examine the condition of the flagstones covering
the entrance stairway, which, owing to the unusual severity of
the weather, had not yet been cemented and planted over.
They observed a crevice between two of the outside flags which
they thought had been caused by frost. This was filled up
again with lime, cement was placed round and over the stones,
and the sweet smell was noticed no more for the time. Immediately thereafter, on 2nd or 3rd June, the flags were covered
with earth, grass was sown, and the railing erected, as already
described.

On 8th September following a curious incident occurred
which was not made public until later. Mr. William Yeats,
advocate, Aberdeen, commissioner on the Dunecht estates and
the family's local solicitor, received that day an anonymous
letter in the following terms:—

Sir,—The remains of the late Earl of Crawford are not beneath
the chaple at Dunecht as you believe, but were removed hence last
spring, and the smell of decayed flowers ascending from the vault
since that time will, on investigation, be found to proceed from
another cause than flowers.                           Nabob.

On receipt of this extraordinary communication, which bore

the Aberdeen postmark, Mr. Yeats at once saw the builder who had constructed the vault, and from what he learned from him, came to the conclusion that the letter was a wicked hoax. He therefore said nothing to the family about the letter, but laid it aside as of no importance.

The works in connection with the mansion-house were still in progress, and on the morning of Thursday, 1st December, one of the labourers, passing the entrance to the vault between seven and eight o'clock, observed that the turf at the mouth of the tomb had been displaced. He at once told the overseer of his discovery, the earl's commissioner was informed, and the police were summoned from Aberdeen. When they arrived in the forenoon it was decided to enter and examine the vault. The soil was found to have been removed from above the flagstone directly over the upper steps and farthest from the chapel wall. The stone itself, a huge block six feet by four feet in size, and weighing 15 cwt., had been raised about eighteen inches on one side, and pieces of wood inserted to keep it in position. Within the railing round the entrance were two iron shovels and a pick, which, as later appeared, belonged to the workmen, and had been left in an ajacent lime-shed on the previous night. Another slab was removed, and the party descended to the crypt. On the stairs they found three iron bars and two planks. Though now anticipating the worst, they were horrified at the sight which awaited them.

The floor of the vault was strewn with planks and sawdust, the three coffins, which at the interment had been placed in one of the niches in the middle tier at the left-hand side of the crypt, were lying open and empty side by side in the middle of the floor, and the body of the dead earl had disappeared. The lid of the outer coffin had been unscrewed in a tradesman-like manner, after which it had been turned over on its side and the leaden coffin rolled out and cut open. The inner coffin had then been opened with some sharp instrument sufficiently to admit of the body being drawn out. Its silver handles, plates,

and mountings were untouched. From the scented sawdust
with which the coffin had been filled came the peculiar
aromatic odour that had been remarked in the previousMay.
The fact that the sawdust was mildewed and the leaden
shell, where cut, oxidised, indicated that a considerable time
had elapsed since the commission of the outrage.

A grim satire, this, on the vanity of "Monuments and
Mechanical Preservations"!

An inquiry into the mysterious circumstances of the case
was at once commenced by the procurator-fiscal, the official by
whom the initial steps of a criminal investigation in Scotland
are conducted. The house and policies were guarded by the
police, and all persons connected with the estate were closely
examined. The new earl, who had been absent from home at
the time of the discovery, was at once informed of what had
occurred, and returned forthwith to Dunecht. An exhaustive
search of the surrounding district was instituted, and was continued diligently for a fortnight, but without result. It was
interrupted by a severe snowstorm which began at that date,
and as the snow remained upon the ground until well on into
the following spring, the search had to be abandoned for
the time. A sensational feature of these attempts to discover
the body was the employment of the celebrated bloodhound
"Morgan," which in 1876 had successfully run to earth Fish,
the Blackburn murderer. Owing, however, to persistent frost
the experiment proved unsuccessful.

Weeks passed, and the public excitement and curiosity
continued unabated and unappeased. The inquiry was conducted in private, the authorities would give no information,
and the gallant band of reporters who attempted to storm the
house of Dunecht were repulsed with heavy loss—of copy. In
the absence of authentic news, all sorts of rumour scirculated in
the press. It was said that the outrage had been committed
the day before the discovery of the rifled tomb, under cloud of
a tempestuous night, by Florentine desperadoes who had tracked

the corpse from Italy. Alternatively, the body had never been in the vault at all, having been abstracted before the coffin left Florence. According to other accounts, the deed had been done by certain Italian painters employed in decorating the interior of the mansion-house, or by some medical students from Aberdeen for professional purposes. Prints of many feet were said to have been found in the sawdust on the floor of the vault and in the earth at the entrance, indicating that several persons had been concerned in the offence. Suspicious characters of varied aspect and nationality had been seen lurking about Dunecht, or pervading the neighbourhood in dubious and elusive dogcarts. Finally, it was confidently reported that the body of the late earl had been taken to Italy in an Italian yacht, the *Speranza,* and was then in Florence.

But those better informed knew from the condition of the vault that the outrage had been perpetrated long before the date on which the violation of the tomb was discovered, while the fact that a number of strangers, perambulating a quiet countryside with an embalmed corpse, would be calculated to attract attention, led to the belief that the body had been abstracted by persons familiar with the locality, and was concealed within a short distance of the house.

Meanwhile, on 4th December the procurator-fiscal published in the local newspapers an advertisement earnestly requesting anyone, who during that year had observed anything having reference to the removal of the remains, to communicate with him or with the Chief Constable of Aberdeen. Mr. Yeats, the commissioner, called to mind his mysterious correspondent of the previous September, and an advertisement was inserted on 9th December as follows:—" NABOB.—Please communicate at once." Any information regarding the affair was to be sent to Mr. Alsop, the earl's London solicitor, who was then at Dunecht. On the 13th a further advertisement appeared:—" Fifty pounds reward will be paid to the writer of the anonymous letter in September last addressed to a person in King Street, Aberdeen, on his furnishing full particulars." Although neither the earnest request of the fiscal nor the offer of the reward were sufficient to tempt "Nabob" to discard his anonymity, that retiring individual was stimulated by these announcements once more to take up his pen, and on 23rd December Mr. Alsop received from him in London a letter in the following terms :—

SIR,

*The late Earl of Crawford.*

The body is still in Aberdeenshire, and I can put you in possession of the same as soon as you bring one or more of the desperados who stole it to justice, so that I may know with whom I have to deal. I have no wish to be assinated by rusarectionests, nor suspected by the public of being an accomplice in such dastardly work, which I most assuredly would be unless the gulty party are brought to justice. Had Mr. Yeats acted on the hint I gave him last Sept., he might have found the remains as though by axedand and hunted up the robers at lsure, but that chance is lost, so I hope you will find your men and make it safe and prudent for me to find what you want.

P.S.—Should they find out thad an outsider knows their secret it may be removed to another place.          NABOB.

On the 30th a notice was published, both in the press and by means of placards and hand-bills, headed " £600 REWARD," which stated that £100 would be paid by Her Majesty's Government and £500 by Messrs. Alsop, Mann & Co., Lord Crawford's London solicitors, to any person unconnected with the police force who should first give such information as would lead to the discovery and conviction of the perpetrators of the offence, and that the Home Secretary would advise the pardon of any accomplice, not being the person who actually committed the offence, who should first give such information as would lead to a like result. Among the bushels of epistolary chaff produced by these advertisements, the authorities with much acumen reckoned the " Nabob " letters alone as genuine grain, and to the discovery of the identity of the writer their efforts were now directed.

As months elapsed without any fresh news, public interest in the case began to wane, and the impression became general that the Dunecht mystery would never be solved; but the police had not relaxed their efforts. On 27th February 1882 it was revived by the announcement that two arrests had been made in connection with the affair. The suspected persons were Thomas Kirkwood, a joiner for many years in the employ-ment of the Lindsay family, and John Philip, a shoemaker, who had been at one time drill instructor of the Echt Volunteer Corps, both of whom were brought before Sheriff Comrie Thomson at Aberdeen, and were remanded for a week. After being judicially examined, both men were discharged. The reason of Philip's arrest was not disclosed; he was later adduced as a witness for the prosecution.

Nothing further was heard of the case for five months, but on 17th July the police, acting upon information received, the nature of which we shall presently learn, apprehended a man named Charles Soutar, forty-two years of age, who followed the occupation of a vermin killer, and resided in Schoolhill, Aberdeen. He had been employed for five or six years as a rat-catcher at Dunecht, but on account of his poaching proclivities had been dismissed some three years before the earl's death.

The same day the prisoner was judicially examined by Sheriff Comrie Thomson, and emitted a declaration. He admitted that the two letters signed "Nabob" were both written and posted by him. On being interrogated, "What do you know of the removal of the late Earl of Crawford's body?" he told the following remarkable tale :—

One night about the end of April or the beginning of May 1881, after eleven o'clock, he was poaching with a net in the Crow Wood, near Dunecht House. On hearing a rustle in the brushwood he thought the keepers were trying to surround him, so he took to his heels, making for the thickest part of the wood. After running about twenty yards, he was tripped up by someone and thrown on his back to the ground, where he was held down by two men, "young-like chaps, of middle size." Their faces were "black," and they wore wincey shirts, but had on neither hats nor coats. They spoke with an Aberdeenshire accent, and seemed common men. They were presently joined by two others, tall men, also hatless and coatless, in white shirt sleeves. These seemed to be gentlemen, and spoke like educated men. The taller of the two appeared to be the leader of the party. Both wore masks. One of them presented a large plated revolver at his breast, and said to one of the men holding him, "Remove your arm, and I will settle him." The other replied, "Hold on; there's more of them." The man who held him rose, and said to the one with the pistol, "It's all right; it's the ratcatcher; he's poaching." Whereupon the speaker conversed in whispers apart with the two tall men. On their return they told the man who was still holding him to let him up, which was done. The man with the pistol then examined his net, and asked what he was doing there, and whether he was alone? He answered that he was "looking for a beast," and was alone, upon which the tall man remarked that it was well for him, as if he had been a spy he would not have seen the light of another day, adding, "Remember what I am going to tell you; you're known to our party, and if you breathe a syllable of what you have seen, I will have your life if you're on the face of the earth." He was then released and told to leave the wood by the way he came. After "hunting for an hour or two" he returned at daybreak to the spot. The four masked men were gone, but looking about, he noticed "a heap of rubbish where they had concealed something." On opening this up he saw a blanket, which he lifted, disclosing the dead body of a man, whom he thought at the time had been murdered. He looked at the face, and covered the body up again as he had found it. There was a strong smell like benzoline, from which he inferred that an attempt had been made to destroy the corpse with chemicals. The same smell stuck to his hands for half a day

17

afterwards. He returned on foot to Aberdeen by the turnpike road.

He further declared that in July 1881, on the day of the local cattle show, he had a conversation at Aberdeen with a plasterer named Cowe, who had been employed at Dunecht. Cowe mentioned that the vault in which the old lord was buried had been closed up, because of "the strange, sweet-like smell" that came from it. On his asking what it resembled, Cowe said it was like decaying flowers, or wine, or benzoline. It then occurred to him that such was the very smell he had perceived on the body in the woods; so a few days afterwards he returned to the spot, and found that a mark he had placed there had not been removed.

In answer to a question by the Sheriff, the prisoner declined to take the police to the place or so to describe it that they might find it for themselves, remarking, "I'll rather wait until you get them that took the body; it will be safer for me then."

In consequence of the clue thus obtained, the search was renewed with fresh vigour, and some twenty keepers and constables, provided with sharp-pointed iron probes to test the nature of any suspected spot, began to scour the wood around the mansion-house. But for the narrowing of its area the search would have been much more hopeless than the earlier one in December, for the ground, which was then bare, was now covered by a thick growth of vegetation, and the chance of discovering the grave would have been small indeed. About mid-day on Tuesday, 18th July, after some eight hours' beating of the wood, as the party were searching the course of an old ditch, the probe rebounded. There was no visible indication of the ground having been disturbed, and the soil at that point was as firm as in any other part of the ditch. A spade was obtained, the earth dug up, and there, at the bottom of the old ditch, about a foot below the surface, lay, wrapped in a blanket, the missing body of the earl. The place was some five hundred yards from the house, close by a gravel-pit.

Before its removal from the grave, the body was inspected by Dr. Ogston, Aberdeen, who prepared reports of its position when found and of its condition when subsequently examined by him. From the state of the wrappings and of the surrounding soil, he formed the opinion that the body, which had suffered no injury, had been buried for a considerable time, and had not since been disturbed. The face was quite recognisable.

The remains of the late earl were in due course removed to Haigh Hall, and were afterwards reinterred in the family vault beneath the Lindsay Chapel, in the parish church of Wigan.

On 21st July the Glasgow police arrested in connection with the case a man named James Collier, who had been a sawyer on the Dunecht estate and had recently left the district. He was, however, liberated in a few days, and, like Philip, appeared later as a witness at the trial.

On 23rd July the prisoner was again brought before Sheriff Comrie Thomson at Aberdeen for further examination, and was informed that Lord Crawford's body had now been found, whereupon he remarked, " I am very glad to hear it; they did not get it through me, at all events." He still declared that he was not concerned either in its abstraction or concealment. Upon the application of the fiscal the examination was then adjourned to Dunecht, and the prisoner was taken to the empty grave in the wood. He was asked if that was the place where he had seen the body of a dead man, and replied, " I cannot say; I am not acquainted with this part of the woods." Asked further if that was the wood referred to in his first declaration, he declined to answer any more questions on the subject. He added that he wrote the first " Nabob " letter for the purpose of unburdening his mind and giving a hint which might be acted on, that he had nothing to do with the lifting of the slab in the end of the previous November, and that he had not been near Dunecht since July 1881.  He further declared that when he found the body there were five or six inches of earth over it, which he removed with his hands.  It was not raining that night, but very cloudy.

The prisoner was then taken to the house of Dunecht, and being shown the earl's body and asked if it was that which he had previously seen, he declared, " It bears some resemblance to the face of the body I saw in the wood."  He recognised the aromatic odour.  This concluded the judicial examination of the prisoner.

On 24th July a petition was presented to the Sheriff for Soutar's liberation on bail, under an Act of 1701 to the effect that all crimes not entailing capital punishment should be bailable at the amount of 300 merks, equivalent to £60 sterling.  The Sheriff found that the offence charged was bailable, and granted warrant for the prisoner's liberation, on caution to that extent being found for his reappearance.  Next day, however, the friends of the prisoner learned that if the bail was forthcoming the authorities were prepared to rearrest him upon a fresh charge on which bail would not be allowed, so the matter went no further, and the prisoner remained in gaol to await his trial.

On Monday, 23rd October 1882, Charles Soutar was placed at the bar of the High Court of Justiciary, Edinburgh, indicted and accused of the crime of violating the sepulchres of the dead and the raising and carrying away dead bodies out of their graves.  Lord Craighill presided.  The prosecution was conducted by the Solicitor-General (Mr. Alexander Asher) and Mr. Æneas J. G. Mackay, Advocate-Depute, the prisoner being represented by the Dean of Faculty (Sir J. H. A. Macdonald, the present Lord Justice-Clerk), Mr. (now Lord) Mackenzie, and Mr. William Hay.  The only official shorthand notes of the trial were taken by Mr. Crabb Watt, K.C., who had not then been admitted to the bar.  These notes were extended verbatim, and

are now in the possession of the Crawford family. The indictment bore that the accused, either by himself or acting in
concert with some person or persons to the prosecutor unknown,
on an occasion or occasions between 1st April and 8th September 1881, broke into the vault, forcibly removed from the
coffins the dead body of Lord Crawford, and carried away the
same. No objection was taken to the relevancy, and the pannel
pleaded not guilty.

The circumstances attending the burial of the earl on 29th
December 1880, the first perception of the odour on 29th May,
and the lifting of the stone on 1st December 1881, the arrest
and examination of Soutar on 17th July 1882, and the discovery
of the body on the following day, all as before narrated, were
duly established by various witnesses. It remains to be told
upon what evidence the Crown relied for proving the prisoner's
connection with the crime.

James Collier, who had been a sawyer at Echt for thirty
years, until he left the district in July of that year, deponed
that he knew the prisoner by sight. On Friday, 27th May
1881, he travelled from Aberdeen by the Cluny coach, which
passes the Broadstrake Inn at Waterton of Echt, about a mile
from Dunecht House. The prisoner was also in the coach. The
witness's attention was attracted by the fact that he knew that
Soutar "was newly out of prison for another offence," the
nature of which does not appear from the proceedings at the
trial. It was, however, stated in the press at the time that
Soutar, in 1878, had been sentenced to eighteen months'
imprisonment with hard labour for participation in a poaching
affray, wherein a police sergeant was fatally injured. The
coach stopped at the inn, where Collier pointed out the prisoner
to a man named Coutts. When Collier got down, half a mile
from Dunecht, the prisoner was still on the coach. Coutts
corroborated. He had seen the prisoner get off the coach at
the inn, but did not notice whether he proceeded by it further.
Mrs. Leith, the innkeeper, who knew the prisoner personally,

said that he arrived by the coach that afternoon at six o'clock. He walked up the road towards the village of Echt about the time that the coach resumed its journey. She saw no more of him that night. Her daughter Barbara gave similar evidence.

Dunecht House lies midway between the hamlet of Waterton of Echt and Echt village, and the evidence of these four witnesses proved the presence of the prisoner in the neighbourhood on the Friday before the Sunday on which the odour was first noticed at the vault.

James Cowe, plasterer, Aberdeen, said he had known the prisoner for three or four years. He did not see him on 21st or 22nd July 1881, during the cattle show in Aberdeen, or about that time. He did not remember ever speaking to him of the removal of Lord Crawford's body, or as to the smell from the vault, nor did he say to him that the smell was like decaying flowers, wine, or benzoline. The last word he never mentioned to him in his life. The evidence of this witness contradicted the statement made by the prisoner in his declaration that he first heard of the matter from Cowe. Mrs. Legatt, a daughter of Mrs. Leith, said that the prisoner arrived at Broadstrake Inn by the Aberdeen coach one afternoon in July or August 1881, when her mother was from home. After having some refreshment he left on foot, going in the direction of Dunecht. There is no evidence as to what he was doing in the neighbourhood on this occasion.

William Lawrie, farmer, Echt, stated that he was introduced to the prisoner by a gardener of Dunecht at Mrs. Livingstone's inn at Echt on 20th September 1881. They had a drink together. The prisoner asked him if any person had disappeared mysteriously thereabouts, and on his replying in the negative, said, " Ay, but there was," adding that he had happened to be on the estate of Dunecht one night, and came across some men with a body. The witness understood the prisoner to mean that a murder had been committed. At the time he thought the story "a parcel of lies"—the jury later arrived at the same conclusion—and paid it no attention. Elizabeth Mitchell, a servant at the inn, deponed that she overheard part of the above conversation. She mentioned the matter to her mistress, who advised her to say nothing about it. There was then no suspicion of any interference with the vault.

John Philip, shoemaker, Aberdeen, said that he had been apprehended in connection with the affair in the end of February, and was liberated on 4th March 1882. Shortly thereafter the prisoner, whom he did not know except "by reputation," accosted him in Aberdeen. The prisoner introduced himself thus: "You must know me, I am Soutar, the ratcatcher, who was at Dunecht when you were drill instructor there," to which Philip made the euphuistic reply, "I remember distinctly a gentleman of your profession having been employed at the policies, although I never saw you." "I added," continued the courteous shoemaker, "that I believed he was the party who should have been where I had come from—meaning the prison." Soutar, so far from taking offence at this observation, proposed adjourning for refreshment. The object of this hospitable offer was to find out if Philip, on his judicial examination, had said anything about him (Soutar). He received the disconcerting answer that Philip, "from information he had obtained," had felt obliged to tell the Sheriff that Soutar was the perpetrator of the outrage. Lord Craighill, in charging the jury, commented on the singular fact that no question was put to this witness from either side of the bar to ascertain upon what knowledge he had made such a statement.

George Machray, who had been gamekeeper at Urie, Stonehaven, when the prisoner was employed as a ratcatcher there, stated that on two occasions prior to the month of March 1882 Soutar said to him that he could tell where Lord Crawford's body was hidden. The witness, who had previously heard of the outrage, "thought nothing about it." On Friday, 14th July 1882, the prisoner invited him into a public-house in

Aberdeen, and requested him to inform one Mr. Cassells, who was then making inquiries on behalf of the Crawford family, that he (Soutar) "could tell where the body was on two conditions, namely, that they would find out the persons who took the body, and give protection to him." He said nothing about a pardon. At that time the reward was advertised in the newspapers. Machray failed to find Cassells, and next day the prisoner again asked him to deliver the message. He tried to do so, without success. On Sunday, the 16th, the prisoner for the third time asked him to see Cassells, and he made another attempt, with the like result. Perceiving that it was useless to contend further with fate, Machray then gave the information to the police which led to Soutar's arrest.

A notable, if not unique, feature of the trial was the fact that none of the witnesses for the prosecution were cross-examined by counsel for the defence, only a single question being put to Machray by the Dean of Faculty, to the effect that the prisoner had said he was "threatened very hard by the men in the wood."

The case for the Crown closed with the reading of the prisoner's declarations. No witnesses were adduced for the defence, and the Solicitor-General rose to address the jury. He submitted that the character of the crime precluded the possibility of presenting direct evidence, unless through the confession of an accomplice. The facts and circumstances of the case all pointed conclusively to the prisoner as at least one of the persons guilty. The outrage was unquestionably committed by someone acquainted with the locality and the circumstances of the family, with the motive of obtaining a ransom for recovery of the body. The prisoner lived in Aberdeen, and knew Dunecht well. The winter of 1880-1881 was a very severe one—there was snow on the ground till late in the spring—and, in order to avoid discovery, the attempt had to be delayed, as indicated by the evidence, till about the end of May. There could now be no doubt that the peculiar odour first discovered on Sunday, the 29th, was connected with the opening of the vault on the 27th or 28th May. The crevice between the flagstones was observed by the masons on the morning of Monday, the 30th. On Friday, the 27th, the prisoner was proved to have gone by the coach from Aberdeen to Waterton of Echt, where he arrived at 6 P.M. He was afterwards seen to go along the road towards Dunecht, and no explanation was offered as to how he spent that night. The cause of the odour was misunderstood, the flags were cemented, covered with earth, and sown with grass, and all trace of the outrage was in a fair way of being obliterated. But the hope of reward depended on its discovery. The prisoner returned to Waterton in July or August, and again there was no explanation of what he was doing in the neighbourhood. No doubt he visited the vault and found that the grass was growing over the entrance, so that accidental discovery was becoming daily more impossible. Therefore, on 8th September, he wrote and sent the first " Nabob " letter, not to the police, to whom he would naturally have looked for protection, but to Mr. Yeats, the agent for the Crawford family, as the source of ransom or reward. Mr. Yeats paid no attention to the letter, and the prisoner then took a bolder step. He returned to Echt, and on 20th September, in Livingstone's inn, told Lawrie that a murdered man was buried in the woods of Dunecht—a hint intended to spread the belief in the neighbourhood that something had occurred, which he hoped would lead to inquiry. But, for his own protection, he made his information too vague, and a more definite step had to be taken for the purpose of attracting attention to the matter. On 30th November one of the flagstones covering the entrance to the vault was displaced. The outrage was at length detected; the body was searched for without success, advertisements were published, and finally a ransom was offered and a pardon promised, but under the, for him, unfortunate condition that the informant must not be the person who committed the offence. In view of this he wrote the second " Nabob " letter to Mr. Alsop, Lord Crawford's agent in London. Again, he did not go to the police for protection, as would have been the natural course if his story were true, but to those who would be the source of a reward. Mr. Alsop having taken no notice of his letter, he attempted to put himself in communication, through his friend Machray, with Mr. Cassells, who, as representative of the Crawford family, was making inquiries at Aberdeen. Again he failed. Cassells was not at home, and Machray informed the police. The declarations emitted by the prisoner after his arrest were altogether incredible, but they at least showed that he was in the wood when the body was buried. The story he told was most cunning and highly dramatic, but was it natural that the four men, surprised in those circumstances, should seize and detain him, instead of allowing him to escape? The date assigned by the prisoner for the occurrence was clearly false. His statement that he only discovered on 21st July 1881, from his conversation with Cowe, that the body he had seen was that of Lord Crawford was also false. Cowe denied that any such conversation ever took place. How, then, could the prisoner know that the body was Lord Crawford's except from guilty participation in the commission of the crime? When he met Lawrie at Livingstone's inn on 20th September, he knew whose body it was, although at that time no one else was aware of the violation of the tomb. Yet he represented the body to Lawrie as that of a murdered man. In conclusion, the Solicitor-General submitted that the admissions of the prisoner, taken along with the rest of the evidence, clearly established that the mystery had at last been solved, and that the prisoner at the bar was one of the persons who perpetrated this outrageous crime.

The Dean of Faculty then addressed the jury for the defence. It was, he said, admitted by the prosecution that this crime could not have been committed by the prisoner alone, and therefore the mystery was only half solved. The prisoner's presence in the neighbourhood on 27th May 1881 was sufficiently explained by the fact that he was a notorious poacher, and had been dismissed from service on this very property on that account. There was no secrecy in what he did; he travelled in a crowded coach in broad daylight, and left it at the inn, not the nearest point to Dunecht. The assumption of the Crown that the crime had been committed that night was not warranted by the evidence. The odour perceived on 29th May, two days afterwards, might, so far as the evidence went, just as well have proceeded from the *arbor vitæ* as from the opened coffin, and might have existed for weeks before it was noticed. It was also a far-fetched argument to say that because the prisoner had endeavoured to spread the report that a man had been murdered and his body buried in the woods, he then knew that it was the body of the earl. His statement that he never knew until his interview with Cowe was not contradicted by that witness, whose evidence amounted at most to *non memini*. The story told by the prisoner in his declaration was quite consistent with all that he had previously said. If a reward were what the perpetrators had in view, it was likely enough that they should seize the prisoner and bind him to secrecy, because his knowledge placed him in a position to obtain the reward and put them in danger of being punished. The prisoner wished to get the reward, and with that object he communicated with those acting for the Crawford family. If he were guilty it was strange that he should make the conditions, first, that the true perpetrators should be apprehended, and second, that he himself should be protected, for he knew from the advertisements that no protection would be given to a principal. If the perpetrators were arrested he would be quite safe, and the fact that he applied to the family agents instead of to the police was no reason for assuming his guilt. If he were not a principal his position was quite intelligible, and the stipulations he made were those of an innocent man. This prosecution was a highly sensational case based upon a number of small points, which, if carefully examined, did not cohere, and it was therefore the duty of the jury to discharge the prisoner.

At the conclusion of the learned Dean's address the proceedings were adjourned till the following day.

At half-past ten o'clock on Tuesday, 24th October, Lord Craighill began his charge to the jury. His lordship at the outset referred to the unfamiliar nature of the crime charged. In former times, he said, bodies had been raised in order to be sold for dissection, but nothing of that kind had occurred for the last half century. There were in this case only two conceivable motives, either to wreak vengeance upon the family of the deceased or to obtain from them a ransom for discovery of the abstracted body. There was here no suggestion of any ill-will towards the family, and the perpetrators were therefore actuated by the hope of reward, yet the offenders must secure themselves from punishment. All the acts of the prisoner from first to last were characterised by an attempt to realise this motive. The competency of the evidence led in support of the charge was not disputed, and the vital question was, not what was its nature, whether direct or circumstantial, but what was its power and effect? It was perfectly impossible that one man alone could accomplish what had been done; probably more than two were concerned. The vault was opened and closed the same night without suspicion being aroused, and not only strength but skill was employed in the perpetration of this offence. The body was removed, the grave was dug, and all traces of these operations were obliterated. Probably these things were not all done on a single night, and certainly one man could not have done them; there must have been others. The guilt of the prisoner, however, if he were concerned, was in law the same as if he had been the sole offender. The question for the jury was whether they were satisfied that the prisoner was art and part in the deed. After the funeral on 29th December 1880, all that was done was to close the entrance of the vault and to joint with lime the crevices between the flags. From that date till 29th May 1881 nothing was heard about the vault. That day the peculiar smell was noticed, and on 2nd June the flags were cemented and grass was sown. The Crown fixed Friday the 27th or Saturday the 28th May as the date of the outrage, because the prisoner was proved to have been in the neighbourhood on the 27th. He came by the coach from Aberdeen to Waterton of Echt; he left it there, and walked towards the village of Echt, Dunecht House being situated between those two places. Where he went or what he did the jury did not know. If the odour noticed was that of *arbor vitæ*, there could be no inference that the body had been removed; but the prisoner had stated that he touched the blanket and perceived a smell which remained on his hands for half a day. The precise time of the outrage was, however, immaterial if the jury were satisfied that the prisoner was concerned in it. With reference to the first "Nabob" letter of 8th September 1881, his lordship observed that the person who wrote it knew that the vault had been rifled, and also where the body lay. The purpose of writing it was to bring the matter to the knowledge of the family, who suspected nothing. The prisoner's conversation with Lawrie on 20th September—one of the mysterious communications made by him from time to time—was an attempt to get the news circulated in the district. As both these acts proved ineffectual, on 1st December the flagstone was raised. His lordship then referred to the various advertisements published on behalf of the Crawford family, and remarked as to the second "Nabob" letter of 23rd December, that it showed the writer knew the place of concealment, and assumed that the body might be removed. The postscript was inconsistent with the idea that the perpetrators knew that an outsider was aware of what they had done. These letters were written by the prisoner, therefore so early as 8th September he knew of the removal, and on 23rd

December he knew that the body was still in the wood. With regard to the prisoner's conversation with Philip in March 1882, his lordship pointed out that if Soutar had been, as he asserted, an innocent spectator of the crime, it was difficult to see why he should be so anxious as to what Philip had said to the Sheriff. Before March the prisoner twice told Machray that he knew where Lord Crawford's body was hidden; he repeated that statement on 15th July, and requested Machray to inform Cassells, evidently for the purpose of obtaining the reward. Was the prisoner's account of his knowledge of these matters a reasonably credible one? The thing *might* have so happened, but apart from its improbability was the further fact that this man, let loose as he was, should return to discover the deed and should so easily find the body. If, as he said, it was then covered with rubbish, the men must have returned later to bury it in the ditch. The prisoner had hunted for two hours, yet he went back, and though, as he said, unfamiliar with that part of the wood, he readily found the spot. If the body was untouched after he first saw it, he could *not* have found it, as there was no external indication on the ditch of where it lay. He got no information from the men as to the identity of the body, yet in September 1881 he knew whose body it was. His story that he learned this from Cowe was disproved by the evidence of that witness. Cowe was sure that the word benzoline was never mentioned, and if such a conversation had occurred, the witness could not have forgotten it. If the jury believed Cowe, then the prisoner had a guilty knowledge derived solely from participation in the commission of the crime.

At the conclusion of his lordship's charge, which occupied an hour and a half, the jury retired to consider their verdict, and after an absence of thirty-five minutes returned to Court with a unanimous verdict of guilty as libelled. Mr. Mackay having moved for sentence, his lordship said that he would be glad if counsel could refer him to any precedents. Mr. Mackay said that he had looked into the precedents, and found that the previous cases were almost all those of body-snatching for purposes of anatomical dissection, generally followed by sentence of imprisonment. The present case was, he submitted, entirely different.

Lord Craighill, in passing sentence, commented upon the peculiar heinousness of the crime of which the prisoner had been convicted, and, referring to the fact that in previous cases imprisonment had been deemed a sufficient punishment, observed, " But when I look at this case, at the coolness, the determination, the perseverance, the continuous heartlessness of the proceedings, when I look at its cold-blooded and mercenary character, and when I remember also the strength of this vault which was violated, I cannot help thinking that, of its class, this is a case by itself, and that what was adequate punishment in those previous cases, where the same character of offence was dealt with, is not, in my opinion, adequate punishment on the present occasion. The sentence of the Court is that you be subjected to penal servitude for a period of five years." The prisoner was then removed, and the Court rose.

Unusual interest had from the first been taken in the trial by the other judges, and it is understood that Lord Craighill acted throughout in concert with the Lord Justice-Clerk (Moncreiff), as is frequently done in difficult cases. Parts of the evidence were transcribed for Lord Moncreiff, and it may be assumed that Lord Craighill in his charge expressed the views of the Justice-Clerk as well as his own.

The Dunecht mystery was, in the words of the Dean of Faculty, only half solved by the verdict of the jury. That Soutar was not alone concerned in the crime is certain ; and while it is satisfactory to know that one of the miscreants who inflicted upon a noble house such long mental agony for so base an end, did not escape retribution, the failure of Justice to detect and punish the other actors in the execrable plot must be a matter of regret. It does not appear that Soutar ever disclosed the identity of his accomplices, but some of these at least were probably his superiors in station and intelligence, for it is difficult to believe that a scheme of this elaborate sort, devised with diabolic ingenuity and executed with a skill and success unequalled in the annals of crime, was the product of the brain and hand of an obscure and illiterate ratcatcher. Was his adoption of the "Nabob" pseudonym due to familiarity with Daudet's work?

On 24th June 1883 an interesting debate took place at Aberdeen before Sheriff Guthrie Smith regarding the allocation of the reward, upon which his lordship was to adjudicate by instructions of the Home Office. The proceedings were conducted in private. It had been announced that as the authorities believed Soutar was not the sole person concerned in the crime, and as others might yet be implicated, only one-half of the Government reward of £100 would be paid. For this there were three claimants, namely, Machray, Philip, and Collier, all of whom had been witnesses at the trial. The two former were represented by agents, the latter appeared in person. After hearing the cases for the respective applicants duly stated the Sheriff gave judgment, finding Machray alone entitled to the £50. It was said by the press to be understood at the time that Lord Crawford would probably hand to Machray one-half of the reward of £500 offered by the family. Be that as it may, one is glad to learn that Machray's claim was recognised, as, but for his action in giving information to the police, the ratcatcher might otherwise have remained uncaught.

Advocates of burial reform have in the Dunecht case a strong argument in favour of cremation. "To be knaved out of our Graves," says Sir Thomas Browne, "to have our Skulls made Drinking-Bowls, and our Bones turned into Pipes, to delight and sport our Enemies, are tragical abominations escaped in burning Burials." The fate of his own skull, had he foreseen it, would probably have confirmed his judgment.

# THE ARRAN MURDER

THE Isle of Arran, as most readers know, lies in the estuary of the Clyde, between the pleasant shores of Carrick and Kintyre. To the north, beyond the Kyles of Bute, are the sea-lochs, moors, and mountains of Argyll; southward the Craig of Ailsa stands sentinel in the wider Firth. The first prospect of the island, whether from the Ayrshire coast or from the deck of some passing vessel in the fairway, is unforgettable—the majestic outline of the serrated peaks, soaring out of the sea to pierce the rain-clouds too often wreathed about their summits, the sunlight gleaming on their granite flanks, wet from some recent shower, and over all, austere and solitary, the great grey cone of Goatfell, "the mountain of the winds." Amid these formidable giants are many glens, some bare and savage as themselves, others domesticated, as it were, by the kindly uses of man; while at their feet lie certain bays whose yellow sands, beloved by generations of children, are, alas! no "undiscovered country" to the excursionist.

At the time of which we write the moral and physical atmosphere of the island was above reproach; wickedness and manufactories were alike unknown. The larger villages boasted each its own constable, who embodied the law in some peaceful cottage, incongruously labelled " Police Station "; but these officers led a life of ease and dignity among the blameless lieges, being only called upon to exercise their functions now and then on the person of an obstreperous tripper. Yet this fortunate isle was to become the scene of a crime, characterised at a later stage as " unprecedented and incredibly atrocious."

On the forenoon of Friday, 12th July 1889, the once famous Clyde steamer *Ivanhoe*, in the course of her daily run to Arran from the upper reaches of the Firth, called at Rothesay, the "capital" of Bute. Among the passengers who then joined the vessel was a party from Glenburn Hydropathic, including a young Englishman named Edwin Robert Rose, a clerk in the employment of a Brixton builder, then spending his fortnight's holiday in Scotland. He was thirty-two years of age, of light build, five feet seven in height, of athletic, active habits, and in the best of health and spirits. On the sail to Arran he struck up an acquaintance with a fellow-passenger, a young man who gave his name as Annandale, and they landed together at Brodick for an hour or so until the steamer's return from Whiting Bay. Apparently they had decided to take lodgings in the village, for shortly after the steamer's arrival Annandale presented himself at the house of Mrs. Walker, Invercloy, and inquired for rooms. Invercloy is the name of the village, Brodick that of the district. It was then the Glasgow Fair week, and the limited accommodation available was taxed to its utmost limits. Mrs. Walker, however, was able to offer a room with one bed, in a wooden structure adjoining her house, having a separate entrance from the outside. Annandale agreed to take it for a week, stating that he came from Tighna-bruaich, and that his room would be shared by a friend who could not remain longer than the following Wednesday. It was arranged that they should occupy the room next day, and that Annandale was to take his meals there, while Rose got his at Mrs. Woolley's tea-shop in the village. They returned together to Rothesay that afternoon, and Annandale accom-panied Rose to the Hydropathic, where the latter introduced him to some of his friends.

Two of these, named Mickel and Thom, who also intended spending the week-end at Brodick, left for Arran by the *Ivanhoe* on Saturday, the 13th, and were joined on board by Rose and Annandale. Mickel and Thom were unable to find rooms, and slept on a friend's yacht in the bay. From the Saturday to Monday the four men saw a good deal of each other, walking and boating together, and occasionally meeting at meals in

Woolley's shop. Mr. Mickel formed an unfavourable opinion of Annandale, who struck him as singularly silent and uncommunicative, and as he could neither find out who that young man was nor where he came from, Mickel more than once strongly advised Rose to get rid of him, even if he had to leave his lodgings, and in particular not to climb Goatfell in his company, as he had proposed to do. Rose promised accordingly, and at half-past three in the afternoon of Monday, 15th July, Mr. Mickel and his friend left by the *Ivanhoe*, Rose and Annandale being on the pier to see them off.

Both Mickel and Thom spoke highly of Rose as a young fellow of agreeable manners, very frank and open, and "ready to take up with strangers." So far as they knew he seemed to have plenty of money. He had a watch and chain, and carried a pocket-book, containing a return half ticket to London, and his luggage consisted of a black leather Gladstone bag. His wardrobe included a chocolate and brown striped tennis-jacket, a grey felt hat, and a white serge yachting-cap.

Mrs. Walker saw nothing further of her lodgers that day, as, from the situation of their room, they could go out and in without her knowledge. At eleven o'clock on the Tuesday morning she knocked at their door. Getting no answer, she entered and found that the visitors had vanished, together with the two bags which they had brought with them when they came. The room appeared to have been occupied overnight by two persons. A straw hat, a pair of slippers, a waterproof, and a tennis-racket had been left behind. Such incidents are probably not unknown to Arran landladies, and the worst that Mrs. Walker anticipated was the loss of her rent. She did not report the matter to the police.

Rose's holiday expired on Thursday, 18th July, on which day his brother went to the station in London to meet him. His relatives, alarmed at his non-arrival, telegraphed to the Reverend Mr. Goodman, the son of Rose's employer, who was staying at Glenburn Hydropathic, from whom they learned that Rose had gone to Arran with an acquaintance a few days before, and had not returned. On Saturday, the 27th, Rose's brother, accompanied by the Chief Constable of Bute, arrived at Brodick. They ascertained that, in spite of Mickel's warning, the missing man had gone up Goatfell on the Monday afternoon with the mysterious Annandale, who had been seen to leave Brodick alone next morning by the early steamer, and it was believed that Rose had never left the island.

On Sunday, the 28th, a search was organised, every able man willingly taking his share of the work, and various parties began systematically to beat the district. No one unacquainted with the nature of the ground can form any idea of the difficulties attending their efforts. Upon the north and west Goatfell is bounded by a congregation of jagged mountain ridges and fantastic peaks, with deep shadowy glens and grim ravines, the bleak sides of which are furrowed by innumerable gullies and abrupt watercourses—a scene in its awful solitude and grandeur so wild, dreary, and desolate as hardly to be matched in Britain. Day after day the search was continued among the barren screes and boulder-strewn corries, day after day the weary searchers returned unsuccessful to their homes, nor till the evening of the following Sunday, 4th August, was the object of their quest attained.

That day the search party, consisting of upwards of two hundred persons, was divided into three portions, one of which was scouring the east shoulder of Goatfell, at the head of Glen Sannox. Francis Logan, a Corrie fisherman, being high up on the mountain-side, near a place named Corrie-na-fuhren, noticed an offensive odour which he traced to a large boulder some distance further up the slope. Built up about its face was a heap of smaller rocks and stones, with pieces of turf and heather inserted between the clefts. On examining this structure more closely, Logan saw among the stones part of a human arm. He at once raised a shout, and Sergeant Munro with others of the search party, including the lost man's brother, were quickly on the spot. When the stones, forty-two in number, were removed, in a cavity beneath the boulder was seen the dead body of a man. The screen of stones which had concealed it, the largest being over a hundredweight, was obviously the work of human hands. Dr. Gilmour, Linlithgow, a summer visitor at Corrie, was sent for as the nearest medical man, and until his arrival the body, which was guarded by the police, remained untouched. When the doctor reached the boulder about eight o'clock he first examined the position of the body, which lay at full length upon its face, and was fully clothed, the skirt of the jacket being turned back over the head, probably to conceal its ghastly appearance while the stones were piled around it. The body was then lifted from beneath the boulder, and having been identified by Mr. Rose as that of his missing brother, a thorough examination was made by Dr. Gilmour. Nothing was found upon the body; all the pockets were empty, and one of them was turned inside out. On examining the head and face, Dr. Gilmour found both "fearfully and terrible smashed." Practically the whole of the face and left side of the head was destroyed and in an advanced stage of decomposition, but the body otherwise was uninjured, excepting a fracture of the top of the left shoulder-blade.

While those who found the body were awaiting the doctor's arrival, a search of the surrounding ground was made. Above the boulder the hill slopes steeply upward to the ridge, at an angle of about 45 degrees, on the line of a deep gully and watercourse, often dry in summer, but in which there was then a small stream. The ground is composed of slabs of granite, rough heather, sand, and gravel, strewn with boulders and loose stones. The following articles, afterwards identified as Rose's property, were found higher up the gully at various distances from the boulder:—a walking-stick, lying head downwards, as if dropped; a waterproof, split into two pieces, "huddled together in a dub, as if they had been trampled upon"; a knife, pencil, and button; and a cap, folded in four, with a large heavy stone on the top of and almost completely concealing it, in the centre of the bed of the stream. On one side of the gully, above where the cap was found, was a clear drop of 19 feet, while on the other side, lower down, above where the knife and pencil were found, was a similar fall of 32 feet.

About nine o'clock the body was placed in a box and taken to the coach-house of Corrie Hotel, where a post-mortem examination was made next day by Dr. Gilmour and Dr. Fullarton of Lamlash, after which it was buried in the ancient and picturesque burying-ground of Sannox, at entrance to the glen. On 27th September the body was exhumed by warrant of the Sheriff, to enable Sir Henry (then Dr.) Littlejohn and Dr. Fullarton to examine more particularly the condition of the internal organs. The conclusion arrived at in the various medical reports as to the injuries which caused death were, that these had been produced by direct violence of repeated blows on the left side of the head, inflicted with some heavy, blunt instrument.

We shall now see what, so far as ascertained, were the movements of the mysterious Annandale on the day of the murder.

From the sea-level at the old inn of Brodick—now used in connection with the estate—on the north side of the bay, the way to Goatfell lies through the grounds of Brodick Castle, past the Kennels, and through the woods to the open moor, whence the climber has a clear view of the task before him. Two relatives of Mrs. Walker, who knew her lodgers by sight, returning from Goatfell that afternoon, met Annandale and Rose in the castle grounds about four o'clock. One of them noticed that Rose was wearing a watch-chain. Shortly there-after the Reverend Mr. Hind, with two other visitors from Lamlash, who had left Brodick about three o'clock to climb the fell, were overtaken on the open hill beyond the castle woods by two young men. One of these (afterwards identified by a photograph as Rose) walked with the party for about half-an-hour. The other kept steadily some yards ahead, and spoke to no one. Rose mentioned that he came from London, and had been staying at Rothesay. A shower coming on, Mr. Hind's party took shelter behind a boulder, but the others, who had waterproofs, continued the ascent. The party could see them going up in front, and when they themselves gained the top about six o'clock, they saw Rose and his companion standing upon the further edge of the plateau from the point at which they reached it. The view from the summit is one of the most extensive and magnificent in Scotland. After enjoying the prospect for about a quarter of an hour Mr. Hind's party descended the mountain by the way they came, reaching Brodick in time for the 8.30 steamer to Lamlash. They saw no more of the young men on the way down, and wondered what had become of them. Two brothers named Francis were photographing on the hill that day; one sat down to rest, while the other went on. After the first reached the top he was joined by his brother, following the two young men, walking in single file. Rose had some conversation with the brothers about the scenery. When they left the summit at 6.25 they saw these young men standing on a boulder, with their backs to Ailsa Craig, and pointing in the direction of Glen Sannox, as if discussing the way down. This is the last that was seen of Rose alive. The brothers, we may here anticipate, at the trial identified the prisoner as his companion.

There are two recognised routes in descending Goatfell— the direct and comparatively easy one to Brodick, which is that usually taken; and the much longer and more arduous descent by "The Saddle," the lofty ridge connecting Goatfell with its giant neighbour Cir-Mhor, and forming the head of the two great glens of Rosa and Sannox, which run almost at right angles from each other. A third way, rarely taken by anyone before this case occurred save by shepherds or others familiar with the hills, is to go straight down into Glen Sannox from the ridge of North Goatfell by the wild and lonely gully of

Corrie-na-fuhren. By either of these last routes the climber, having descended into Glen Sannox, follows that glen eastward to its entrance at Sannox Bay, three and a half miles from the ridge, returning to Brodick by the coast road and the village of Corrie, a further distance of seven and a half miles.

At half-past nine o'clock that Monday evening a shepherd named Mackenzie was talking to two servant girls near the old burying-ground of Sannox, when he saw a man coming out of the glen and going in the direction of Corrie. Mackenzie remarked at the time that the man was "awful tired and worn-out like, and seemed to have had a heavy day's travelling on the hills." This is the first that was seen of Rose's late companion after they were left together upon the mountain top shortly before half-past six. A few minutes after ten o'clock a visitor standing at the bar of Corrie Hotel was accosted by a stranger, who asked the visitor to order a drink for him, which he could not get himself as it was after closing time. The barmaid supplied him with some spirits in a bottle, which he took away with him, remarking that he had to walk the six miles to Brodick. He was afterwards identified by his impromptu host.

Next morning (Tuesday, 16th July) Mary Robertson, who had been staying in Invercloy, went to Brodick pier at seven o'clock to take the early steamer to Ardrossan. Between the village and the pier she overtook a man, whom she later identified, carrying two bags, one black, the other brown, on his way to the boat. It happened that on the Saturday before the murder Mickel and Thom had introduced Rose and Annandale to a friend named Gilmour. By a curious chance Mr. Gilmour was returning to Glasgow that morning, and on going on board the *Scotia* at Brodick pier the first person he saw was Annandale, wearing a grey felt hat. They travelled to Greenock together, and Mr. Gilmour offered to help Annandale to carry his luggage. He noticed particularly the black leather bag, which his companion took into the compartment with him when they left the steamer at Ardrossan. This, so far as the evidence goes, was the last that was seen of Rose's bag.

On Saturday, 6th July, ten days earlier, a young man, whose card bore the name of " John Annandale," had taken a room for a fortnight in the house of Mrs. Currie, in Iona Place, Port Banna-tyne, Rothesay. His luggage consisted of a brown leather bag. On Friday, the 12th, he told his landlady that he was going to Arran for a few days, and left, wearing a straw hat and taking the brown bag with him. On the afternoon of Tuesday, 16th July, he reappeared at Port Bannatyne, wearing a grey felt hat and carrying a paper parcel containing, as his landlady afterwards found, a white serge yachting-cap and a chocolate and brown striped tennis-jacket. These articles he wore during the remainder of his stay. He talked " quite pleasantly " to Mrs. Currie about his visit to Arran, saying that he had been up Goatfell and had enjoyed himself. His time expiring on Saturday the 20th, he asked her to have his bill and dinner ready at one o'clock. He went out, however, in the forenoon and never returned ; all that Mrs. Currie got for his fortnight's board and lodging was the yachting-cap and a pair of tennis shoes, which were afterwards identified as Rose's property.

Even as Mrs. Prig, on a certain historic occasion, boldly expressed her disbelief in the existence of the immortal Mrs. Harris, so may the discerning reader have had his own mis-givings regarding the genuineness of Mr. Annandale. These may now be justified by the statement that this name had been temporarily adopted, for what reason does not appear, by a man named John Watson Laurie, twenty-five years of age, employed as a pattern-maker at Springburn Works, Glasgow. Since 8th June of that year he had been living in lodgings at 106 North Frederick Street there, until he went to Rothesay on 6th July. While at Rothesay he met an acquaintance named Aitken, who knew him as Laurie. To him Laurie pointed out Rose as a gentleman with whom he was going to Arran. Aitken saw him again on Sunday, the 20th, when Laurie was leaving Rothesay for Glasgow. He was then wearing a yachting-cap which struck Aitken as very like the one he had seen Rose wear. Aitken asked, "How did you and your friend get on at Brodick?" to which Laurie replied, "Oh, very well." He returned to his Glasgow lodgings and resumed his work as usual on 22nd July. He mentioned to a fellow-lodger that he had a return half ticket to London. On Wednesday, 31st July, Aitken met him accidentally in Hope Street. That week the fact of Rose's disappearance had been published in the Glasgow newspapers, and Aitken accosted Laurie with the startling question, "What do you know about the Arran mystery?" Laurie "hummed and hawed"; and Aitken said, "Dear me, have you not been reading the papers? Was not Rose the name of the gentleman with whom you went to Brodick?" Laurie said it could not be the same man, as his Mr. Rose had returned with him and had since gone to Leeds. Aitken then strongly advised him to communicate what he knew to the authorities, and asked him whose cap he was wearing when they last met at Rothesay. Laurie replied, "Surely you don't think me a . . . ," and did not complete the sentence. He excused himself for leaving Aitken at the moment, as he saw someone approaching whom apparently he wished to avoid, but at Aitken's request he agreed to meet him at his office that evening at six o'clock to give him further particulars. Laurie did not fulfil the engagement, and Aitken never saw him again. Four days later Rose's body was found, and Aitken, so soon as he learned the fact, gave information to the police.

Evidently realising that Glasgow was now no place for one in his peculiar circumstances, Laurie that day applied to the foreman at the Springburn Works for his wages, saying that he was leaving to be a traveller in the grain trade. He also informed a fellow-worker that he was going to Leith as an engineer, that he had a return half ticket to London, and that he had been spending his holiday at Brodick with a friend whom, he euphemistically added, "he had left

in Arran." The same day he sold his pattern-maker's tools
to a broker in the Commercial Road for twenty-five shillings,
and disappeared from Glasgow. His landlady there, more
fortunate than those who had enjoyed his patronage at
Brodick and Port Bannatyne, received on 3rd August a
letter from him, posted at Hamilton, enclosing a remittance
for rent due. "There are some people trying to get me
into trouble," he wrote, "and I think you should give them
no information at all. I will prove to them how they are
mistaken before very long." She afterwards communicated
with the police, and delivered to them certain articles which
Laurie had left in his room.

Laurie was next heard of at Liverpool, where, on Tuesday,
6th August, he took lodgings at 10 Greek Street, paying a
week's rent in advance. On the morning of Thursday, the
8th, however, he informed his landlady that he was leaving
that day, as he had got a situation in Manchester as a
traveller in the cotton trade. He left behind him a box
he had brought from Glasgow which, when taken possession
of later by the authorities, was found to contain some white
shirts, identified as Rose's property, having the name "John
W. Laurie" impressed thereon with a stamp, also found in
the box. It does not appear from the evidence led at the
trial why Laurie left Liverpool so suddenly, but the
*Liverpool Courier* that day published the fact of his identity
with "Annandale," together with an account of his recent
movements, which plainly showed that the police were upon
his track.

Since the discovery of the body, the Glasgow newspapers
had been full of "The Arran Murder," and the hunt for the
perpetrator had been followed with keen interest, so when
the *North British Daily Mail* received and published a letter
from the wanted man, the local excitement was intense.
This letter was dated 10th August, and bore the Liverpool
postmark. "I rather smile," he wrote, "when I read that

my arrest is hourly expected. If things go as I have
designed them I will soon have arrived at that country
from whose bourne no traveller returns, and since there
has been so much said about me, it is only right that the
public should know what are the real circumstances. . . .
As regards Mr. Rose, poor fellow, no one who knows me
will believe for one moment that I had any complicity in
his death. . . . We went to the top of Goatfell, where I left
him in the company of two men who came from Loch Ranza
and were going to Brodick." He admitted that he himself
returned by way of Corrie, and had been in the hotel there
about ten o'clock.

The renewed outburst of newspaper articles and correspondence produced by the publication of this letter drew a further
protest from the fugitive. In a second communication, dated
27th August and bearing to have been posted at Aberdeen,
addressed to the *Glasgow Herald*, he complained of the "many
absurd and mad things" appearing about himself in the
papers, which he felt it his duty to correct. "Although I
am entirely guiltless of the crime I am so much wanted for,"
he wrote, "yet I can recognise that I am a ruined man in
any case, so it is far from my intention to give myself up.
. . . When I saw from an evening paper that Mr. Rose had
not returned to his lodgings, I began to arrange for my
departure, for I had told so many about him. Seemingly
there was a motive for doing away with poor Rose; it was
not to secure his valuables. Mr. Rose was to all appearances
worse off than myself; indeed he assured me that he had
spent so much on his tour that he had barely sufficient to
last till he got home. He wore an old Geneva watch with
no gold albert attached, and I am sure that no one saw him
wear a ring on his tour. . . . As I am not inclined to say
any more, I hope this will be the last the public will hear
of me." Both letters were signed "John W. Laurie," and
were proved to be in his handwriting.

It is difficult to see what induced Laurie to write these letters. He seems to have lost his head at finding himself the subject of so much of the popular attention which, that August, was divided between himself, Mrs. Maybrick, then on her trial at Liverpool, and "Jack the Ripper," whose mysterious crimes were horrifying humanity. Be that as it may, the first letter enabled the police to get the box left by him at Liverpool; but they considered that the posting of the second at Aberdeen was intended as a blind, and that Laurie had returned to his old haunts, as he was reported to have been seen at Uddingston and also at Coatbridge. How much money Rose actually had upon him at the time of his death was never proved, but at least there must have been enough to enable his murderer so successfully to elude the vigilance of the police during the five weeks which elapsed between his absconding and apprehension.

On Tuesday, 3rd September, a man entered the railway station at Ferniegair, which is the first out of Hamilton on the Lesmahagow branch of the Caledonian line. He was about to take a ticket, when he saw a police constable on the platform; he at once left the station and made for the Carlisle road. The constable followed, as the man resembled Laurie whom he had previously known. Laurie, for it was he, realising that he was being shadowed, began to run; crossing a field and the railway, he reached the Lanark road, and running along it till he came to a wood called the Quarry Plantation, near Bog Colliery, about three miles from Hamilton, was lost sight of by his pursuer. The constable who had been joined by some of the workmen from the colliery, got them to surround the wood, which he himself began to search, and presently found Laurie lying under a bush, with an open razor beside him and a superficial wound in his throat. His hand had been less certain than at Corrie-na-fuhren. He was then arrested, and having received the usual caution said, "I robbed the man, but I did not murder him." On the following day the prisoner was taken to Rothesay, where he was examined before the Sheriff on the charge of murdering Rose, upon which he was duly committed for trial, and was removed to Greenock prison. There on the 11th he was further examined before the Sheriff. In his first declaration the prisoner admitted his identity, adding, "I have nothing to say to the charge in the meantime." In his second, being shown the cap, waterproof, and other things found near the boulder, he declared, "I wish to say nothing about any of these articles."

The trial of John Watson Laurie for the murder of Edwin Rose took place before the High Court of Justiciary at Edinburgh on Friday the 8th and Saturday the 9th of November 1889. So greatly had public interest been excited and sustained by the unusual and mysterious character of the crime, the circumstances in which the body was found, and the subsequent hue and cry after the murderer, that long before the opening of the doors the entrance to the Court was besieged by a crowd, estimated by the *Scotsman* of the day to consist of about two thousand people. Specially stringent regulations, however, had been made regarding admission to the Courtroom, and only a privileged few were able to witness the proceedings when the Lord Justice-Clerk (Lord Kingsburgh) took his seat at ten o'clock. There appeared for the Crown the Solicitor-General, Mr. (afterwards Lord) Stormonth-Darling, assisted by Mr. Graham Murray (now Lord Dunedin) and Mr. Dugald M'Kechnie, Advocates-Depute; the counsel for the defence were the Dean of Faculty, Mr. John Blair Balfour (the late Lord Kinross), and Mr. Scott Dickson.

According to the theory of the prosecution, Laurie, who was familiar with the locality, having induced Rose to descend by Corrie-na-fuhren, struck him down by a blow with a stone upon the left side of the head, delivered from above and behind, as they clambered down the steep incline; then, as he lay on the ground, his face and head were furiously battered so as to prevent recognition, the injury to the top of the shoulder-blade being caused by a blow which missed the head and struck the top of the shoulder. Laurie had thereafter rifled the body and buried it beneath the boulder, close to which the deed was done. Why he did not also conceal in the same hiding-place the cap and other articles found in the gully the Crown failed to explain. Possibly he overlooked them until he had finished building up the turf-and-stone dyke about the body, when even he may have hesitated to re-open the cavity, preferring to place the cap under the large stone in the stream where it was found, and let the rest take their chance of discovery. The waterproof was split up the back into two pieces. No reason was given for this, but it looks as if it had been thus torn from the body (for Rose when last seen alive was wearing it) and then rolled up and trampled into the pool. The stick, knife, pencil, and button were either dropped, unnoticed by Laurie, during the assault, or thrown away by him after he had searched the pockets of his victim.

The theory of the defence was that all the injuries to the body were produced simultaneously as the result of a fall over one or other of the steep rocks before referred to, further up the gully. On the left side, above the place where the cap was found, as already mentioned, was the 19 feet drop, 156 yards beyond the boulder; the 32 feet drop was on the other side, 40 yards lower down, above where the knife and pencil were found. The former fall was that favoured by the defence. There was no indication on the body or clothes of its having been dragged from thence down to the boulder, which, looking to the nature of the ground, must, if done, have left unmistakable signs of the process. Indeed, the only injury to these, apart from the head, was that of the shoulder-blade, with corresponding damage to the flesh, the clothing, and the waterproof. If killed further up the gully, the body of Rose must therefore have been carried down to the boulder. The prisoner in his letter to the *Mail* had stated that he left Rose on the top of the mountain with two men from Loch Ranza, and the defence maintained that Laurie never saw him again, alive or dead. Even if the death were the result of an accidental fall, the robbing and elaborate burial of the body and the folding and concealment of the cap proved the presence of another person, and the defence could do no more than deny, with the prisoner, that these acts were the work of his hands. The unlikelihood of any third party finding and robbing the dead body, and thereafter running the needless and fearful risk of burying it, is obvious, while the suggestion of the learned Dean that the stone (which, by the way, weighed between seven and eight pounds) might have been carried down by a freshet, was negatived by the witnesses who saw its position upon the folded cap.

On the first day of the trial the prosecution was mainly concerned to prove that Rose met his death by murder; on the second, they sought to establish the prisoner's connection with the crime. The members of the search party who had seen the body found, one and all denied that the descent was dangerous or specially difficult, or that a man going down by the left side of the gully, which was the natural way, would have any occasion to go near the steep rocks at all. In cross-examining the police witnesses, the Dean elicited the curious fact that, after the post-mortem examination on 5th August, the boots removed from the body were taken to the shore at Corrie and there buried below high-water mark. The constable who had done this was severely pressed by the Dean as to his reason for so disposing of them, the Dean holding that their condition as regards nails and heels was most important with reference to the question at issue, but the witness could give no more satisfactory answer than that he had been ordered by his superior officer "to put them out of sight." It has been said that the object of this irregular act was to prevent the dead man's spirit from "walking," which, if true, would seem to imply some deficiency of humour on the part of the authorities.

The medical evidence as to the cause of death was the real battle-ground of the case. The skilled witnesses for the Crown were Drs. Gilmour and Fullarton, who saw the body at the boulder and performed the post-mortem examination, and Sir Henry (then Dr.) Littlejohn, who examined the body later on its exhumation. Into the ghastly details of the injuries to the head and face it is unnecessary here to enter; it is sufficient to say that the three medical witnesses concurred in stating that these had been produced by direct violence, in the manner alleged by the prosecution. The limbs and extremities were free from fractures and dislocations, and there was no indication of blood either upon the body or clothes. The injured parts were horribly decayed, and the fact that the highest of the cervical vertebræ was lying loose when first seen by Dr. Gilmour was attributed by that gentleman to the advanced decomposition of the neck. The whole of the upper jaw was detached in one piece. These injuries, in his opinion, must have been due to repeated impacts, whether by blows or falls. All the injuries were confined to the left side; and in the case of a sheer fall the injuries to the face would not, he said, be present. Dr. Fullarton stated that the extent and severity of the fractures were the result of repeated blows with a blunt instrument; he had never seen a head so smashed except by a machinery accident. The injury to the shoulder confirmed his view, for any conscious person falling would have had his hands before him, and the injuries, which in this case were all localised on one spot, would have been different. He thought the first blow had been given while the man was standing, and the others when he was on the ground. Dr. Littlejohn stated that the condition of the cranium as seen by him was at once suggestive of direct violence by blows. A heavy stone in the hand would be an instrument likely to have caused the injuries. The severity of the bruises would stop hemorrhage, and the absence of hemorrhage would account for the speedy decomposition. The detachment of the cervical vertebræ, as described

19

in the first medical report, might be consistent either with dislocation or decay of the tissues. A fall would not have inflicted such localised violence without producing severe injuries to the extremities and to the internal organs of the abdomen, which in this case were intact and uninjured, and the latter remarkably well preserved. He had considerable experience of falls from heights such as the Dean Bridge and the Castle Rock, Edinburgh, but he never saw injuries like these so caused. A fall of such severity must have implicated the liver, the condition of which was normal, and there would also be other injuries not present in this case.

The medical experts for the defence were Sir Patrick (then Dr.) Heron Watson and Drs. M'Gillivray and Alexis Thomson, none of whom had the advantage of seeing the body. They were therefore called to give their opinion solely upon the medical reports and evidence adduced for the Crown. Dr. Heron Watson stated that the injuries which he had heard described were, in his view, more consistent with a fall than with repeated blows, and he considered that they had been produced instantaneously. All the probabilities were in favour of a fall upon the vertex. The vertebræ of the neck were probably broken, and there would be little bleeding, which, in the case of blows, would have been copious. The fact that the liver was not ruptured did not affect his opinion. He described, as the result of certain grisly experiments, the difficulty of fracturing the human skull by blows, so as to produce the extensive smashing present in that case. He suggested that Rose had slipped on the slope, and, turning round before he reached the edge, fell over the cliff headlong, backwards, and leftwards. If the head alighted on a granite boulder on which there was a nodule of some size, this would account for the injuries to the face and shoulder. The other two medical witnesses for the defence concurred generally in the opinion of Dr. Heron Watson as against that of the Crown doctors.

With regard to the conflict of medical testimony, it is note-

worthy that upon cross-examination neither side absolutely
negatived the possibility of the other's theory; and it occurs
to the lay mind that perhaps, as Mr. Mantalini remarked in
another connection, they may "both be right and neither
wrong," in the sense that Laurie may have first pushed Rose
over the rocks, and, having stunned him, then completed the
deed with a stone.

The several chapters of the story which has here been
briefly told were elicited from the various witnesses.  The
identity of the prisoner and "Annandale" was clearly established; the property of the dead man found in his possession
was duly identified by relatives and friends; and his movements, as well before as after the murder, were traced beyond
all manner of doubt.  It was proved that to go from the top
of Goatfell to the boulder took half an hour, and that to walk
at an ordinary pace from the boulder to Corrie Hotel took an
hour and forty minutes, while the prisoner had spent four
hours upon the way.  In addition to their medical men the
defence called only four witnesses: one, an Italian fisherman,
to give expert evidence as a guide regarding the dangerous
character of the descent by Corrie-na-fuhren; another, a girl
who had known Laurie at Rothesay, to say that she found him
"chatty and agreeable" on his return from the excursion to
Arran.  It appeared, however, on cross-examination, that the
guide, who had only been three years in the island, had never
been in Glen Sannox till after the body was found; while the
girl admitted that on her asking Laurie how long he had taken
to climb Goatfell, he avoided the question and made no reply.
The other two witnesses called were the servant girls who had
been with Mackenzie at Sannox burying-ground.  They did not
remember Mackenzie's remark as to the man, but admitted that
it might have been made.

At a quarter past five on the second day of the trial the
Solicitor-General rose to address the jury on behalf of the
Crown.  After drawing their attention to the exceptional

features of the case, he remarked, that if this was a murder, it was undoubtedly one of a peculiarly atrocious character. The salient facts of the case were these : Two young men went up the hill together. Only one came down. The other was found, after an interval of weeks, with his body horribly mutilated, hidden away among the rocks of the hillside, and all his portable property removed. The survivor was seen within a few hours of the time when the death of his friend must have been accomplished. He returned to the place from which they both started, and gave no sign or hint of anything having happened to his friend, or that he had not returned with him. The next morning he left Arran and resumed his ordinary occupation, which he continued until the hue and cry arose. Then he fled, and when he was about to be arrested, attempted to cut his throat. The Solicitor-General then reviewed the evidence led for the Crown bearing upon the movements of the prisoner, from his arrival at Rothesay under a false name and his subsequent association with Rose until his return to their Brodick lodgings alone. Laurie spent the night in the room which he and his friend had shared, and left next morning by the first available steamer, before the people of the house could see him, without paying his bill, and leaving the room in such a state as would suggest that it had been occupied by two persons. When he left, he obliterated every trace of Rose except the tennis-racket, which, as it bore Rose's name, would have been awkward to take with him. He returned to Rothesay wearing Rose's hat and carrying other property of his in a parcel, while certain things which also had belonged to Rose were found in the trunk left by the prisoner at Liverpool. The watch and chain and pocket-book, which Rose was known to have upon him, were missing, and though they did not know how much money he had in his possession, it must have been sufficient to pay his way during the remainder of his holiday. The question was, Whose hand rifled the pockets and put the body under the boulder ? He thought they would have little difficulty in coming to the conclusion that the prisoner was with Rose down to the end. The suggestion of the defence that these two parted on the top of the mountain was excluded by the facts of the case. If, then, the prisoner robbed and buried the body, was his the hand that caused the death ? The supposition that Rose's death was the result of an accident, and that the robbery and secretion of the body was the work of the prisoner, was so inherently, so wildly improbable that, even apart from the medical evidence, the jury must hesitate to give it credence. If such were indeed the fact, it indicated a depravity of mind but little removed from that which led to murder. The Solicitor-General then discussed the nature of the *locus* and the character of the injuries to the body, and examined the conflict of medical testimony. The prisoner's own behaviour, he said, afforded the readiest solution of what had really happened. He asked them to apply to it the ordinary standard of human conduct, and to say if any man could have so acted who was not the murderer of Rose. As to motive, the prisoner probably expected to get more by the murder than he actually got, but having done it, he had to go through with it. Finally, counsel submitted that the prosecution had established beyond reasonable doubt that the prisoner at the bar was guilty of the crime with which he was charged.

The Dean of Faculty then addressed the jury for the defence. He agreed with the prosecutor that if the case were true, this was a murder unprecedented and incredibly atrocious. If so, the onus of proof was all the heavier upon the Crown. Every probability, he might say every possibility, was against it. Even if they came to the conclusion that murder had been committed, of which he hoped to show there was no evidence, they must consider whether there was sufficient proof that the murder was committed by Laurie. They would bear in mind that suspicion was not proof. Before they could arrive at a verdict of guilty, they must be clear in their minds upon both these points. He then described the injuries to the body, and pointed out that there were no signs of any struggle or of the body having been dragged, nor was it suggested that any instrument had been found in the neighbourhood to which the infliction of the injuries could be attributed. All these were upon the left side. No right-handed man would have attacked Rose upon that side, and it was not suggested that the prisoner was left-handed. He argued that the fractures of the skull and the injury to the shoulder, involving as it did the clothing, together with the severance of the highest joint of the back bone, all supported the theory of the defence. Near the spot they had two declivities such as would bring about these results if a man fell over either of them. He did not know where the Crown said the murder was committed. If at the boulder, how came the various things at the places where they were found ? Concealment could not have been the object, for they were left lying perfectly open, and their position was much more consistent with Rose's pitching over the rock and the things flying in all directions. His first point against the Crown was that they had failed to prove a murder, and that the probability on the medical testimony was that the injuries were due to causes other than wilful infliction of violence. With regard to the prisoner's conduct, the Dean remarked that there was nothing in Laurie having called himself "Annandale" when he went to Rothesay; he was not then aware of Rose's existence, and he was seen and known as Laurie there by other persons. Their meeting was casual, and the visit to Brodick in company was, in the circumstances, quite natural. Laurie could then have had no murderous design. The reticence of the prisoner, as described by some of the witnesses, was due to his suffering from toothache. There was no evidence that Rose and Laurie were ever together in this world again from the time they were seen on the top of Goatfell. Whoever removed the body, the jury would understand that their verdict must not proceed upon the suggestion of the Solicitor-General that it was the theory of the defence that the prisoner had done so. No one knew by whom it was done, but at those Fair holidays there were plenty of other people on the island who might have robbed the body and put it where it was found. That the prisoner alone and unaided could have lifted, carried, and piled the heavy stones upon it was most unlikely; two men would be required to do that. When Laurie arrived at Corrie Hotel he had no appearance of being a red-handed murderer, but if the Crown case were true there must have been some traces of the deed upon him. He left the island next day, and it was proved that he improperly took away with him some things belonging to Rose. He made no secret of it, for he wore these things at Rothesay among people who knew them both. If this were a charge of theft, these circumstances might be important; but what connection had they with the murder of Rose? Not one article which Rose had with him on the day of his death had been traced to the prisoner. If he had murdered his friend would he have gone back among people who had seen them both together, and afterwards have quietly returned to his work? Not until Aitken showed that he suspected him did Laurie realise that, having been seen with Rose in Arran, he might himself be held responsible for his disappearance. If he had expected this charge he would not have waited till 31st July before leaving Glasgow. He would realise later that his disappearance then had only tended further to compromise him, so he continued in hiding, and when about to be captured he attempted to cut his throat. When he said, "I robbed the man, but I did not murder him," it was certainly not a confession that he had rifled the body, but had reference to the things which he had taken away from the lodgings. In conclusion, the Dean maintained that the Crown had failed to prove, first, that there was any murder, and, secondly, if there had been, that Laurie was the murderer. He asked the jury to return a verdict which would acquit the prisoner of that most terrible and appalling charge.

At twenty minutes to nine o'clock the Lord Justice-Clerk
began his charge to the jury.  His lordship described the
case as one of the most remarkable that had ever come
before a Court of Justice.  Both the theories which had
been set up presented points almost inconceivable to the
ordinary mind.  As this was a case of purely circumstantial
evidence, he proposed in the first place to go over the facts
as to which there was no doubt.  His lordship then reviewed
the evidence as to the movements of Rose and Laurie till
they were last seen together on the top of the mountain.
It was proved that the deceased was then wearing his
watch-chain, and they also knew that he had in his
pocket-book a return half ticket to London.  It was quite
certain that neither of them descended by the same way
as they came up.  They took a route which, though not the
ordinary one, was proved not to be dangerous to any person
taking reasonable care.  Now, on the way down Rose
unquestionably met his death by violence of some kind,
and after death his body was carefully hidden by someone
under the boulder.  If he died by falling over one or other
of the rocks further up the gully, it must have been a work
of great labour and difficulty to bring the body down to the
boulder and conceal it with the stones.  His cap was found
folded up, with a heavy stone placed upon it, his waterproof, cut
in two, was rolled together near the burn, his pockets were
rifled, his watch, money, and return ticket were gone.  All
that must have happened within a few hours of a summer
evening.  The prisoner was seen coming out of the glen at
half-past nine, and again at Corrie Hotel about ten o'clock.
He returned to Brodick, and, without any intimation to the
people of the place, left the next morning, taking with him
Rose's bag, and wearing his grey felt hat.  On his return to
Rothesay the prisoner was seen wearing Rose's tennis jacket
and yachting-cap.  His lordship then referred to the incident
of the prisoner's conversation with the witness Aitken, to

the fact that Laurie had stated to others that he had a return half ticket to London, to the circumstances of his flight to Liverpool with a box containing property proved to have belonged to Rose, to the letters which he addressed to the newspapers, and finally to his apprehension and attempted suicide. These were facts about which there could be no doubt, and the Crown said they all pointed to the prisoner as having committed the crime with which he was charged. The defence was that the death of Rose did not take place in presence of Laurie, that they, having gone up Goatfell together, did not descend together, although the one met his death on the way by Glen Sannox to Corrie, and the other reached Corrie by way of Glen Sannox. Laurie must have been surprised to find that his friend did not return to their lodgings, but the effect which Rose's non-arrival had upon him was, that without saying a word to anyone, he went off with his own and Rose's luggage. The defence maintained that Rose had fallen over one of the rocks at a considerable distance from the boulder, and that it would have been impossible for one man to have brought the body down and buried it. His lordship was afraid there were two views as to that, for the Crown's contention was that Rose was done to death by blows with a stone, which could have happened close to the boulder. The Dean had asked, if Rose was killed there, how came the various articles to be found below the rocks further up the gully ? Again his lordship was afraid that if Rose in fact was killed at the boulder, the person who put him to death might so have disposed of the articles as to suggest that Rose had fallen over a precipice. His lordship pointed out that the hiding of the cap and the cutting up of the waterproof must have been done by a human hand after Rose's death. The defence being that Laurie and Rose were never seen together after they left the top of the hill, it was extremely remarkable that the prisoner did not reach Corrie Hotel till ten, while the witnesses who left the top at the same time reached Brodick before half-past eight. The jury must consider if they could reconcile all these facts with the idea that Laurie was not present at Rose's death. If he was, there was no escape from the conclusion that his was the hand that folded the cap, cut off the waterproof, and hid the body; and then they would have to consider could these acts possibly have been done by a man who had witnessed a terrible and accidental death. With regard to Laurie's possession of a return ticket to London, it was in evidence that Rose had such a ticket in his pocket-book. It had been urged for the defence that the prisoner openly wore the coat and hats of Rose, and that no person anxious to conceal a crime would have done so, but it was his duty to point out that such rashness on the part of criminals often formed the very threads of the web of justice. They must take the whole facts of the case together, and say whether it led to a conclusion that was reasonable and just. His lordship then reviewed the medical evidence, and observed that those who saw all the details and examined them were necessarily in a better position to give their evidence and opinions than those who merely based their statements upon evidence which they heard. It was not the province of the jury to decide between the medical opinions, but to find what, taking the whole facts and incidents along with that evidence, was the most probable cause of death. If they came to the conclusion that the prisoner was present and that his hand buried the body, that would tend very much against the theory of the defence. The case was purely one of facts, and it was the jury who had the responsibility and duty of coming to a conclusion on those facts which would commend itself to their consciences as reasonable and experienced men.

At a quarter to ten, on the conclusion of the judge's charge, the jury retired to consider their verdict, and after an absence of forty minutes they returned to Court, when the Foreman announced that their verdict was " Guilty, by a majority." It was afterwards ascertained that the verdict was arrived at by a majority of one, eight voting for "Guilty" and seven for "Not Proven." So soon as the Lord Justice-Clerk had pronounced sentence of death the prisoner, who stood up to receive judgment, turned round in the dock and, facing the crowded benches, said in a clear, firm voice, "Ladies and gentlemen, I am innocent of this charge!" His lordship at once intimated that the prisoner could not be allowed to make a speech. Laurie was then removed to the cells below, and the Court rose at twenty minutes to eleven o'clock.

No one who witnessed the closing act of this famous trial can forget the impressive character of the scene. Without, in the black November night, a great crowd silently awaited the issue of life or death. The lofty, dimly-lighted Court-room, the candles glimmering in the shadows of the Bench, the imposing presence of the Justice-Clerk in his robes of scarlet and white, the tiers of tense, expectant faces, and in the dock the cause and object of it all, that calm, commonplace, respectable figure, the callous and brutal murderer whom Justice had tardily unmasked.

On Monday, the 11th, the convict was conveyed from Edinburgh to Greenock, where the sentence was to be executed on 30th November. This was a distinction which the magistrates and citizens of that town viewed with anything but satisfaction, for since its creation as a burgh of barony in 1675 only four executions had taken place there, the last being in 1834, and it was hoped and expected that the sentence would be carried out in Edinburgh.

A movement was at once set on foot in the Coatbridge district, where Laurie's relatives were well known and respected, to obtain a commutation of the death sentence. Various meetings were held, and a petition to Lord Lothian, the Scottish Secretary, was adopted. Apart from the stereotyped objections to the verdict common to such documents, the petitioners stated that there had been, and then was, insanity in the convict's family; that he himself had shown from infancy decided symptoms of mental aberration, which accounted for the extraordinary and eccentric character of his conduct both prior and subsequent to the 15th of July; and that the petitioners were prepared to adduce proof of such aberration if required. This petition, which was widely signed in Glasgow and the West of Scotland, was duly despatched to Dover House on Friday, 22nd November. Meanwhile, pending the result of this application, the Greenock magistrates proceeded to make the necessary arrangements for carrying out the sentence, and thriftily borrowed the Glasgow scaffold. Laurie, who still maintained the cool and calm demeanour which he had preserved throughout the trial, was said to be confident that his life would be spared.

On Saturday, the 23rd, on the appointment of Lord Lothian, the convict was visited by Sir Arthur Mitchell, K.C.B., Dr. Yellowlees, of Glasgow Royal Asylum, and Professor (afterwards Sir William) Gairdner, of Glasgow University, with a view to examining and reporting upon his mental condition. It was stated in the newspapers at the time that Laurie had himself written a letter to Lord Lothian to the effect that Rose was killed in his presence by an accidental fall from a rock, and that his (Laurie's) subsequent actions arose from his dread that he would be charged with murder, and, owing to the absence of witnesses, might be unable to prove his innocence. This was at least a more plausible explanation than that afforded by the defence at the trial; but it is understood that the line of argument then taken was the prisoner's deliberate choice, and was adopted by his counsel at his own request.

On Thursday, the 28th, two days before that fixed for the execution, the local authorities were informed by telegraph that in consequence of the Medical Commission having reported that the convict was of unsound mind, the Secretary for Scotland had felt justified in recommending a respite. The terms of the Commissioners' report were not disclosed.

The death sentence having been formally commuted to penal servitude for life, Laurie was removed on 2nd December to Perth Penitentiary, the scaffold was returned to Glasgow, and the Greenock magistrates were left to pay the bill.

The *Glasgow Herald* of 3rd December 1889 published an interesting account of the unfavourable impression made by Laurie upon those who were in close contact with him during his confinement, from which the following passage may be quoted:—"His references to Rose were not marked by any exhibition of sympathy for that unfortunate gentleman. On the contrary he spoke of him as a vain, proud man, always boastful of his money, and desirous of making his hearers believe that he was wealthy. The significance of Laurie's comment upon this point is striking; with singular callousness he added that Rose had not very much after all."

Four years elapsed before public attention was again directed to the Arran murderer. On 24th July 1893, Laurie, who had been removed to Peterhead Convict Prison, made a bold bid for freedom. He was employed as a carpenter, his behaviour had been exemplary, and, having a good voice, he was, as a newspaper reporter records, "the mainstay of the Presbyterian choir, leading the praise with great enthusiasm." But the old Adam was not wholly eradicated. That morning a gang of convicts under a civil guard was early at work upon an addition which was being made to the warders' houses outside the prison walls, and Laurie was carrying planks for the scaffolding. There was a dense sea fog; so, seizing his opportunity, he leapt a fence and made for the public road. He was then seen by the civil guard, but before the latter could fire the fugitive had disappeared in the fog. An alarm was instantly raised, and guard and warders started in pursuit. One warder, mounted on a bicycle, speedily overtook the running man. He struggled violently, but other warders arriving on the scene, he was quickly handcuffed and marched back to prison. On the way, says our reporter, "Laurie characterised his captors in language wholly inconsistent with the ecclesiastical office which he fills." Human nature was too strong for the precentor.

In 1909, on the completion of twenty years of his sentence, echoes of the old story were heard in the press, and persistent rumours were circulated that the convict was about to be released. But on 28th April 1910 Laurie was removed from Peterhead to Perth Criminal Asylum, where he still remains (1913).

In the ancient burying-ground of Sannox, briers and brambles have striven to conceal the granite boulder which, with a somewhat painful propriety, marks the resting-place of Edwin Rose; and year by year the tourists visiting that beautiful and lonely spot leave, with better intention than taste, their calling-cards upon the stone.